From Teacher to Trainer

Matthew T Ellman
and Peter Lucantoni

CAMBRIDGE
UNIVERSITY PRESS

University Printing House, Cambridge CB2 8BS, United Kingdom

One Liberty Plaza, 20th Floor, New York, NY 10006, USA

477 Williamstown Road, Port Melbourne, VIC 3207, Australia

314–321, 3rd Floor, Plot 3, Splendor Forum, Jasola District Centre, New Delhi – 110025, India

103 Penang Road, #05–06/07, Visioncrest Commercial, Singapore 238467

Cambridge University Press is part of the University of Cambridge.

It furthers the University's mission by disseminating knowledge in the pursuit of education, learning and research at the highest international levels of excellence.

www.cambridge.org
Information on this title: www.cambridge.org/9781108827072

First published 2022

20 19 18 17 16 15 14 13 12 11 10 9 8 7 6 5 4 3 2 1

Printed in Great Britain by CPI Group (UK) Ltd, Croydon CR0 4YY

A catalogue record for this publication is available from the British Library

ISBN 978-1-10882707-2 Paperback
ISBN 978-1-10882711-9 eBook

Contents

Acknowledgements

The authors and publishers acknowledge the following sources of copyright material and are grateful for the permissions granted. While every effort has been made, it has not always been possible to identify the sources of all the material used, or to trace all copyright holders. If any omissions are brought to our notice, we will be happy to include the appropriate acknowledgements on reprinting and in the next update to the digital edition, as applicable.

Key: Int = Introduction, U = Unit

Text:

Int: Quote reproduced by kind permission of Donya Estafanous; **U3:** Extract taken from 'Metaphors we work by: EFL and its metaphors' by Scott Thornbury, *ELT Journal*, Volume 45, Issue 3, July 1991, Page 200, https://doi.org/10.1093/elt/45.3.193, by permission of Oxford University Press via Copyright Clearance Center; **U6:** Jim Scrivener for the text adapted from '16- Next Steps' by Jim Scrivener, *Learning Teaching*. Text Copyright © 2011 Jim Scrivener. Reproduced by kind permission of Jim Scrivener; **U9:** Quote reproduced by kind permission of Bahar Gün; Design variables taken from 'Teacher education: Factors relating to programme design', by Martin Parrott, *Applied linguistics and English language teaching*. Copyright © 1991 Modern English Publication and The British Council. Published by Macmillan Publishers Limited. Reproduced by kind permission of The British Council; **U10:** Quote reproduced by kind permission of Allen Davenport; Text taken from 'British Council Continuing Professional Development (CPD) Framework for Teacher Educators'. Copyright © 2021 British Council. Reproduced by kind permission; Association of Teacher Educators for the text taken from 'Association of Teacher Educators standards'. Copyright © 2021 Association of Teacher Educators. Used with permission. All rights reserved; Quote reproduced by kind permission of Walid Shawky; **Notes:** Text taken from *Evaluating professional development* by Thomas R Guskey. Copyright © 2000 Corwin Press. Reproduced by permission of Corwin Press.

Photography:

U1: skynesher/E+/Getty Images; **U2:** Westend61/Getty Images; **U3:** Reproduced by kind permission of Sandy Millin; **U4:** d3sign/Moment/Getty Images; Images of book cover and inside page from *Meanings into Words Upper-intermediate Workbook* captured by Peter Lucantoni, Professional Learning and Development Manager, Cambridge University Press and Assessment.

Cover Photography by Jon Feingersh Photography Inc/DigitalVision/Getty Images.

Video:

Pre-lesson observation: Theresa Dyer (teacher) and Peter Lucantoni (trainer); **Lesson observation:** Theresa Dyer (teacher), Peter Lucantoni (trainer), Anna, Dunia, Gaia, Jessica, Óscar, Francesca (students) and Globally Speaking; **Post-lesson observation:** Theresa Dyer (teacher) and Peter Lucantoni (trainer).

Trainer Voices: Allen Davenport; Andrea Tolve; Anil Bayir; Bahar Gün; Chris Thorn; Claire Ross; Fabio Galvanini; Nahla Al Malki; Olha Madylus; Rawya Zakzouk; Ricardo Morales; Scott Thornbury; Zhenya Polosatova.

Typesetting:

QBS Learning

URL:

The publisher has used its best endeavours to ensure that the URLs for external websites referred to in this book are correct and active at the time of going to press. However, the publisher has no responsibility for the websites and can make no guarantee that a site will remain live or that the content is or will remain appropriate.

Thanks

Heartfelt thanks to our friends and colleagues at Cambridge University Press, particularly Jo Timerick and Karen Momber, without whom this book would not exist. Tremendous thanks also to Alex Tilbury for his insightful comments and ideas, and to Greg Sibley for his splendid editing.

We are indebted to our trainer friends who contributed their voices and wisdom on video and in print, as well as to those who helped create our lesson videos: Nicole and Michelle at Globally Speaking in Rome, Sarah Ellis, and especially Theresa Dyer for volunteering to be our teacher.

Matt: I was very lucky to have outstanding trainers when I was learning to teach, and I'm pleased to have this chance to thank Andy Cox, Dave Rea, Steven McGuire and Kate Leigh for all they taught me. Thank you to Olha Madylus, Chris Thorn and Sangeeta Sathe for reading drafts and for being brilliant co-trainers and friends. Big thanks to Peter for inviting me to join this project and for being a pleasure to work with. Finally, thank you and much love to Donya for all her support, encouragement, ideas and endless patience.

Peter: A huge thank-you to my co-author, colleague and friend, Matt, who helped make the idea of this book become a reality. Without his enthusiasm and input the journey would have been far more difficult and the result far less impressive.

Foreword

In our many encounters with teachers, we – Peter and Matthew – have often been asked for advice on how to get into teacher training. It's not unusual for the question to be asked with a sense of frustration, and sometimes there even seems to be an underlying assumption that becoming a trainer is more like joining a secret society than making a perfectly logical career move.

The advice we give is quite straightforward (if there is a secret society for teacher trainers, we haven't been invited!) – to become a teacher trainer you need two things: opportunities to work with teachers, and the skills to perform well when you get those opportunities. We can't provide you with the opportunities (although we show you where to look for them, in Chapter 10), but what we can do is help you develop the skills, so that you're ready to seize whatever chances you come across.

We have written this book to support and guide your journey towards becoming a teacher trainer. There are plenty of methodology books for teachers available, as there are coursebooks for students; there is also a number of resource books for more experienced trainers. But this book is intended to bridge the gap between teacher and trainer, and to provide a comprehensive foundation for your training career, whether you are aspiring to it or already supporting teachers as part of your work. Many of the skills involved in effective teaching are also part of effective teacher training. We try to build on your experience as a teacher and help you to use your existing skills as fully as possible, while also providing you with the techniques and know-how that are more specific to teacher training.

Our goal is not only to help you transition from the classroom to the training room. Crucially, we aim to help you become a trainer whose interventions have a lasting, positive impact on what teachers think and do when they teach. Being effective as a teacher trainer means effecting change in your trainees' teaching practice, ultimately to achieve better student learning outcomes. We hope, therefore, that the importance of achieving this kind of impact through your training runs through the whole book.

Between us we have more than 50 years of experience in teaching, training, writing and academic management, in countries across the world. Both of us work with and support teachers in different contexts, face-to-face and online, on a daily basis. We have designed and delivered training programmes to large institutions and ministries of education, and we also train trainers, often working side-by-side on the same course.

We hope you enjoy and benefit from using this book, and that the teachers you work with will benefit as well. Training teachers is challenging, but it's also varied, fun, fascinating and richly rewarding. We wish you good luck as you take your first steps from teacher to trainer!

Introduction

When you become a teacher you get training, and if you go on into management there are training courses for that, but no one ever tells you how to do teacher training because it's just seen as another kind of teaching, just telling people what you know because you're a good teacher.

Donya, teacher trainer, UK

Many experienced teachers will find themselves in the situation Donya describes at some point in their careers. In management roles or simply respected by their students and by their peers, they may be asked to deliver workshops, observe colleagues or act as a mentor. But they're often expected to do that on the basis of their teaching skills alone, and while teacher training can certainly be considered 'teaching of teachers', there is more to being a successful trainer than simply knowing how to teach, in the same way that there is more to being a good language teacher than simply knowing how to speak the language.

Why we wrote this book

Like Donya, we see that there is a lack of practical help available to experienced teachers who hope to take on more of a training role – in other words, to move from teacher to trainer. The problem is that even if opportunities to start training are available, opportunities for learning *how to become a trainer* are often very limited, and in certain contexts may be non-existent. Even the teachers who are lucky enough to have access to guidance as they begin their careers as trainers may find the task more daunting than anticipated, or feel that the guidance they receive is inadequate.

This lack of support inevitably makes life difficult for new trainers, who have to find their way through trial and error, but it also increases the risk that the training they deliver will have limited impact, or even the wrong impact: one teacher describes how, tired of attending training sessions that didn't meet his needs, he has 'on more than one occasion, . . . skipped an offered session, opting for *elopement* over *development*' (Kirkham, 2015, p. 4)! It's understandable that the transition into teacher education isn't easy. Moving from teaching to training doesn't just entail doing things differently, or even doing entirely new things; it involves 'a transformation of perspective on the educational process' (Wright, 2009, p. 104), and that is a challenge. But at the same time, experienced teachers have a wealth of classroom know-how that they can tap in to when they begin training, and right through their training careers – *if* the right support is provided.

Who can benefit from this book

Anyone who is moving from teacher to trainer, even in an unofficial manner, should be able to take something from this book. It does not assume that you have had any experience of delivering training, nor do we believe that 'one size fits all'. We are very aware that every educational context is different, and that different solutions are needed for different challenges. However, we do believe that there are certain universal principles that all trainers can benefit from, and we will address these in the initial chapters.

So this book is for you if you are, for example:

- an experienced teacher who is called upon to support colleagues, either one-to-one, or by delivering workshops

- a trainer-in-training on a course such as Cambridge English Train the Trainer, or as a tutor-in-training to deliver the Cambridge CELTA or equivalent

- a co-ordinator or manager who is required to guide, observe or train staff

- a practising teacher trainer who wishes to review or develop their knowledge and skills

- a supervisor or inspector, required to observe teaching and deliver feedback

- a teacher receiving a trainee in their class as part of an initial teacher training programme

We expect that you will be an experienced language teacher, and that you will broadly place your skills at either Proficient or Expert level on the Cambridge English Teaching Framework (see Appendix 1). In addition we expect that you will have been through a certain amount of formal teacher training yourself during your career, which you will be able to draw upon as you read through the book. Although our focus is principally the training of English language teachers and the examples we use will reflect that, there is no reason why trainers of teachers of other languages can't benefit from the book too, or even those training teachers of other subjects – the principles of teacher learning that we present are drawn from research undertaken in a wide range of educational contexts.

Our approach

A key part of our approach is the belief that new trainers can and should draw extensively on their teaching experience as they make the transition into teacher training. There are many skills and habits that can be transferred from the classroom to the training room, and our experience suggests it is very much the case that 'experienced teachers make effective teacher educators if their experience is acknowledged and built upon' (Vilches, 2015, p. 286).

At regular points, therefore, you will see tasks that require you to look back at your teaching career and draw out memories and insights that can inform your work as a trainer. You'll see these labelled as **From teacher . . .** tasks. In addition to these, you'll also want to check your understanding of the concepts that you encounter, to gauge your progress and to help you absorb and retain new ideas. To do that we have also created **. . . To trainer** tasks. We have provided suggestions and responses to most of the tasks in the Notes on tasks section in the back of the book (where we haven't, the response is either unique to you or covered in the text that follows the task), but these should not be seen as 'answers'. Instead, we hope they will serve as prompts that encourage you to reflect on your context and draw your own conclusions.

One of the best ways to develop your training skills is to learn from skilled trainers. We are extremely lucky to have been able to draw on the experience of colleagues around the world who have kindly provided their insights through case studies, helping to demonstrate how principles are put into practice. Their input has meant that this book includes a wide range of examples and contexts, and we have been able to highlight the differences (but also the similarities!) that exist between training contexts around the globe.

We feel that there's tremendous value in hearing directly from some of these trainers, in order for you to develop an understanding of how widely training contexts can differ, of how trainers solve some of the problems that their contexts present and of how the trainers moved from the classroom to the training room. So at certain points in the book you will see that there are video resources to supplement the text. Some of these appear as part of a task, while others serve to elaborate on what we have described, and are referred to in the **Trainer voices** sections at the end of each chapter. The videos are indicated by the ▶ icon and can be accessed by scanning the QR Code in each section. This is followed by **To find out more** sections with recommendations for further reading.

Lastly, we strongly believe that teacher trainers have a responsibility to build bridges between educational research and classroom practice by ensuring that the concepts and practices they foster in trainees are evidence-based. Where possible we do that in the book by providing references in the text to (1) show that there is a theoretical basis or research evidence for our claims and (2) guide you towards further reading. There is a growing body of research literature on teacher training and how teachers learn, and we feel that it is important that new trainers are introduced to it.

How to use this book

The book is loosely divided into four parts. The first is Chapter 1, which introduces the theoretical background to teacher training and many of the concepts that are referred to in discussions of training practice later in the book. Chapters 2–4 deal with planning and delivering training sessions, Chapters 5–8 deal with mentoring and observing teachers and giving them feedback on teaching, and finally Chapters 9–10 focus on bringing it all together when planning programmes of training and your own development as a trainer.

This book can be read cover-to-cover for a comprehensive introduction to language teacher training, but just as effectively you can jump to the part that is most relevant to your immediate needs. Where possible we encourage you to read Chapter 1 first, to get a sense of the ideas that underpin the rest of the book and to help re-orient your perspective towards that of a trainer.

What we don't cover in this book is the content of a teacher training course. In other words, we are not going to tell you what to teach your trainees. Our concern here is with the processes of teacher training, which include making decisions about what trainees need to learn, and we hope to provide you with the tools to make those decisions yourself. As an experienced teacher you will already be familiar with many principles of effective language teaching, and there are many other excellent resources available that outline foundational skills and knowledge, such as Penny Ur's *Course in English Language Teaching* (Ur, 2012).

From Teacher to Trainer is standalone: in other words, you can use it as a self-study guide as there are suggested responses and solutions to the tasks we set. However, if you are in a situation where others are also moving into the role of trainer, most of the tasks in the book can be shared and discussed, and it will be helpful to work through them with others who are also on the journey from teacher to trainer.

Terminology

We use *teacher education* as the umbrella term for *teacher training* and *teacher development* (Freeman, 1989). Broadly speaking, we see teacher training as any learning process led by a trainer, while teacher development is a learning process led by the teacher. For any teacher, at any career stage, both are necessary for effective, sustained professional learning, and they should be seen as complementary. Our main concern in this book is teacher training, and our definition of it means that we see it as a diverse activity. Being a trainer also means being a coach, mentor, counsellor, and tutor (to name just a few of the different hats trainers wear).

We use *trainer* to refer to those who plan and/or deliver workshops or teacher education programmes, provide feedback on teaching, or mentor teachers. If you are doing these things then consider yourself a trainer, whatever your formal job title! In certain contexts, such as online or on CELTA courses, the term *tutor* is used to mean the same thing.

We use *teacher*, *trainee* or *participant* to refer to those who learn from, or are guided by, the trainer. For some, *trainee* refers to teachers at the beginning of their careers, or on preservice courses. Here we have chosen to use it to refer to teachers of all levels of experience who are learning with the help of a trainer.

We refer to the people learning language in teachers' classrooms as *students* or *learners*.

A *session* is the broad term we use for a teacher training workshop, and we use *training rooms* to refer to the places where those take place, whether physical or virtual. When we talk about what teachers do in their *classrooms*, we use the term *lesson*, and when we talk about what teachers do as part of their professional lives in general, in and out of the classroom, we use *teaching practice*, or just *practice*.

The verb *to train* often carries connotations of repetitive activity, and of having habits 'drilled in'. It's common to hear people talk, for example, about *training in the gym* or of *having a personal trainer*. Sometimes training means learning how to operate machinery, as in being *a trained pilot*. And animals are often the objects of training: you might *train a dog to sit*, or make sure that it's *toilet trained*. Training in this sense – of being taught to act a certain way in particular situations, or to respond a certain way to particular cues – sometimes carries over into discussions of teacher training, and it is associated with the idea of training as a process of instilling practical techniques or routines for use in the classroom. Helping teachers form good habits is indeed a part of what trainers do, but it is far from the complete picture, as we hope to show you. The classroom is not a piece of machinery that functions in predictable ways, and our goals as trainers go beyond showing trainees 'which buttons to press'; trainers want teachers to understand what they're doing and why they're doing it:

> Teachers need to be *trained* in practical techniques, but must also be *educated* to see those techniques as exemplars of certain theoretical principles and therefore subject to continual reappraisal and change. This is necessary in the interests of the learner. If teachers are not educated in this sense then they cannot derive expertise from experience.
> (Widdowson, 1984, p. 88)

Ultimately, we all want our training to lead to better outcomes for our trainees' learners, and we also want our trainees to be able to continue to grow and develop once they leave the training room. So, our use of the verb *to train* indicates much more than the formation of good habits in teachers: we want them to understand the rationale for the techniques we train them in, when to use them, and why. While we could probably identify other terms that reflect these goals better (such as *teacher educator*, *facilitator*, or *teacher of teachers*), we've found that by far the most widely understood title for what we do is *trainer*, so that is what we've used in this book.

 ## TRAINER VOICES

 Scan the QR Code and watch the videos 'Starting out' and 'Trainer profiles' to hear trainers talk about how they got started and where they work now.

 ## TO FIND OUT MORE

Woodward, T. (1991). *Models and metaphors in language teacher training: Loop input and other strategies.* Cambridge: Cambridge University Press. (At the very beginning of this book Tessa Woodward considers the roles of trainer, teacher, student, etc. and how the relationships between them are important to teacher training.)

1 From teaching learners to teacher learning

Here we consider:

- Different teaching and learning contexts and how they affect teaching
- What effective teachers do
- What effective teachers know
- How expert teachers acquire that knowledge and skill
- The implications of teacher learning for trainers

I think we're always learning as teachers and trying to do better, and we should be.

Claire, teacher trainer, Cyprus

Teaching and learning contexts

It's not uncommon for professionals in several fields to perform their roles in a variety of different situations. Footballers, for instance, have to play home and away, and will play in dozens of different stadiums in the course of a season, each with its own characteristics. The demands of a league game differ to those of a cup game, and a match in the early stages of a cup competition may have a very different feel to a match in the knockout stages, when it's a case of 'winner takes all'. But despite these variations, the rules of the sport are always the same, and so is the objective: score more goals than your opponent.

Language teachers sadly don't enjoy professional footballers' wages, but we need to be similarly adaptable. You probably teach in several different classrooms in an academic year, and each one will differ in terms of size, layout, resources and ambience. You may have a weekly timetable that includes classes of young children, teenagers, university students and working professionals, particularly if you work for a private language school. Learners in those groups will have different motivations for attending classes, and even when the same group meets, the group dynamic can vary. But like footballers, teachers can rely on the 'rules' remaining constant – all learners, for example, need extensive exposure to the target language, and benefit from opportunities to practise sustained, meaningful speaking (Ellis, 2005) – and improved proficiency is an objective for all students, even if it is not always the principal objective.

All teachers, then, share similar goals but need to be able to work within a variety of teaching contexts on the way to achieving those goals. Probably we immediately think of a typical classroom as the most obvious context, but teaching and learning can take place almost anywhere, particularly when digital technology is involved. We should also include here as part of the context not only *where* teaching and learning take place, but also *what* will be learned and any materials used to facilitate the process (the curriculum, materials and the resources), as well as *who* is involved (the number of participants, their background and motivation, knowledge and skills, etc.) and *how* this is done (the teaching approach, interaction patterns and techniques).

Two characteristics of teaching and learning contexts are particularly important, because they shape what teachers do when they teach. The first is that every teaching and learning context is different. This is true even if you teach the same students, in the same room, using the same coursebook, every day of the week. People will respond differently at different times to the same things, and in many ways this is what makes our profession so interesting and, at the same time, so challenging. The second is the fact that many aspects of context are usually outside the control of a teacher. For instance, we – Peter and Matthew – have visited schools and universities where students' desks are bolted to the floor, and students sit four or more on a shared bench; others where learners' parents sit at the back of the classroom during lessons and complain if they don't like what they see; and others where all books were replaced by tablet computers that later proved to be faulty. Such factors are the result of decisions made outside the walls of the classroom, attributable to individuals, to school culture, or to the wider social culture surrounding the institution. So the limitations on a teaching context often originate from beyond the walls of the classroom, but affect what goes on inside it.

CASE STUDY 1.1: MATTHEW

I remember my first teaching context quite clearly, a small private language school in London. Classrooms were small, with 12–16 adult students of various nationalities, who came for daily three-hour lessons. There was a coursebook that I had to use, but also a lot of freedom to select other materials and take advantage of being in London. Having a multilingual class of mixed nationalities presented fantastic opportunities for students to talk about their home countries and cultures, and because there was no shared first language, English was the natural way of doing that. So in several ways it was quite a gentle introduction to teaching! But there were challenges, too: each week new students joined the group while others left, resources were very limited, and I had 30 teaching hours a week, so there was very little time for professional development.

> ## TASK 1.1
>
> **From teacher ...**
>
> Think about your current teaching context and answer these questions:
>
> - What does the context look like?
> - Where are the teacher(s) and the student(s) located?
> - What materials and resources are available? Are any mandatory?
> - What materials and resources are *not* available?
> - How much space and time is there for learning?
> - What goals are there? Who set them?
>
> If possible, share and compare your answers with another teacher's.
>
> *For notes see page 211*

All this means that teachers constantly need to make choices as part of their work, and these choices should be based on their intentions for a particular lesson. In other words, teachers work within local limitations to select the *what* and *how* in order to achieve particular goals, while recognising that they may have little control over the *where* and *who*. Some of these choices can be made before the lesson starts, but others will be made during the lesson itself, in response to what unfolds in the classroom. As Jim Scrivener points out, 'all effective teaching requires an active moment-by-moment processing of the current situation and a flexible ever-changing reflection as to what might be the best thing to do next' (Scrivener, 2012, p. 2). So one view of teaching is as improvisation; an ongoing balancing act between the intended learning outcomes of the teacher and the opportunities and limitations presented by the teaching context. Unsurprisingly, then, a significant part of learning to teach 'involves understanding what the characteristics of the teaching context are and how they shape the nature of teaching and learning' (Richards & Farrell, 2011, p. 32).

Therefore it is essential that, as a trainer, you ensure your trainees are mindful of context as they develop their ideas about teaching. Even when training and subsequent teaching occur in much the same context, it isn't unusual for trainees to find that the reality of day-to-day teaching doesn't quite equate to what they experienced in the training room. Most of us have probably experienced this 'gap of applicability' (Freeman, 2009, p. 15) in our own training at some point, sitting in a workshop thinking 'nice idea, but it won't work in my classroom!' That's not to say that trainees shouldn't be encouraged to give new ideas due consideration, but it is also true that one size does not fit all, and all educators need to be aware of this. That applies to teachers as much as it does to trainers – Sharon Childs writes that:

> While teacher education cannot prepare . . . [trainees] to
> be ready to teach in every context, it can prepare them to
> understand that context is a powerful mediator that can
> shape or be shaped by how they conceptualize teaching. It is
> incumbent on teacher professional development programs to
> ensure that teachers leave with this understanding. (Childs,
> 2011, p. 85)

In practice, this means encouraging trainees to consider how they can apply or adapt ideas, approaches, activities and techniques to their own specific context, usually through guided reflection (see Chapter 3).

One of the problems trainers face is that they may never see the precise contexts their trainees go on to work in, particularly if most of their work is with preservice trainees. As a trainer you may work with teachers in their own classrooms, you may work with them in a dedicated training venue, or you may deliver training online. Whatever your training situation, you will need to be mindful of your trainees' teaching contexts (or likely future teaching contexts) when you plan, deliver and give feedback as part of training activity. What may be highly effective in one context may be counterproductive in another. Adrian Doff suggests that 'most people involved in teacher education are aware of the existence of two separate worlds' (1996, p. 8), comparing well-resourced private teaching contexts with small class sizes to 'the world of most other teachers': those who work with large groups of students in state schools or universities, often with limited and out-of-date resources. This latter world is much larger, meaning that the teaching profession is primarily made up of teachers working in mainstream schools and universities, with relatively large groups of students. Globally, most teachers work in these more restricted environments, where syllabuses and materials are decided by committees, teachers' views are often not considered, and there is little opportunity for teachers (and their learners) to experiment. Evidently, approaches to training teachers for work in these diverse contexts must take such differences into account.

In addition to considering the trainees' teaching contexts, trainers have their own teaching and learning context to manage: the training room. This will have its own affordances and limitations to be aware of, but as a trainer you will need to consider how to best explore and exploit not only your training context, but your trainees' teaching contexts too. The vast differences that exist between Doff's 'two separate worlds' impact significantly on what teachers and students can and cannot do in the classroom. There is an equally significant impact on how teacher development might be structured, and on how appropriate and applicable ideas and methods are in one context versus another. As trainers of teachers, we need to be familiar with a wide range of teaching contexts in order to be confident and effective in our role.

TASK 1.2

...To trainer

Consider the different teaching contexts in photos A and B, and then answer the questions.

What might be the main opportunities and limitations of each context?

What could the teacher in A do that the teacher in B could not?

What could the teacher in B do that the teacher in A could not?

For notes see page 211

What effective teachers do

As we've seen, teaching and learning contexts provide the *where* and the *who*, but what happens in those contexts – the *what* and the *how* – is of more interest to us, because that's the part our trainees have some control over. Why is it important to start by thinking about what language teachers do and how they do it? Because if we can understand what is required of teachers in the classroom, and what it is that highly-skilled teachers do to meet those demands, we can begin to think clearly about what our trainees need to learn in order to be effective. As Donald Freeman points out, 'how we define language teaching will influence, to a large extent, how we educate people as language teachers' (1989, p. 28).

Defining 'language teaching', and particularly 'effective language teaching' is actually very difficult, because what is effective will differ from context to context. Different cultures also have different ideas about what good teaching entails. So this is an area that is difficult to research: 'to date, there are no precise benchmarks of what constitutes effective second language teaching in all settings, nor are there agreed effective strategies that teachers should implement in their classes' (Farrell, 2015, p. 81). But what we can do instead is look at expert teachers, those we know to be highly effective, and examine their practice for clues about the kinds of expertise that non-expert colleagues should aim to develop. Expert teachers are often those with many years of experience, although experience alone doesn't guarantee expertise. Studies into teacher expertise usually rely on several additional indicators to identify expert teachers, such as recommendations from managers, colleagues and students, teaching awards, and student exam results.

One way of seeing what makes teachers experts is to look at 'snapshots' of them at work. As we see what expert teachers do while planning, teaching and after lessons, we can compare their activities to those of novice colleagues. Table 1.1 gives some examples of how expert and novice teachers work differently before, during and after they teach. In general, the contrast between the actions of novices and experts indicates that expert teachers are able to draw on patterns of student behaviour they recognise from experience, along with tried-and-tested classroom routines, to give themselves time to focus more on student learning and on the bigger picture of the learning journey. This is not unlike learning to drive (Weston & Clay, 2018; Woodward, 1991): new drivers are initially so overwhelmed with the need to juggle steering, changing gear, controlling speed, and checking mirrors that paying attention to the road is the least of their priorities, but they eventually learn to handle many of those demands automatically and concentrate on driving safely. There is just as much, if not more, for teachers to manage in a classroom, but similarly, with time and experience most teachers develop routines that allow them to deal with certain aspects of teaching with a degree of automaticity so that they can prioritise student learning over managing behaviour, resources, administration and so on.

Snapshots, however, don't give us the full picture. They don't tell us how the skills on display were developed, which is what distinguishes teachers who are genuine experts from those who have simply been doing the job for a long time. To return to our driver analogy, what is it that makes the difference between a motor racing champion (an expert driver, in other words) and someone who passed their driving test 20 years ago and drives to work every day? Both are experienced drivers, but only one is an expert. Clearly there is more to expertise than experience, and just looking at snapshots of how experts operate doesn't tell us what makes the difference. So we can look at expert teachers in another way, with a 'behind the scenes' view of expertise that focuses on the process of becoming an expert.

Looking at expert teachers in this way reveals that it is *what you do with experience* that determines whether you become an expert. Gaining experience as a teacher means building a repertoire of classroom activities and routines, knowing how students will react to them, developing language awareness and so on, over time. Novice teachers need to devote time and attention to all of these areas, but more experienced colleagues can draw on their experience to carry out the same tasks with less effort. That alone doesn't make them experts, though. Instead of resting on their laurels, experienced teachers become experts when they are able to recognise where they need to learn more, and 'reinvest the resources freed up by the use of routines to tackle more advanced problems and to problematise what appears to be the unproblematic and routine' (Tsui, 2009, p. 194). In other words, expert teachers are always working behind the scenes to improve their teaching, hence the old adage that there's a big

Table 1.1: Expert versus novice teacher behaviours, as reported in Tsui, 2009

	Experts	**Novices**
Before lessons	○ Can make decisions about what to exclude/add/adapt to lesson procedure	○ Follow procedures, rules and curriculum guidelines
	○ Anticipate problems and plan solutions for them	○ Are much less able to anticipate potential problems
	○ Plan more efficiently, incorporating insights from similar lessons in the past, and plans are shorter. Make long-term plans for objectives and content	○ Spend a long time planning and plans are more detailed. This leaves less time for longer-term planning
	○ Demonstrate an integrated knowledge base, linking each lesson to others in the course	○ Tend to view each lesson in isolation
	○ Start their lesson planning with knowledge of the students and their needs, as a group and as individuals	○ Focus on their teaching objectives with relatively little attention to how students might respond
During lessons	○ Recognise patterns in classroom events very quickly, and interpret them in meaningful ways	○ Can easily be overwhelmed by classroom events and struggle to interpret them in relation to each other
	○ Are selective about what needs their attention in the classroom, whether immediately, or later on	○ Attend more to classroom events relating to behaviour, and less to those related to learning goals
	○ Have better improvisational skills: they can draw on established routines to give examples and explanations effortlessly, addressing emergent needs without the lesson derailing	○ Have difficulty addressing questions without losing track of the lesson, and tend to cope by ignoring student needs and focusing on the immediate task
	○ Can justify their practices in a principled manner	○ Are not able to justify practices with reference to principles
	○ Focus more on language (the subject)	○ Focus on classroom management
After lessons	○ Focus on what students learned and what they can do to enhance learning	○ Reflect on their own performance in the classroom rather than on the students'

difference between 20 years' experience and one year's experience repeated 20 times. This process of continual adaptation to the demands of the teaching context, even after many years of experience, is the defining feature of 'adaptive experts', and distinguishes them from experienced non-experts, or 'routine experts' (Hatano & Inagaki, 1986).

As trainers, we need to recognise how the practices our trainees demonstrate relate to their levels of experience, and help them use the experience they gain to develop the habits that will make them adaptive experts, not just routine experts. That means developing teachers who are 'evaluative practitioners' (Weston & Clay, 2018, p. 3), who are able to continually assess how effective their teaching is and direct their own learning and development towards the skills and knowledge that will have the most impact in their specific teaching and learning context.

CASE STUDY 1.2: MATTHEW

Reflecting now on what I was doing in my lessons during my first year of teaching, I think my main preoccupation was with making my classes interesting and enjoyable. I wanted my students to learn, of course, but I had the idea that learning had to be fun, which I think was a misunderstanding of the student-centred approach that I had learned on my initial training course. I also tended to plan lessons alongside my colleagues, and borrow ideas from them, particularly if they sounded dynamic and exciting! So taking my students and their needs as the starting point for planning wasn't something I was doing then, partly because I was a novice but also partly because the context made that difficult, with students coming and going each week.

TASK 1.3

From teacher ...

Think back to different periods of your teaching career. Do you recognise the traits of novice and expert teachers in your own development as a teacher?

For notes see page 212

What effective teachers know

Several of the actions of expert teachers mentioned above involve specialist knowledge that sets skilled teachers apart from novices. Some of this knowledge is highly contextualised, such as understanding of the learners and their needs, but other elements are transferable across contexts, such as language awareness or techniques for checking comprehension. Understanding the knowledge that underpins effective teaching is important for teacher trainers, because developing that knowledge will form a key part of successful training.

Knowing about, Knowing how, Knowing to

Angi Malderez and Martin Wedell (2007, p. 18) discuss three different types of teacher knowledge: *Knowing about* (things), *Knowing how* (to do things) and *Knowing to* (use appropriate aspects of the other kinds of knowledge when teaching). More specifically, *Knowing about* includes things that teachers have knowledge of and use in their profession, such as knowledge about language, of how learning takes place, information about students and their backgrounds and needs, and even things such as school policies. *Knowing about* also includes an understanding of how a teacher might manage their own professional development and obtain access to resources or support – knowing where to go for help. Malderez and Wedell point out that 'concept development' is an important aspect of *Knowing about*. What this means is that even if you learn a new idea and it becomes part of your *Knowing about*, there is probably still room to develop that knowledge, as even apparently simple ideas can hide complexity and require a deeper professional understanding over time. For most teachers this will mean revisiting concepts and refining their grasp of them in a cyclical process of 'iterative development' (Weston & Clay, 2018, p. 6). Encountering an idea once is not enough to really understand it and apply it.

Knowing how refers to the development of skills – knowledge of how to do things – such as selecting an appropriate lesson aim, getting the attention of a noisy class, or correcting a student's pronunciation. These skills will be underpinned by appropriate *Knowing about* – creating a lesson aim, for example, involves knowing what the students are currently capable of, judging (from experience) what can be achieved in the allotted lesson time, and so on. There is an element of conscious intent in the development of *Knowing how*. Developing any skill takes time and effort, so *Knowing how* requires the awareness of a skill and the inclination to learn it. After making some progress there may be then a point at which the teacher decides to prioritise the development of a different skill, at least for the time being. Such decisions will depend on the teaching context. As a case in point, one of the authors of this book, having tried somewhat unsuccessfully to use drama activities in the classroom, made a conscious decision that this was not a skill area that he needed to develop and improve. This decision has not changed over the years, mostly due to contexts in which the author has found himself. On the other hand, conscious decisions have been made to seek out expert help to develop other skills, for instance to become more literate in the use of digital technology in teaching and learning.

Finally, *Knowing to* is the skill of classroom improvisation mentioned above; the expertise that a teacher has to know when to use what they know, 'intuitively and instantaneously' (Malderez & Wedell, 2007, p. 25), to support learning in the classroom. This automaticity is not something that can happen without the existence of the expertise described in *Knowing about* and *Knowing how*. *Knowing to* is demonstrated when a teacher notices something in the classroom (for example, students' body language, or a particular response or question from a student) and through evaluation and interpretation makes a decision about what to do next in order to progress students towards whatever goals have been identified. The jazz musician Charles Mingus famously said 'you can't improvise on nothing', and it is only with carefully considered experience and professional knowledge that a teacher can be expected to make such important on-the-spot decisions about student learning. Improvisation in this sense is not about 'winging it'; it is about exercising adaptive expertise, or what David Tripp calls '"professional judgement": those expert guesses which result from combining experience with specialist theoretical knowledge' (Tripp, 1993, p. 7). But for an expert teacher it might feel like working on intuition or just doing what feels right.

What does this mean for us as trainers? In the words of Julian Edge, it means 'training is more than training' (Edge, 1985, p. 115). That is to say that we are aiming to develop not just teachers' knowledge and skills, but also awareness and sensitivity to their individual teaching contexts. *Knowing how* and *Knowing to* perhaps stretch the meaning of the verb 'to know' outside its standard definition and into the realm of skills and actions, such as those outlined in Table 1.1 on page 13. But the distinction between the three types of knowledge is useful, because the development of each one happens in different (albeit overlapping) ways.

CASE STUDY 1.3: MATTHEW

If I compare my knowledge then to knowledge now . . . I certainly had a much weaker understanding of language, which meant that a lot of my planning time involved reading up on the language points I was teaching. It also made me less discriminating, in that I simply taught whatever was in the coursebook, whereas now I might adapt things, or skip certain items altogether if I don't feel they will be useful.

I also had very little understanding of how students would react to the tasks I planned. I remember one of my very first lessons involved a simple grammar gap-fill exercise from the coursebook, for which I allowed 15 minutes. When it came to the lesson, the students completed it in what seemed like seconds! It seems obvious in hindsight, but at the time I had no way to gauge how long that kind of task would take my students to complete, because I didn't have enough classroom experience.

How teachers learn

Expert teachers exhibit all the skills and knowledge described above, but, crucially, they all had to learn those skills; no one is born with them. So how did they do it?

Beginnings and scope

It is worth thinking about where we all began our training as teachers: not on a preservice training course, but as children, in school. All of us spent thousands of hours in classrooms as students before we began to learn how to teach – sometimes referred to as the 'apprenticeship of observation' (Lortie, 1975) – which creates a very powerful sense of what it means to behave as a teacher that can be hard to change. Of course, as a child you are not interested in teaching methodology, but children do become aware of routines and patterns, and of similarities between different classrooms and different teachers. Some of these 'ghosts of teachers past' (Weintraub, 1989) can then reappear involuntarily when trainees step in front of students for the first time, and often persist beyond that time, whether they are effective or not. In the ever-changing, complex world of the classroom it is easy to revert to instinct, to the type of teaching we are most familiar with: the way that we were taught ourselves as children, whether it is helpful or not. You may even be able to think of times when you've found yourself doing this.

For trainers, this means two things: firstly, that not all teacher education revolves around us! Besides the apprenticeship of observation, teachers can learn things that impact their practice while they are planning or teaching, while chatting with colleagues in the staffroom, from educators they encounter in other walks of life and even from things they read or watch that may appear to have nothing to do with language teaching. But the training we are involved in should aim to help trainees draw coherent insights from this bigger picture as much as possible: if trainees are presented with ideas and practices that are consistent across the different teacher education experiences they take part in (including those that do not involve a trainer), then their paths towards expertise will be more direct (Childs, 2011).

Secondly, we need to be aware that no trainee, even those on preservice courses, comes to the training room as a 'blank slate'. They all have notions of what good teaching is, of the sorts of activities that take place in a classroom, of what it means to act as a teacher and as a student, and more. Some of these preconceptions will prove to be useful, while others will need to be reformulated or discarded. Trainees' beliefs and assumptions about teaching play a crucial role not just in determining what decisions they make as teachers, but in how they react to new ideas we present to them in our training. A good example of this is provided by Zoltán Dörnyei and Maggie Kubanyiova (2014), who describe how two trainee teachers conducted the same activity, with the same materials, to very similar groups of students, but with starkly contrasting results. The main reason for the difference was most probably the trainees' differing beliefs, which 'shaped their vision of themselves as classroom practitioners – determining how they related to the learners and how they acted out the teacher's role' (Dörnyei & Kubanyiova, 2014, p. 24). For one of the trainees, beliefs and practices were aligned, which led to a successful class, whereas for the other, the practices the teacher was expected to demonstrate did not align with their beliefs, leading to a lack of student engagement and learning. It is absolutely essential, therefore, that teacher trainers are able to elicit teacher beliefs and encourage trainees to reflect on how well they align with teaching theory and research, as well as with their own classroom practice.

The right conditions

Earlier in this chapter we quoted Adrian Doff: 'most people involved in teacher education are aware of the existence of two separate worlds', and we believe the variation in contexts he describes affects not just teaching, but also teacher learning. Successful teacher learning at any level requires certain essential conditions, many of them the same as the conditions we would hope to create in our own language classes, such as:

- **Time**, both in the sense of (1) time out of a busy schedule to attend training, and (2) repeated opportunities over a longer period of time to work on developing an area of knowledge or skills

- **Clear objectives**, with a degree of trainee **autonomy** in setting those objectives

- Access to relevant **resources** and **expertise**

- A **supportive**, **collaborative** environment

This last point should not be underestimated. We all need to feel comfortable in our surroundings in order to learn, whether we're students in a classroom or teachers in training. Activities for building group cohesion are therefore an important means of creating the right conditions for teacher learning. We feel it is important to make sure that the teachers we are working with are familiar with each other and with who we are, not only to highlight how we can all help each other, but also to build up a relationship of mutual trust.

TASK 1.4

...To trainer

Imagine that you and a group of trainees are all meeting for the first time. Think of two 'getting to know you' (GTKY) activities that you could do: one for the teachers to get to know you, and one for them to get to know each other.

In what ways do your activities differ from GTKY activities in a language lesson?

For notes see page 213

Unfortunately, not all teachers are in a context that offers them all of these conditions, although the reality is perhaps not two separate worlds but a spectrum of teacher learning conditions, some more nurturing than others. The role of trainer includes fostering all of the conditions above, although time is almost always in short supply!

How teachers move from novice to expert

We've seen that teaching knowledge and skills can be viewed in three categories: *Knowing about*, *Knowing how*, and *Knowing to*. How is each of these types of knowledge developed?

Knowing about in teacher education often means knowing the terms we use to talk about teaching practice, and understanding the ideas those terms refer to. Training sessions are well-suited for introducing these. Some concepts you present to trainees might be entirely new (particularly if they are preservice trainees), for example the elicitation of target language. In those cases, it makes sense to demonstrate – or model – the concept for trainees, so that they experience it and reflect on it before putting a name to it, but the resulting knowledge is still *Knowing about*. In other cases, your training may focus on an area that trainees have some experience of, but which they still need to develop, such as error correction. In those situations, it makes sense to begin by discussing what the trainees do to correct their students' errors, and from that discussion draw out concepts and terms for them (e.g., reformulation).

Attention is a pre-requisite for learning: trainees won't learn what they don't notice. So creating a need to name and explain or discuss elements of teaching is a good way of encouraging trainees to attend to new concepts, and you can do that by (1) inviting them to talk about what happens in their classrooms, or their beliefs and assumptions about what should happen, or (2) having trainees experience concepts and practices in the role of 'students'. Either way, the subsequent learning process then becomes one of aligning teachers' beliefs and personal experience with ELT knowledge and theory, rather than simply presenting theory in isolation.

Knowing how has to build on first *knowing about*, because to be able to perform a skill it is usually necessary to have seen or experienced it being performed first. The next step towards developing that skill comes from trying it out and evaluating the results. In learning how to correct students' errors, for example, *knowing how* might develop through practice in the training room with fellow trainees (who offer feedback), trying new techniques in teaching practice (with feedback from students and/or an observer), or trying new techniques in front of real students (and self-evaluating). In all these situations there is someone to say what you did well and what you could improve, and on the basis of these comments you go and try again. That person needs to help you understand what the goals are, because you may be judging your actions against different criteria to the ones they're using. In many cases, developing teaching skills is a process of raising trainees' awareness of an aspect of teaching that may have been automatic, providing or eliciting principles for more informed action (*knowing about*) and then helping the teacher consciously apply those more informed actions in practice (*knowing how*).

Knowing to requires drawing on *knowing about* and *knowing how* as required by the teaching and learning context, so true development of *knowing to* needs to take place in that context. Often this means that the onus is on teachers to apply what they have learned in the training room once they return to their classrooms, but it may be possible for you to work with trainees in context too. What is most important here is trainee reflection during or after the lessons they teach, considering which teaching decisions and actions were effective (in terms of student learning), which were not, and why – and based on that reflection, trying to improve over subsequent lessons. These are the same sorts of actions that expert teachers take in order to continually improve and refine their teaching, and the result is effective professional judgement, or adaptive expertise.

You'll see that learning each type of knowledge involves repetition and, for certain teaching concepts, the process of moving from *knowing about*, to *knowing how*, through to *knowing to* will need to be repeated too, in order to understand concepts at a deeper level. Teachers who are more experienced and further along the path to expertise may find that process more difficult, because revisiting *knowing about* for any given concept involves noticing new elements of it, and experienced teachers have developed particular ways of looking at classroom activity that might make that harder. Similarly, many teaching routines developed as part of *knowing how* may have to be 'unlearned' in order to refine techniques that may have become automatic. That is not easy to do: 'try to keep a lesson running smoothly while trying to consciously override an existing habit or pattern of thought – that's extremely difficult' (Weston & Clay, 2018, p. 28). One solution is the 'intentional destabilisation' (Lubelska & Robbins, 1999, p. 8) of teachers who might be resistant to change, along with well-supported reflection on teaching, but that kind of work is more suited to mentoring or observation situations. So there are some additional challenges for experienced teachers who are trying to develop their skills, because instead of learning new skills they're trying to change existing skills that have already developed to the point of automaticity.

 **CASE STUDY 1.4: MATTHEW**

That first school in London offered me no formal professional development; there was no opportunity for it in the timetables we were given. But I learned a huge amount in that first year of teaching from discussions with colleagues in the staffroom: activities and techniques they used, their approach to planning lessons, useful supplementary resources (both on the staffroom bookshelf and online) and how I could have managed some of the many classroom situations that didn't go according to plan. Schools I worked at later on gave me access to methodology books and regular training sessions and observations, but never with quite the same collegiate atmosphere in the staffroom. I'm sure that a lot of my passion for teaching emerged from those discussions, which was important, because it's a difficult job when you are a new teacher.

Very broadly then, getting trainees from *Knowing about* to *Knowing how* and *Knowing to* involves two changes: firstly, a move from working in the training room with a group of teachers towards working in the classroom with an individual teacher, and secondly, a move from trainees being very reliant on you, the trainer, for information and guidance on a given topic to a situation where trainees can work on that topic more autonomously.

We've covered quite a lot in this chapter, but we can encapsulate much of what we've discussed here in the relatively simple model that follows, which is applicable to every area of training activity.

Balancing the three Ps

One way of looking at the trainer's role is through what we might call the three Ps of training: the Personal, the Professional and the Practical. We use these terms here in specific ways, and we return to them in future chapters. The Practical relates to what teachers *do* in their teaching contexts, and our ultimate goal is to make these actions and decisions as effective as possible in order to maximise student learning. But to do that we need to work not only with what we see teachers doing in the classroom or the staffroom, but also with the Personal: the existing knowledge, experience, beliefs, assumptions, feelings and personalities that they bring to the training room, because those are the foundation for the decisions and actions teachers take. In addition, a large part of our role is to demonstrate how the Professional – the body of knowledge provided by research, theory and other practitioners – can inform or alter the Personal so that teachers can make practical decisions that are as effective as possible in their own contexts. For our training to be successful and have an impact on what teachers do in their classrooms, all three of these Ps need to be present. We discuss how you can ensure that they are as we go through the book.

For now, let us emphasise that the trainer's job is not to simply pass on theories, nor to just demonstrate activities. Those alone will not lead to lasting changes in classroom practice that will stimulate better learning. What we should aim for is 'an approach that considers teacher learning as theorizing of and from practice' (Farrell T. S., 2018, p. 5), which might include:

1. Talking about an aspect of teaching through the beliefs and experiences of the trainees, and providing them with experience of teaching techniques if necessary.

2. Helping trainees develop 'a professional language of teaching drawn from relevant conceptual tools (theories) . . . to talk and think about these experiences' (Malderez & Wedell, 2007, p. 22).

3. Supporting trainees as they weigh up their current practices in relation to the chosen aspect of teaching, and possible (more effective) alternatives.

4. Providing trainees with opportunities to try out those alternatives in the training room, and then in the classroom.

5. Guiding trainees as they reflect on the results in terms of student learning, and perhaps try again.

Obviously, this kind of approach takes time, and it is important to remember that changes in teaching won't happen overnight. To do all this, trainers must be able to:

- Help teachers develop an appropriate knowledge base for teaching, incorporating *Knowing about*, *Knowing how*, and *Knowing to*.

- Build on trainees' prior knowledge and beliefs where appropriate, and challenge beliefs that stand in the way of effective professional learning.

- Act as mediators of research and teaching literature, selecting and interpreting relevant insights to ensure that the knowledge that trainees develop is current, evidence-based and effective.

- Help trainees to tailor their professional learning to the teaching contexts they find themselves in, so they can be effective in a wide variety of teaching situations.

- Support trainees to notice classroom events and the connections between them, balancing the perspectives of teacher and student.

- Nurture trainees to become effective evaluators of their own impact on student learning, so that they can continue to learn and develop once they have left a training or mentoring programme.

This might seem like a tall order now, but remember how you felt as a new teacher and how far you have come since that time. By the end of this book you should feel much more confident in your ability to do all these things!

Summary

We have seen that teaching and learning takes place in a range of contexts, and that the work of the teacher is both limited and enabled by context. We have also considered what constitutes effective teaching, and looked at what teachers need to know in order to be able to get the best learning outcomes from their students. Finally, we have seen how these three areas – teaching context, teaching expertise, and teacher knowledge – impact on how teachers learn and what that learning process involves. Our takeaway from all this is the three Ps model, which we can apply to training sessions, work with individual teachers and the design of courses and programmes. We explore the three Ps in more depth as we look at each of these areas in subsequent chapters.

TASK 1.6

...To trainer

Think about your move from the role of teacher to the role of trainer. What have you read in this chapter which you believe will be the most useful as you transition from one role to the other? Is there anything that you found surprising in this chapter? If so, what and why?

 **TRAINER VOICES**

 Scan the QR Code and watch the videos 'Becoming an expert teacher' and 'Learning to teach' to hear trainers discuss how they developed their teaching skills. How do their experiences affect their training now? Then watch 'Preservice vs. in-service training' to hear the trainers' thoughts on how these differ.

 **TO FIND OUT MORE**

Lubelska, D., & Robbins, L. (1999, November). Moving from teaching to training. *IATEFL Teacher Trainers' SIG Newsletter*, 7–9. (This short article is an excellent comparison of how teacher training differs from teaching, aimed at new trainers.)

Malderez, A., & Wedell, M. (2007). *Teaching teachers: Processes and practices*. London: Continuum. (The first part of this book gives a thorough description of the *Knowing about, Knowing how, Knowing to* model and useful discussion of teacher learning.)

Weston, D., & Clay, B. (2018). *Unleashing great teaching: The secrets to the most effective teacher development*. Abingdon: Routledge. (The early chapters of this book give a neat overview of how teachers learn.)

2 Training sessions: Designing an outline

Here we consider:
- How trainers think about context when designing sessions
- How context helps determine session aims
- The ingredients of a good session outline
- The principles of session design

My starting point is always to try and make sure I understand the training context and its needs in the first place.

Chris, teacher trainer, UK

In the first of three chapters on designing and delivering training sessions, we begin by looking at how to plan an outline for your session. Taking a bird's-eye view in this way before dealing with activities and tasks in detail ensures that the session meets the needs of your trainees, and that it fulfils the principles of effective professional learning.

Your starting point

You're going to design a teacher training session. Where do you begin? In this chapter we use case studies that describe the situations and thought processes of three trainers each designing a session. They begin by describing their training circumstances.

TASK 2.1

From teacher ...

Think back to some of the training sessions you have attended as a participant. Why did the trainer choose to focus on the area covered by the session?

If you have already delivered one or more sessions, how did you decide what to focus on?

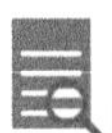

CASE STUDY 2.1: EMAD, THE TRAINING CO-ORDINATOR

I teach English for Academic Purposes (EAP) to students on a foundation year, but part of my job is to provide training for my colleagues here at the English Language Centre in the university in Saudi Arabia where we work. There is a training day once a month, and there are a lot of English teachers working here, so I am part of a team of 4–6 trainers. Unfortunately, we do not have a lot of time for planning because we have teaching responsibilities, so trainers take it in turns to plan the sessions each month and share the materials. This month it is my turn, and the topic is 'giving feedback on academic writing'. This is something that the teachers have asked for help with because the students here find academic writing in English particularly challenging, so I want to make sure it's really useful for them.

CASE STUDY 2.2: MARIE, THE CELTA TRAINER

I work as a CELTA tutor at a small private language school in Ireland, as one of two full-time trainers. Most of the CELTA courses we deliver are intensive four-week courses, so there really isn't very much time to think about the sessions once the course has started – we have a bank of session plans and materials that are ready to use, and every course has more or less the same structure, so I've delivered all the sessions many times now. Nearly all of our trainees are native speakers of English with no teaching experience, and that makes it quite easy for us to know what they will need to learn. Something we've been meaning to do for a while is to add more sessions on teaching young learners (YLs), because many of our trainees seem to be going on to jobs in private language schools where they need to teach children. So I'm in the process of planning a session to introduce some ideas and techniques for doing that.

CASE STUDY 2.3: SOFIA, THE ONLINE TUTOR

I've had a range of teacher training jobs but at the moment I'm working as an online trainer on a country-wide high school teacher training programme for a ministry of education. The teachers have a mixture of face-to-face and online training over a 12-month period, and my role involves running online discussions and virtual seminars (webinars), and liaising with the face-to-face trainers to make sure the programme runs as a coherent whole. Many of the teachers have only had limited training in language teaching so the content of the course is pitched quite low. Right now, we're beginning a new section on developing reading skills, so I need to plan and deliver a webinar that will kick off this part, focusing on the staging of reading lessons.

The trainers in these three case studies have a range of different starting points. Marie has identified a training need based on feedback from former trainees, Emad is fortunate to have had direct requests for training on a particular area, while the driving force behind Sofia's choice of session topic is the course she is delivering. None of the trainers, then, has had to conjure up the focus of the session they are designing from thin air, and you will often find that as a novice trainer, the *what* of a training session is chosen for you, or chooses itself to some extent. Your answers to Task 2.1 may have identified any of the following, all of which point the trainer towards a particular topic area: a request (from teachers, management, or even students), a training course curriculum, a change faced by teachers (e.g., a new course, coursebook or exam) or a programme mandated by an educational authority or ministry of education. Even if a trainer delivers a session based on practices they have recently been experimenting with or learning about, the scope of that session is usually fairly clear from the outset of the design process. The process itself involves narrowing the focus and deciding how to present it in a way that will help trainees teach better, and to start doing that you will need to consider two things: your aims for the session and what we call the training habitat.

TASK 2.2

From teacher ...

What factors do you take into consideration when planning a language lesson for your students? Think about:

- your institution
- the course
- the students

Which of the factors would apply to designing a training session for trainees?

For notes see page 216

Session aims

All sessions should aim to lead to changes in teaching practice amongst trainees, whether those sessions take place as standalone events, or as part of a series or course. Ideally those changes in teaching practice then lead to improved student learning outcomes. A change in practice may not necessarily be classroom-based: modifications to lesson or curriculum planning, to assessment practices or to reflective practice, for instance, are equally valid outcomes, but they would be put into practice outside lessons. At the most modest level, some trainees may leave a session more secure in the knowledge that their current practice is effective, so that they keep doing what they're doing. That is also a valid outcome, but it's far from the best outcome. We're sure you've been a trainee in sessions that were fun and interesting but which had no impact on your teaching – we certainly have. But if teaching and student learning remain completely unaffected following a session, what was the point of it? Most teachers are too short of time to sit in training sessions that don't teach them anything, as David Weston and Bridget Clay point out: 'teaching is a demanding job; it is imperative that professional learning has impact' (2018, p. 25).

Given, then, that the main aim of teacher training is 'to effect changes in teaching so that it results in enhanced students' learning' (Richardson & Díaz Maggioli, 2018, p. 7), session aims must aspire to change behaviour, not simply transfer knowledge. This principle should be familiar to you as a language teacher, especially if you have written aims starting with the words 'by the end of the lesson, students *will be able to . . .* '. There is an expectation that the lesson will lead to demonstrable changes in learners' skills, and the same expectation applies to training sessions with teachers.

There are two differences when it comes to trainees: firstly, unlike students in the language classroom, the change in skills can't be implemented until after the session is over and the trainees go back to teaching. Secondly, the precise nature of lasting changes to teaching practice will take time to establish: trainees will probably need to experiment to see what works and what doesn't within their context, and developing teacher knowledge from *Knowing about* to *Knowing how* and *Knowing to* takes time, trial and error, and reflection. For that reason, we suggest that you write two aims for your training sessions, one relating to what trainees will know as a result of the session, and one describing what they will do in their lessons when they go back to them. You could use the following prompts for this:

> *As a result of the session, trainees will know . . .*
>
> *Following the session, trainees will . . . in their classrooms/ staffrooms*

It can be difficult, of course, to know how or whether a session has affected trainees' knowledge and classroom practice, and this has implications for evaluation (Chapter 4) and training course planning (Chapter 9).

The training habitat

What do the trainers mention when they explain their *what, where, why* and *who* in Case studies 2.1, 2.2 and 2.3? We can break down their descriptions into three main areas:

- the trainees' teaching context, e.g., EAP courses (Emad), or YL classes in private language schools (Marie)

- the training context, e.g., online in-service training (Sofia), or an intensive preservice course (Marie)

- the trainees themselves, both individually and as a group, e.g., inexperienced native speakers (Marie), a large group of teachers under a single ministry of education (Sofia)

As we saw in Chapter 1, your training context and your trainees' teaching contexts will play a big role in how you design your session, and now we see a third element entering the picture: the trainees themselves. Together we think of these three areas as the training habitat. In the natural world, the amount of sun, rainfall and the type of soil all have an effect on which plants will be most successful in a particular habitat. Similarly, the trainees' teaching context, the training context and the trainees themselves should all have an influence on how your session design grows and develops from the initial choice of topic, and on how successful it will be.

There are other ways of thinking about the training situation too; for example, Woodward (1991) breaks it down into tangible factors, intangible factors, people factors and course factors, and you might be able to think of other ways of chopping it up. The key thing, though, is to be aware that these 'parameters' (Woodward, 1991) exist and that they should shape your design decisions, in the same way that teaching context affects teachers' lesson planning decisions. Some parameters can be frustrating – we often wish that we have a bit more space or slightly smaller groups of trainees – but they should also be seen in positive terms too: as 'an interesting design problem rather than a restriction or obligation' (Woodward, 1991, p. 176).

To think about ways your session design might adapt to the training habitat you first need to map out that habitat, and Table 2.1 below lays out the questions that might help you do so. The profile of the trainees, and their needs, are obviously major factors in deciding on the content of a training session. As we saw in Chapter 1, even preservice trainees have firmly established views on teaching, and these need to be considered even when introducing fairly elementary teaching concepts. It is also true that experienced teachers may be very familiar with a particular context but need training to adapt to a new one in which they may have no experience at all, so a considered approach to assessing participants' knowledge and experience is essential. Whatever their level of experience, the approach of the trainer 'should be that it avoids a deficit view of learning, and goes out to meet the learner and accepts what the learner brings to the classroom as being of value' (Edge, 1985, p. 115) – an approach that treats participants as 'blank slates' will almost never be appropriate.

Insights into the trainees and their needs can come from various places. If possible, speak to the trainees themselves to answer the questions in Table 2.1. If that isn't possible, conversations with the academic manager (in in-service training scenarios), with other trainers who are familiar with the training context, or with former trainees, can help to give you an idea of what to expect.

Table 2.1: Initial questions for understanding the training habitat

Teaching context	○ How many students are in a typical class? ○ How are classrooms laid out, and what resources are available? ○ How many hours of teaching do students get each week? ○ What materials are available? Which materials are mandatory? ○ What exams are students expected to sit?	*These questions should help you to work out the parameters of the trainees' contexts, and to think about what **solutions** will be most appropriate to them.*
Training context	○ How many trainees will be present? ○ How will the training room be laid out? ○ How long will the training session(s) last? ○ What materials and resources will be available? ○ Is the session standalone or part of a course? ○ Are other trainers involved?	*These questions will help you with the practicalities of your session design; to think about **what is possible** during the session.*
Trainees	○ What qualifications and experience do the trainees have? ○ What is the trainees' level of English? ○ What needs have been identified on behalf of the trainees? ○ What needs and wants have the trainees identified? ○ How much time do the trainees have for teacher development activity beyond the training session(s)? How do they spend it? Is it paid?	*These questions will help you understand the **needs and motivations** of the trainees, and to think about how the session might fit into the bigger picture of their development.*

Writing your aims

Creating your aims for the session and understanding the training habitat go hand in hand. You may begin with the questions in Table 2.1 and then move on to writing your aims, but you will probably flick between the two tasks as you refine your thoughts about each one. Clarifying the training habitat allows you to identify the gap in trainees' practice that the session will seek to fill, so it makes sense to start with the questions in Table 2.1.

When you've considered those, you should be able to formulate your aims by answering these questions:

1. What is it that trainees should be able to *do* differently as a result of the session?

2. What do the trainees currently do in or out of their classes (if anything) to meet the same need?

3. What do the trainees need to know in order to make the desired change(s) to their practice? What *Knowing about* is essential for the *Knowing how* that you hope trainees will go away with?

4. How will the session provide opportunities for the trainees to experience new practices, and to try them out?

This approach requires you to keep in mind two objectives, one for the end of the session and one for when the teachers return to their classrooms. It's a bit like walking: you watch where you're putting your feet while also keeping an eye on the path ahead. If you can maintain both viewpoints while designing and delivering your session, you will have a good chance of helping teachers improve not just their knowledge, but their practice too.

You may need to return to your analysis of the training habitat after writing your aims to confirm that they are realistic and achievable. For instance, you will need to adapt expected outcomes to the time available in order to be able to deal with the session topic in adequate depth. It is often a good idea to limit the scope of a session and examine a relatively specific area in more detail than to try and squeeze in too much and provide only superficial treatment of a topic.

TASK 2.3

...To trainer

Based on the case studies you read earlier, what aims do you think each of the trainers might set for their sessions? What will each one hope to achieve by the end of the session?

CASE STUDY 2.4: EMAD, THE TRAINING CO-ORDINATOR

As a result of the session, trainees will <u>know</u> a range of evidence-based techniques for giving feedback on academic writing and the principles behind them.

Following the session, trainees will <u>use</u> a range of contextually appropriate evidence-based techniques in their teaching for giving feedback to students on writing.

My goal is to present the teachers who attend the session with a range of techniques that they can use for giving feedback on academic writing. I want them to understand the ideas behind these techniques so that they can decide which ones will work best for them, and how they can adapt them if necessary.

CASE STUDY 2.5: MARIE, THE CELTA TRAINER

As a result of the session, trainees will <u>know</u> how teaching YLs differs from teaching adults, some routines and activities for YL classes, and how to plan a lesson from YL coursebook materials.

Following the session, trainees will <u>use</u> YL-appropriate routines and resources when teaching YL classes, and will <u>seek to develop</u> further if required to teach YLs.

I have tried to be realistic about what is possible in a single session: the trainees should be able to *survive* a YL lesson after this session, but teaching a course will need a lot more training. They will probably have access to a coursebook or other published materials in their future contexts, so I have included some planning work with a representative coursebook. This session is a way in to the topic – no one expects them to be proficient YL teachers after 90 minutes. But it also indicates what teaching skills are transferable to YL classes and what might need to be learned, which is also a door to further development in this area.

CASE STUDY 2.6: SOFIA, THE ONLINE TUTOR

As a result of the session, trainees will <u>know</u> the stages of a typical reading lesson, the rationale behind each stage, and how these stages are typically represented in course materials.

Following the session, trainees will <u>plan</u> reading lessons that are appropriately staged, and <u>adapt</u> course materials where necessary to ensure appropriate staging of reading lessons in their classrooms.

To be honest, one of my main aims is to keep the trainees motivated and engaged with the whole training programme, so one thing I really wanted to do was make the session as relevant as possible, but also as practical and useful as possible. I had to think carefully about how to manage some of the activities because there are things I can't do online that we could do if the session was taking place face-to-face.

Session shapes and the three Ps

Understanding the training habitat makes it possible to start designing ways of maximising the opportunities it presents and overcoming any limitations. For instance, the number of participants in a session plays a part in the types of activities that will work best: smaller numbers allow for more attention to be paid to individuals' contexts, beliefs and needs, and are more suited to interactive, participant-led work. That doesn't mean that such activities can't be used with larger groups – it is a myth that the only suitable format for a large audience is a one-way lecture – but they may need to be set up and managed differently (for suggestions as to how, see Chapter 3).

Before thinking about individual activities and tasks in more detail, however, you will need to sketch out a basic outline of your session. As a teacher you are probably familiar with the concept of lesson shapes, which provide a template for lessons that can be used when planning. Common lesson shapes are Presentation-Practice-Production (PPP), Test-Teach-Test (TTT), or Jason Anderson's Context-Analysis-Practice (CAP) (Anderson, 2017). From a lesson planning perspective, these are useful outlines that help teachers to start thinking about how they can plan and sequence classroom activities in order to achieve their lesson aims. Essentially, each lesson shape involves dividing lesson time into separate building blocks, each with its own aim. The same principle can be applied to the process of designing a training session, but different building blocks are needed because we are teaching teachers, not language students.

We saw in Chapter 1 that successful teacher learning requires trainers to deal with three building blocks of teacher training – the three Ps – for any given topic: the Personal, which concerns teachers' beliefs, assumptions, prior experience and knowledge; the Professional, which involves theories, research and terminology; and the Practical, which consists of the teaching practices that trainees need to adopt or change. To make sure that all these are dealt with as part of a session, we can use each one as building blocks for a session outline. Then we can construct our session shapes from them in various sequences. Let's first see how the trainers in our case studies did this, before thinking about what each building block means in more detail:

CASE STUDY 2.7: EMAD, THE TRAINING CO-ORDINATOR

i. *Trainees evaluate a teacher's feedback on a student essay (PRACTICAL / PERSONAL)*

ii. *Trainer presents key principles from research into feedback techniques on writing (PROFESSIONAL)*

iii. *Based on that, trainees mark a sample of student texts (PRACTICAL)*

iv. *Trainees compare results and reflect (PERSONAL)*

I am using some real student writing as the basis for this session. We only have an hour but I thought it was important to spend time discussing what the teachers' main problems and concerns are and some research findings, and then some time actually giving feedback on the examples I have. The scope of the session is quite narrow so that we can do something useful in only sixty minutes that the teachers will be able to implement straight away.

CASE STUDY 2.8: MARIE, THE CELTA TRAINER

i. *Trainer delivers a model lesson to trainees based on a story (PRACTICAL)*

ii. *Trainees reflect on how language was presented and practised, and how the classroom was managed (PERSONAL)*

iii. *Trainees examine differences between teaching adults and YLs (PROFESSIONAL)*

iv. *Trainees complete a partial lesson plan based around a YL coursebook (PRACTICAL)*

I start by treating the trainees as learners, running through a short lesson sequence, starting with a vocab warmer (using ELT terms as the vocab; the wider context for this session is an intensive preservice course, so I felt it was important to revise some of the concepts we've been working on), then presenting and practising simple language from a story. Then I'm going to get them to reflect on what happened in three separate groups, before an activity to focus on the differences between teaching adults and YLs. The last part is a guided planning activity, so that by the end of the session they will have covered both teaching and planning for YL classes.

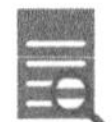

CASE STUDY 2.9: SOFIA, THE ONLINE TUTOR

i.   Trainer delivers a looped reading demonstration lesson (reading about the stages of a reading lesson) (PRACTICAL / PROFESSIONAL)

ii. Trainees reflect and discuss the lesson and the text (PERSONAL)

iii. Trainees comment on some texts from their coursebook and suggest how they could adapt them in the light of the principles they've seen (PRACTICAL)

I've tried to use loop input for this session because I thought it would be motivating for the trainees and an effective use of the time we have. What that means is that the topic of the session is how to stage a reading lesson, and I am going to open with a mini reading lesson using a text on how to stage reading lessons! There's quite a lot to unpack from all that so we'll spend some time discussing it, and then finish by looking at the teachers' coursebooks to see how they might be able to adapt them based on what they've learned.

Practical

Practical session content has two possible aims: either to present teaching practices (and perhaps provide a window into a particular teaching context, as Marie plans to do), or to provide opportunities for trainees to gain hands-on experience of particular teaching practices. So it's not surprising to see Practical stages both at the beginning and at the end of the trainers' sessions because they serve slightly different purposes. For example, Emad has his trainees assessing writing during the opening and closing stages of his session, before and after they consider how they could do so differently. Similarly, Marie's opening stage involves modelling YL teaching practices by treating the trainees as 'students'. At the end of her session, she incorporates another Practical stage, but this time with the trainees in the role of 'teacher', as they try to use what they've learned to plan a lesson.

This all seems quite straightforward, but there are a few considerations for trainers that apply to any Practical stage. Firstly, switching between 'teacher' and 'student' roles like this can be quite a challenge for trainees. It's a change that should be signposted quite clearly, and it takes a moment to sink in. In particular, acting as 'students' requires trainees to participate in the tasks the trainer is modelling but also to pay attention to what is happening so that they can emulate some of the same practices in their own teaching. So a lot of attention is required and the cognitive demands on trainees are high. Nevertheless, the value of modelling good teaching practice in this way cannot be understated, and is a key principle of training (Bailey, 1996; Edge, 1985; Wallace, 1991; Woodward, 2003).

Secondly, an essential element of Practical session stages is reflection. More specifically, trainees should be encouraged to discuss what took place during Practical stages, especially if they were in the role of 'students' during those stages, when cognitive demand is highest. Then they should be guided towards consideration of the aims of the practices they've experienced, whether those practices would support those aims in their own classrooms, and if not, how they could adapt them in order to do so. We can see that all three trainers have done this in their sessions. This reflection incorporates elements of the Personal, and is an important catalyst for bringing *Knowing about* closer to *Knowing how*, so it's not an optional extra. In fact, when activities are demonstrated in the training room it is usually sufficient to demonstrate only part of the activity, and call a halt to it midway through in order to move onto reflective discussion. It's counterintuitive, but the most vital part of Practical stages isn't the practical content, it's the time spent critically evaluating and reflecting on that content!

Thirdly, there is a school of thought which argues that what teachers want from training sessions is practical ideas they can take and use in the very next lesson. Practical applicability is undoubtedly an essential quality of training sessions, but changes in practice need to be *sustained* if they are to have an impact on student learning. So practical ideas – teaching techniques and activities – need to be presented in a way that means they can be absorbed and then applied as part of a principled approach to teaching. Presenting trainees with a succession of activities is indeed practical, and may affect their classes over the subsequent week, but is unlikely to foster lasting change in their teaching. That's where Professional stages come in.

TASK 2.4

From teacher ...

Think back to some of the training sessions you've attended. How many of them:

- put you in the role of student to experience activities and techniques?
- encouraged you to reflect on how you could apply new practices to your own classroom?

How much do you feel the inclusion of modelling and reflection affected the effectiveness of those sessions?

For notes see page 217

Professional

Professional stages provide teachers with the concepts, language and research insights that inform the teaching practices that are covered during the session. In doing so, these stages don't just develop teacher knowledge but also the ability to take part in conversations about teaching, whether in the training room, the staffroom, at teacher conferences, or through the pages of a methodology book. Professional stages therefore provide a platform for further learning once trainees leave the session, in addition to developing trainees' understanding of the teaching practices they are led towards.

All the trainers have included Professional elements in their sessions, either as standalone stages (Emad and Marie) or incorporated into a Practical stage (Sofia). They follow these with further Practical work, in order to give trainees a chance to try applying principles or theories in their own teaching. For many trainees, it's not really clear how Professional content relates to their work until they can 'feel' it in action in this way.

We believe that one of the most important roles of second language teacher trainers is to provide a connection between the teaching profession and research into language and education; to act as mediators between theory and practice by making research and theory intelligible and meaningful to teachers. There are several reasons for this:

1. First of all, we have a responsibility as educators to strive for the best learning outcomes amongst students, and our trainees want those too. That means continuing to evaluate theories of teaching and learning, and updating our training accordingly. The concept of learning styles, for example, and particularly the idea that students are primarily visual, auditory or kinaesthetic learners, has now been disproved, and should no longer be advocated as a basis for teaching practice (Kirschner, 2017; Willingham, Hughes, & Dobolyi, 2015). Many teachers remain unaware of this change or other recent developments, and generally don't have the time to read research papers, or don't have access to them (Borg, 2009), but as a trainer it is part of your role to keep in touch with new findings and pass them on to teachers so that they can take advantage of educational research.

2. Another reason for mediating between research and teaching is that understanding the theoretical foundations for teaching practices enables teachers to apply them flexibly, and to find what will work best in their unique teaching context. As trainers, we are not aiming to prescribe what teachers *should* do based on the results of studies, but to help them understand what *might* work and why. As Woodward states, 'trainers are perhaps in the business, not of changing people but of adding choices and options to their trainees' repertoire' (Woodward, 1991, p. 134). Of course, this means that effective trainers need both breadth and depth of knowledge.

3. Teacher training that does not include a commitment to the Professional begins to look more like folklore – practices and ideas are passed down from one generation of teachers to the next without the principles underpinning them, and as that happens they can become diluted, misunderstood and

ineffective, a phenomenon termed 'lethal mutation' (Leahy & Wiliam, 2012, p. 55). A good example of this is the concept of active learning: one of us once attended an online session in which colouring in pictures was recommended as a strategy for active learning because it 'keeps students busy for ages'. Not only was this a misrepresentation of the concept (for an accurate portrayal of active learning, see www.cambridgeinternational.org/Images/271174-active-learning.pdf), it gave validity to a teaching practice that is more likely to impede language learning than to promote it. Trainers who are familiar with the research that underpins teaching practices are able to avoid this pitfall.

4. Finally, the inclusion of research insights can help to ensure that sessions include meaningful takeaways for more experienced trainees. It's not uncommon for new trainers to worry that they won't have anything new to offer trainees with many years of experience, and although that is not often the case, including recent research findings can help to shed new light on almost any technique or activity. They also provide a signpost towards further information, if trainees want to learn more.

An example of the last point comes from our own professional learning. At the very end of a preservice training course one of us attended, the trainer took a few minutes to 'sum up', and mentioned, quite informally, some books that the trainees might like to explore once they had gained some teaching experience. One of these books was *Uncovering Grammar*, by Scott Thornbury, and for one of us this led to a fundamentally different way of viewing language and language learning, and to further reading on subjects as diverse as chimpanzees, child language acquisition and chaos theory (perhaps not that diverse if you are a parent!) So even minimal Professional input can have far-reaching effects on teaching practice, because it opens the door to much more than can be covered in a single session.

Reliable references on language teaching are widely available from leading academic publishers such as Cambridge University Press, and are on reading lists for courses such as the Cambridge Delta or MA TESOL programmes. But you may be wondering where to get hold of more specific or more recent research findings to support your sessions. The most trustworthy sources are likely to be academic journal articles and books, but there are some excellent resources that are more accessible online too. We discuss how you can develop this side of your training in Chapter 10.

Personal

All the trainers in our case studies aim to find out what their trainees currently do as part of their teaching, and why they do it – what knowledge, experience, beliefs and assumptions underlie the decisions they take. Inevitably, the responses from each trainee will be different, hence the description of these stages as Personal. There are a few complementary aims in doing this:

- For less experienced teachers (and perhaps for some more experienced ones too), who might still be guided by the ghosts of teachers past we saw in Chapter 1, Personal stages are a way of unpicking those habits and beliefs that may be appearing unconsciously. The rationale here is that 'improvement in teaching comes when teachers can turn actions that are automatic and routine into ones that are considered' (Freeman, 2016, p. 221).

- For experienced teachers, Personal stages are an opportunity to draw out and share the expertise they've gained from experience, and to integrate new learning into that experience.

- Finally, all teachers need to take charge of their own development and also assimilate insights from teacher training into that development. So Personal stages in training sessions help trainees to 'systematically explore their beliefs and classroom practices so that they take responsibility for their own development throughout their careers' (Farrell, 2018, p. 4).

We have already seen that Personal content forms a part of Practical stages, in the form of reflection on practice. In those stages, the subject of reflection is teaching practices that trainees have just experienced, such as Marie's initial lesson demonstration. In Personal stages, the subject of reflection is more likely to be trainees' past experience of teaching or their current classroom practice, or material presented by the trainer designed to elicit trainee beliefs and assumptions. So there's a subtle difference involved: in Practical stages trainees are reflecting on experiences in the same session, in which they were in the role of students. Whereas in Personal stages they are reflecting on time they have spent and will spend in real classrooms, both as teachers and as learners.

One of the key elements in Personal stages is *support* for trainee reflection. It can be difficult to delve into your thoughts and uncover beliefs and assumptions about teaching, and even more difficult to then share them with peers. The process can feel threatening because there's no single correct answer, confusing because it is new, and frustrating because it is always a challenge to make tacitly held ideas explicit. But we want our trainees to develop skills in reflective practice so that they can become the evaluative practitioners we discussed in Chapter 1. It is therefore important during these stages that trainers provide plenty of support to trainees during Personal stages, by modelling what is expected, providing clearly staged tasks to work from, and offering plenty of encouragement (activities for doing this appear in Chapter 3).

Staging your session

The main questions behind the content of each type of stage – Personal, Professional or Practical – are given in Table 2.2. The answers to these questions should emerge in the session itself.

Table 2.2: Questions for deciding on content

Practical	○ What relevant techniques or activities might teachers use in the classroom? How do they relate to Professional content? ○ What relevant procedures might teachers use before or after teaching? How do they relate to Professional content?
Professional	○ What theories and frameworks of language, language learning, or language teaching are relevant to the topic? ○ What is the evidence underpinning these? ○ What are the key terms used by teachers to discuss the topic?
Personal	○ What do trainees already know about this topic? ○ How do they use that knowledge as part of their teaching practice? ○ What beliefs and assumptions around the topic do trainees hold, and how do these influence their teaching practice? ○ What opportunities and constraints are presented by the trainees' teaching contexts in relation to this topic? ○ How might the trainees adapt practices they see in the session for their own specific context and teaching style?

In designing your session outline, you'll need to decide on the order of Practical, Professional and Personal stages, and on the balance between them. Below are the three trainers' outline session designs. The details of each session procedure have been omitted for now (activities and training practices are given in Chapter 3) so that we are able to focus on the broader aims and shape of each session. As you read these, bear in mind that the session plan format is there to help guide your thought processes as you design your own sessions – once you become more familiar with designing and delivering sessions you won't need to write them out in full, or perhaps at all (novice teachers go through a similar process in relation to lesson plans).

TASK 2.5

From teacher ...

All the trainers have used the same template to write out their session designs. What elements of the template do you recognise from a typical language teaching lesson plan?

Based on those similarities, what principles of language teaching can be applied to training language teachers (for example, *set learning outcomes*)?

Is there anything that you don't recognise, or that you feel is missing?

For notes see page 217

<table>
<tr><td colspan="2">Emad's EAP session</td></tr>
<tr><td>Title</td><td>Giving feedback on academic writing</td></tr>
<tr><td>Profile</td><td>Multiple groups of up to 20 in-service teachers of EAP in a university context</td></tr>
<tr><td>Time</td><td>60 minutes</td></tr>
<tr><td>Resources</td><td>Student texts on handouts, projector</td></tr>
<tr><td>What trainees will know</td><td>As a result of the session, trainees will know a range of evidence-based techniques for giving feedback on academic writing and the principles behind them.</td></tr>
<tr><td>What trainees will do</td><td>Following the session, trainees will use a range of contextually appropriate evidence-based techniques for giving feedback to students on writing.</td></tr>
<tr><td>Procedure</td><td>Here's a text. What do you think of the teacher's feedback? (PRACTICAL)

What feedback would you give, how and why? (PERSONAL)

Theories of feedback on writing (PROFESSIONAL)

Based on that, mark this text. Compare and discuss. (PRACTICAL)

Reflect on main takeaways. (PERSONAL)</td></tr>
</table>

Figure 2.1: Emad's session outline

<table>
<tr><td colspan="2">Marie's YL session</td></tr>
<tr><td>Title</td><td>Introduction to teaching young learners</td></tr>
<tr><td>Profile</td><td>12 preservice trainees, all native speakers of English. They are nearing the end of an intensive 4-week course on the basics of communicative language teaching to adults. This is the first session dealing with YLs.</td></tr>
<tr><td>Time</td><td>90 minutes</td></tr>
<tr><td>Resources</td><td>Storybook and flashcards for the lesson demo

Pre-prepared cards for the sorting activity

Selection of YL coursebooks</td></tr>
<tr><td>What trainees will know</td><td>As a result of the session, trainees will know how teaching YLs differs from teaching adults, some routines and activities for YL classes, and how to plan a lesson from YL coursebook materials.</td></tr>
<tr><td>What trainees will do</td><td>Following the session, trainees will use YL-appropriate routines and resources when teaching YL classes, and will seek to develop further if required to teach YLs.</td></tr>
<tr><td>Procedure</td><td>Model lesson (PRACTICAL)

Reflection in small groups on: Presenting language, Practising language and Managing the classroom (PERSONAL)

Differences between teaching adults and YLs (card sorter) (PROFESSIONAL)

Using YL materials to plan a lesson (PRACTICAL)

Trainees share their plans and reflect on the planning process. (PERSONAL)</td></tr>
</table>

Figure 2.2: Marie's session outline

<table>
<tr><td colspan="2">Sofia's online session</td></tr>
<tr><td>Title</td><td>Staging reading lessons</td></tr>
<tr><td>Profile</td><td>Up to 200 in-service trainees attending through individual webinar connections. They can see and hear the trainer but the trainer can only see text messages from trainees in a chat box as part of the webinar.</td></tr>
<tr><td>Time</td><td>60 minutes</td></tr>
<tr><td>Resources</td><td>Slideshow, downloadable reading text</td></tr>
<tr><td>What trainees will know</td><td>As a result of the session, trainees will know the stages of a typical reading lesson, the rationale behind each stage, and how these stages are typically represented in course materials.</td></tr>
<tr><td>What trainees will do</td><td>Following the session, trainees will plan reading lessons that are appropriately staged, and adapt course materials where necessary to ensure appropriate staging of reading lessons in their classrooms.</td></tr>
<tr><td>Procedure</td><td>Looped reading demonstration lesson (reading about stages of a reading lesson) (PRACTICAL / PROFESSIONAL)

Reflective discussion about the lesson using teacher quotations as prompts (PERSONAL)

Trainees to comment on some texts from their coursebook and suggest how they could adapt them in the light of the principles given (PRACTICAL)

Reflective task – what can you implement in your next lesson?</td></tr>
</table>

Figure 2.3: Sofia's session outline

What do we learn about session shapes from the three outlines? All of them include Practical, Professional and Personal elements, and they all 'sandwich' Professional and Personal content within Practical stages. In general, the opening Practical stage is expository – trainees are allowed to experience the teaching practices that are the focus of the session. The closing Practical stages, on the other hand, are there to allow trainees to put into practice what they have learned, and to set them up for applying appropriate changes in their professional contexts. Despite these similarities, there is flexibility, too: Sofia incorporates the Professional element in her opening Practical stage, and of course other options are possible: Emad, for instance, could start his session by providing the evidence-based feedback techniques to trainees before they look at the example feedback.

His reason for not doing that is probably to do with engaging and motivating the trainees. All the session outlines engage trainees from the very beginning of the session by involving them in practical activity. Edge highlights the value of this: 'at each level of training, most units should begin with a practical classroom event, usually based on a piece of current teaching material. This establishes immediate relevance in the mind of the trainee' (Edge, 1985, p. 115). Starting with an activity also means that within the first few minutes trainees have a tangible 'takeaway' from the session – as long as the activity is new to them!

The other similarity between all the session outlines above is that each one ends with reflection. This is slightly different to the reflective activities that appear earlier in the sessions because it is principally forward-looking – for that reason it might be better described as 'preflection'. Trainees consider what they have learned during the session and its relevance to their upcoming classes. The aim is for the trainees to make a specific plan to implement new practices and see how well they work in their own teaching contexts.

Summary

Let's try and distil what we've seen in this chapter into a handful of key principles of session design.

Principle 1: Sessions are shaped by the training habitat

As we have seen, trainers consider the trainees' teaching contexts, the training context and the characteristics of the trainees themselves when designing sessions. This means the needs of participants (both as teachers in their classrooms and as learners in the context of a programme) and the resources available have an impact on design decisions. A good trainer will take these parameters into account in order to ensure that the session is as relevant and useful to trainees as possible.

Principle 2: Sessions aim to have an impact on classroom practice

We are aiming to improve student learning outcomes by developing our trainees' teaching practice. This means that there is a behavioural change on the part of trainees, and this should be captured in the aims we aspire to in designing sessions. Trainers need to think about what they want to achieve by the end of the session, but also remember that trainees don't have a chance to demonstrate meaningful learning until they've got back into the classroom.

Principle 3: Sessions balance the three Ps

Various session shapes can be described in terms of the Practical–Professional–Personal model introduced in Chapter 1. Each element has its own internal principles:

- **Practical** – practices are modelled, not described, and followed by critical reflection. Where possible trainees are given opportunities to try things out.

- **Professional** – training is evidence-based, bridging theory, research and practice, and develops trainees' ability to engage in professional discourse.

- **Personal** – guided exploration of trainees' prior experience, beliefs and assumptions about teaching is a central part of sessions.

All the trainers here have chosen a 'sandwich' session shape, with Practical stages as the 'bread' and Professional and Personal stages as the 'filling'. This is not the only possible design, but we find that it works well.

Principle 4: Start with a bang, end with reflection

A practical start to the session engages participants and can set out the topic area. 'Preflection' at the end ensures that learning doesn't stop when people leave the training room, and that it is carried into subsequent teaching. This principle gives you a useful place to start outlining the session procedure, because you can immediately allocate ten minutes at the end of the session for reflection tasks, and start thinking about how to open the session in a practical way.

Once you have an outline for your session, it's time to start thinking in more detail about what you and the trainees will do at each stage. That's the focus of the next chapter.

 **TRAINER VOICES**

 Scan the QR Code and watch the videos 'Planning a training session' and 'Adapting to the training context' to hear how trainers put the principles we've looked at into practice.

 **TO FIND OUT MORE**

Holmes, A. (2017). Training is teaching. *ET Professional, 111*, 49–51. (This article suggests an alternative shape for training sessions: a *Purposeful introduction>Experiential phase>Reflection phase* model.)

Hughes, J. (2015). *A practical introduction to teacher training in ELT.* Hove: Pavilion. (In this book John Hughes proposes a *What?>Why?>How?* model for planning training sessions.)

Woodward, T. (1991). *Models and metaphors in language teacher training: Loop input and other strategies.* Cambridge: Cambridge University Press. (Includes a useful discussion of training context in Chapter 19.)

3 Training sessions: Activities and materials

Here we consider:
- Activities and materials for Practical stages
- Activities and materials for Personal stages
- Activities and materials for Professional stages
- Activities to end a session
- How to decide what to include in the session

When training teachers, we need to practise what we teach.

Rawya, teacher trainer, Egypt

In this chapter we build on the three Ps model of Chapter 2 to outline what materials and tasks can be used at each stage of a training session. If you need to design your own sessions, you should have a much clearer idea of how to develop new tasks by the end of this chapter. If you mostly deliver sessions designed by someone else, you'll be able to critically evaluate them and make changes if necessary.

Practical

Practical stages aim to demonstrate teaching practices or have trainees experience practices in order to then reflect on them. If possible, they also aim to provide opportunities for trainees to implement those practices and get feedback on them. Here's how the trainers we met in Chapter 2 chose to realise the Practical stages in their sessions:

 ### CASE STUDY 3.1: EMAD, THE TRAINING CO-ORDINATOR

My session has two Practical stages which are at the beginning and at the end. In both of those the trainees will look at a piece of student work and they will have to give feedback on it. So the session shape is like Test-Teach-Test in a teacher's lesson plan.

For the first Practical stage I will give the trainees two pieces of material: the student writing, and some sample feedback. Then they have to discuss if they believe the feedback is effective or not, and why. I was going to just give them the student writing and ask them what feedback they would give, but I decided that it was too intimidating. Some of the teachers are very experienced but others are very new, and I thought that the new ones would be afraid to explain their ideas. If they only have to comment on the feedback of someone else then it is easier and faster.

In the second Practical stage the trainees will give feedback on a different piece of writing. They will compare their comments and opinions, so I hope that they will all feel more confident then.

CASE STUDY 3.2: MARIE, THE CELTA TRAINER

I'm starting my session with a mini-lesson, because I want the trainees to feel how different a young learner class is from what they've been studying up to now. The content isn't totally authentic because I'm using a vocab game – backs to the board – as a warmer to recycle some of what we've already covered on the training course, and you wouldn't teach words like *realia* to young learners! I feel that I have to do this though because there is so much to get through on the course. For the rest of the demonstration the trainees will be in the shoes of YL students, so they'll see how I use a story to present language and then some activities for practising it. Obviously, there's not time to run through a whole lesson so I will cut most of the activities short – the important thing is that they get a sense of how it all works, and there is enough for me to demonstrate some classroom management techniques too.

I've also designed a Practical stage to finish the session, but this time the trainees are doing the work: they need to plan a young learner lesson using some coursebooks that I've collected. I think it'll be challenging, but I plan to have them doing this in groups so that they can support each other, and I'll be there as they're doing it to help, too.

Staffroom practices

Not all teaching practices take place in the classroom. Some of what teachers do, such as planning lessons or marking student work, happens elsewhere. Both Emad and Marie have incorporated these 'staffroom practices' into their training sessions: Emad is focusing on assessment of writing, and Marie is dealing with planning. In both cases the trainees are doing teaching tasks with teacher materials, so these activities are directly applicable to their professional lives. The difference in the training room is that they have more support with these tasks as they complete them.

Emad provides support to his trainees by presenting a model of writing assessment, and then later in the session inviting teachers to mark a piece of writing based on the techniques he presents. They have the chance to compare their opinions and discuss them at the end. Marie provides support to her trainees with their planning task by selecting suitable materials for them, having them plan in groups, and making herself available during the planning stage to answer questions and provide guidance. Supporting teachers in these ways means that routine teaching tasks become training tasks because the trainees have access to alternative approaches and ways of thinking, as well as feedback on their efforts. Table 3.1 lists some of the materials and tasks that could be used as part of training on staffroom practices. Combining these in various ways creates a wide range of task options for trainers.

Table 3.1: Materials and tasks for training staffroom practices

Planning practices	Materials: ○ Sample lesson plans ○ Coursebook material ○ Supplementary material ○ Authentic texts (video, images, etc.)	Possible tasks: ○ Analyse a lesson plan ○ Evaluate a lesson plan ○ Improve a lesson plan ○ Complete a lesson plan ○ Adapt a lesson plan for different contexts ○ Create a lesson plan
Assessment and feedback practices	Materials: ○ Samples of student work (marked or unmarked) ○ Lesson transcripts ○ Recordings of student talk	Possible tasks: ○ Evaluate feedback on marked work ○ Mark student work and give feedback on it ○ Give feedback on students' performance in a speaking task

TASK 3.1

...To trainer

What are the advantages and disadvantages of using staffroom practices in your session instead of classroom practices?

For notes see page 218

Classroom practices

Trainees can occupy various roles as part of Practical stages. They might be acting as students, as trainee teachers, or as teachers putting learning into practice. Similarly, the content that trainees work with might be student content (i.e., the same materials that students would use in the classroom), trainee content (focused on learning to teach), or teacher content (e.g., a lesson plan or teacher's book). If we plot these various possibilities on a spectrum as in Figure 3.1 below, we get a good overview of the activities and tasks that might go into a Practical stage (this is an extension of ideas outlined by Woodward (1991)).

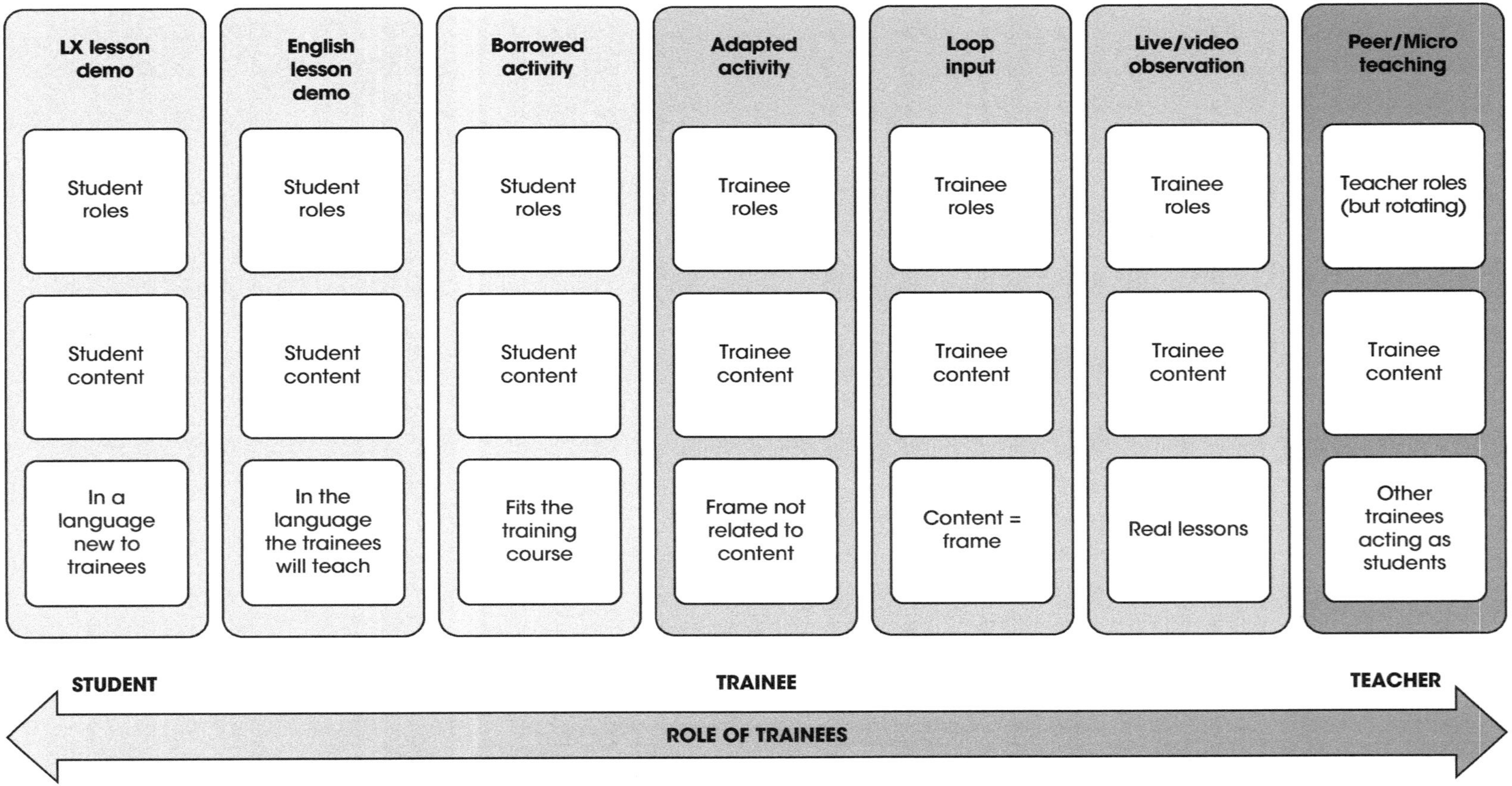

Figure 3.1: Possibilities for presenting classroom practices

Presenting teaching practices

Procedures that involve trainees in the role of student or trainee are ideal for *presenting* teaching practices:

LX lesson demonstrations are a relatively common feature of preservice courses. The group of trainees is given a lesson in a language unknown to all of them ('LX' is used here as a value-neutral alternative to 'L2' or 'foreign language' (Dewaele, 2018)), and the lesson is usually followed by trainer-led discussion. These demonstrations can be a useful way of helping trainees to empathise with their students and they tend to be well received, but they are somewhat artificial: the trainees probably have no particular desire to learn the chosen language, they may not expect to teach complete beginners, and – perhaps most importantly – they may already have plenty of experience as language learners.

An **English lesson demonstration** (assuming that the trainees are teachers of English) is perhaps the most common approach we see to presenting practice. In fact, many teachers take their first steps into teacher training because they have activities to share that they've found to be particularly effective, and they do that by demonstrating them with trainees in the role of students – this approach needn't be used with a complete lesson. Two things are important from the trainer's point of view: managing the shift from 'trainee' to 'student' and back again, and managing the reflective discussion that follows the demonstration. We have found the following procedure helpful:

- Tell the trainees they're now 'students'. They need to wear two hats: They're going to participate in language learning activities, but they will discuss them with their teacher hats on afterwards.

- The trainer carries out the activity/lesson exactly as they would in the classroom. The only difference is that it may not be necessary to let it run to its conclusion. If the trainees have experienced enough of each activity to have a clear idea of how it works (two to three minutes), the session can move on.

- Tell trainees to put their teacher hats back on. They should work in pairs or groups to discuss these questions:
  - What happened? What did the teacher do? What did trainees do? Why?
  - What is the aim of the activity? When would it be useful?
  - What preparation did the teacher need to do for the activity?
  - What would be an effective way of following up on the activity?

- ○ Would the activity work in the trainees' contexts?

- ○ If not, how could it be adapted so as to be useful?

- Trainees will need a record of the activity/lesson and the discussion – this might be a handout or they may need time to make notes.

This routine can be used whenever teaching practices are demonstrated with trainees in the role of students. The initial questions about what happened are important, because it is very difficult to participate as a student in the demonstration and at the same time take note of what is happening in the room. Once trainees are clear about what took place, they can begin to reflect on it with the help of the remaining questions.

Along the same lines, a **negative model** can sometimes be quite effective. This follows the procedure above but instead of carrying out the lesson as they would in the classroom, the trainer deliberately models ineffective teaching. In the subsequent discussions the task for trainees is to consider how the techniques they saw could be improved upon. This kind of demonstration can be an effective way of encouraging trainees to think more critically about what they see in classrooms, including their own.

A **borrowed activity** is simply the appropriation of a classroom activity for the training room, when chosen learning outcomes coincide. The most common examples are icebreaker or getting-to-know-you activities at the start of a course – these can be transplanted directly into the training room because the goals are the same. Other examples might be activities for raising trainees' language awareness, which may be the same as those used in class with learners. Although trainees will benefit from the activity as it is (e.g., by bonding with peers or with increased language knowledge), borrowed activities are also an opportunity to develop teaching skills if the reflective discussion procedure above is followed.

An **adapted activity** is the use of an activity format from the language classroom, but with content relevant to trainees. Marie does this in her session (Case study 3.2) when she demonstrates a vocabulary revision game that is relevant to teaching young learners (the focus of her session), but uses it to revise terminology that her trainees have learned at other points during the course. Again, the reflective discussion procedure should be followed afterwards, perhaps with emphasis on how trainees could adapt the activity to their own contexts.

Loop input is the term coined by Woodward (1991) for practical activities in which the content of the activity mirrors the process that trainees go through. Sofia has chosen this approach for her online session:

 **CASE STUDY 3.3: SOFIA, THE ONLINE TUTOR**

I want the trainees to leave the session with an understanding of the stages of a reading lesson. So I am going to begin the session by actually teaching a short reading lesson, and the text I'm using is about the stages of a reading lesson. Before reading, the trainees have to predict which activities will be mentioned in the text. Then they read to find out if they were correct. Then there are some True/False questions they have to answer about the text, and finally there is a group discussion task, although sadly that will be very brief because we are limited to discussion that is typed into the chat box. So the trainees learn about staging reading lessons in two ways: from the text that they read, and from the stages of the demo lesson that they actually take part in.

> **TASK 3.2**
>
> **...To trainer**
>
> What do you think the pros and cons of using loop input for teacher training might be?
>
> *For notes see page 218*

Loop input can be used for a wide range of session topics (for examples, see Woodward, 1991). Although trainees don't have to deal with a change in role, the reflective discussion is important for teasing apart content and process, and for helping trainees consider how student content would work as part of the same process.

Live observation can be an excellent way of presenting practices, but in our experience is often underused. It has one significant advantage over the techniques above, which is that trainees are not in the role of students, so they are able to observe real student behaviour. That's important for all trainees, but particularly for novice teachers, who naturally focus more on teacher actions than on evidence of student learning. The challenge with observation is the extraordinary amount of information it presents to trainees; focusing on one student during one activity offers plenty of food for thought, let alone a whole class of students for an entire lesson. Trainers, therefore, need to support trainees by directing their attention to particular features of the lesson through tasks.

If you are observing the lesson alongside the trainee(s), instant messaging (e.g., Skype, Slack) is a good way of doing this, because tasks can be given in response to events in the room, and the resulting text can provide useful feedback to the teacher afterwards. If you are not in the classroom then a pre-prepared task will be necessary – for an excellent range of examples see Wajnryb (1992).

Video observation is of course very similar but has the additional benefit of providing much more focused 'bursts' of observation because specific clips can be chosen to exemplify particular classroom behaviours. These clips can be re-watched multiple times, and tasks can be prepared that are closely tailored to what takes place. When the focus is on classroom interaction, **audio 'observation'** may be just as useful, with the benefit of focusing attention more strongly on classroom talk because there are no visual distractions. **Transcripts of lesson** activity can also work for this, although with no visuals or paralinguistic cues so much is lost that they are rarely the first-choice resource.

With all these forms of observation for presenting practice, trainee reflection is really taking place throughout (guided by the tasks set by the trainer), so although there will be some post-observation discussion, it may be shorter than similar phases that follow some of the techniques above. It may also be more trainee-driven, as there are often points of interest raised by trainees that fall outside the topic chosen by you.

Trying out teaching practices

Providing hands-on experience in the training room is more difficult than just presenting practices. Staffroom practices can be tried out easily, as Emad and Marie show, but classroom practices need students. Of course, one way that trainees can apply new classroom routines is in teaching practice (see Chapter 6), but there will be times when you want to offer more immediate opportunities for trainees to 'get stuck in'.

Microteaching is perhaps the most familiar technique for doing that. As the name suggests, it is small-scale teaching: groups of no more than five or six (most often other trainees acting as the students), and 'lessons' of no more than ten minutes or so, with an appropriately scaled-down learning outcome. In most contexts nowadays trainees will take turns to microteach each other during the session. In its original form, they taught volunteer students, microteaching sessions were videotaped to allow trainers to give immediate feedback to trainees, and students also provided feedback. The microlesson would then be delivered again (Fortune, Cooper, & Allen, 1967).

The important thing is to consider what roles trainees will play (will they all act as students when not teaching, or will some observe?), who will give feedback to those teaching and how (video-supported, or student-supported), and what the intended outcome is in terms of teaching practice. We have found microteaching works best when trainees are able to work in groups of four or five, rotating the role of the teacher with other group members as students. In this way, all trainees in a fairly large group can gain practical familiarity with a technique in only an hour. What is especially important is that there is a particular teaching skill being focused on (e.g., teaching three or four vocabulary items; managing a choral drill; monitoring pair discussion in order to give language feedback) – the format is far less effective when the instruction to trainees is simply 'teach for ten minutes'.

In certain situations, particularly online or with large groups of trainees, the training context is such that it is very difficult, or even impossible, to provide trainees with hands-on experience of new teaching practices during the session, there in the training room. One solution is to simply describe activities and techniques, or to invite the trainees to brainstorm and share practices that they are familiar with, perhaps through peer presentations. Another possibility is to use lesson plans as a form of 'observation through text', relying on trainees' imaginations and knowledge of the classroom to bring them to life. Rod Ellis asks if, with these various substitutes for hands-on practice, we can 'really influence what teachers *do* in the classroom by making them *think* about the principles and practice of teaching in sessions remote from the classroom?' (Ellis, 1990, p. 27). The answer, in our experience, is yes. But in order for that to happen it is vital that teachers carry out the hands-on practice of new teaching ideas in their own classrooms. The final reflection stage (see below) of the session is essential to make sure that that happens.

Personal

The activities that support the Personal aspects of teacher education all share one thing in common: discussion. As an experienced teacher, you might feel quite comfortable with these stages of your sessions – they can seem very similar to language lessons, with the satisfying sound of people working energetically together in pairs or groups. But it's important to remember that discussions in the training room have quite different aims, because in most situations we're not trying to teach language. Instead, training room discussions are an opportunity:

- for trainees to share and reflect on how they do what they do

- to elicit teacher beliefs and assumptions, and challenge them if necessary

- for trainees to consider how they could apply concepts to their own teaching contexts

- to build trainees' identities as teachers, and to help them develop autonomy over their professional learning and development

- to model ways of setting up and managing speaking tasks

Let's see how the trainers in our case studies set up Personal stages and exploit these opportunities in their sessions:

CASE STUDY 3.4: EMAD, THE TRAINING CO-ORDINATOR

I am going to elicit what the teachers do and their beliefs with one question that follows their evaluation of the marked writing sample.

Do you give feedback in the same way? Why / why not?

I will do this as a Think-Pair-Share: the teachers can consider their answers individually first, then discuss them in pairs, and finally share them in plenary. By the end of the discussion we should see what the teachers do to give feedback on writing, and the beliefs and aspects of context that lead them to take those actions.

CASE STUDY 3.5: MARIE, THE CELTA TRAINER

My trainees are going to discuss the YL lesson that I model for them, and there's quite a lot for them to talk about. So to focus the discussion, and to allow them to explore topics fully, I'm dividing the class into three groups. Each group has a different topic, and what I want the discussion to focus on is a comparison of what they saw in the model lesson and what they have learned so far on this course – basically similarities and differences between teaching adults and teaching kids.

Every group has a flipchart, and I'm going to ask them to put their ideas onto the flipcharts and use that to report back to the whole class when the discussions are over. I'll be moving around the room listening as they talk, and if I hear any misunderstandings I'll probably intervene to help unpick them. Then after the session I'll share photos of each of the flipcharts and some comments with the trainees so that they've got a record of the discussion.

CASE STUDY 3.6: SOFIA, THE ONLINE TUTOR

In my face-to-face training, I really enjoy discussing the teachers' reactions and feelings to what they are learning. So this part of the session was very hard for me to design, because we cannot talk, we can only type into the chat box during the online session. And if teachers are confused, or if they disagree with the approach I'm showing them, it's really easy for them to withdraw and stop participating during this stage, and I don't want that.

I know that for many of the teachers, a reading lesson means reading the text aloud with the class, and then translating it word by word. What I decided in the end was to anticipate their concerns about adopting a more communicative approach and represent those concerns with quotes from teachers that they can rate according to how much they agree. I've made up the quotes, of course, but I think the teachers will still feel that it makes their concerns valid and be more open to discussing them.

Formats for discussion

Setting up discussions is a routine task for experienced teachers, and the same formats that you use in your language lessons can be used in the training room too (Table 3.2).

Table 3.2: Classroom discussion formats that can be used in the training room

Format	How it works	What it's good for
Jigsaw	Trainees in initial groups (AAA, BBB, CCC) each discuss different topics, then regroup (ABC, ABC, ABC) to exchange findings.	Covering several different related topics in a relatively short space of time (e.g., discussion of several different methods in a session on methodology).
Mingle	Trainees stand and mingle, speaking to as many peers as possible.	Sharing a wide range of viewpoints and experiences.
Think-Pair-Share	Trainees spend one to two minutes thinking about the task, then share their thoughts with a partner. Finally, they share the main points of their discussion with the class.	More in-depth questions that require reflection and careful thought.
Plenary	A whole-class discussion, chaired by the trainer.	Questions about the topic shared by many trainees in the group; insights that the whole group should know to achieve the learning outcomes for the session.
Groups	Discussion in groups of four to six trainees. It is helpful to nominate a note-taker.	Tasks that require trainees to reach a consensus, or to brainstorm ideas.
Debate	Debate with class divided into 'for' and 'against' the motion.	Questions of practice with no clear answer (e.g., should teachers write their aims on the board at the start of the lesson?)

Uncovering beliefs

As part of Personal stages, trainers want to elicit teacher beliefs about teaching in order to work with them in the training room. To do that, you can ask people what they believe, but this is usually not a very helpful strategy. Quite often respondents are not sure what their beliefs are, or they tell you what they think you want to hear, which is of no use if you want to understand what is underpinning their decisions in class. Or they may simply not want to answer. After all, there is plenty of potential for embarrassment, particularly if colleagues are in the room.

So a more useful way of approaching teacher beliefs is with a prompt of some kind that trainees can react to. Usually their reactions reveal far more than a direct question would, and offer an easier route to more in-depth discussion. Sofia's lesson is the best example of this – the online context means she is more removed from her trainees, and the large number of attendees makes it easy for more reticent teachers to hide away, but she has planned a task that makes it as easy as possible for trainees to discuss their beliefs, without necessarily revealing that they are *their* beliefs.

Emad takes actual teaching practice – an example of marking – as his prompt, but brings the trainees' own practice into the discussion. Marie also prompts her trainees with actual teaching practice – her demo lesson – but is also interested in encouraging the trainees to contrast it with the practices they've seen on her course so far (remember that they have very limited practice of their own to explore). So the pattern with all these examples of Personal stages is:

Figure 3.2: The process of eliciting beliefs

Prompts for discussion

Teacher or student **opinions** are excellent prompts because they present varying perspectives on teaching clearly and without requiring trainees to put their own beliefs or practice to the group for judgement. Like Sofia, you can make them up yourself, but you might find that as you work more with teachers you collect some quite useful real quotations. There are also plenty of good quotations online, too, of course. Here are some examples (quoted in Mayne, 2019):

> 'Listen and repeat' is no good for practising pron. You have to get physical.

> Textbooks are a good idea. Somebody took the time to plan a course not just so that you don't need to but because you couldn't do a better job AND teach at the same time.

> The 'subject knowledge' that English teachers are supposed to be experts in is LANGUAGE.

Get creative with how you present these opinions, and try to model the principle of presenting language in context. For example, you could provide trainees with a dialogue overheard in a staffroom, a letter to a newspaper, a text message between students, a teacher's email to parents, a cartoon strip, and so on.

Images can be excellent sources of discussion, particularly images of teaching and learning situations or artefacts. They can often be so thought-provoking that trainees will begin discussing what they see without having been set a specific task. Figure 3.3 is an example of an image to prompt discussion on the topic of boardwork:

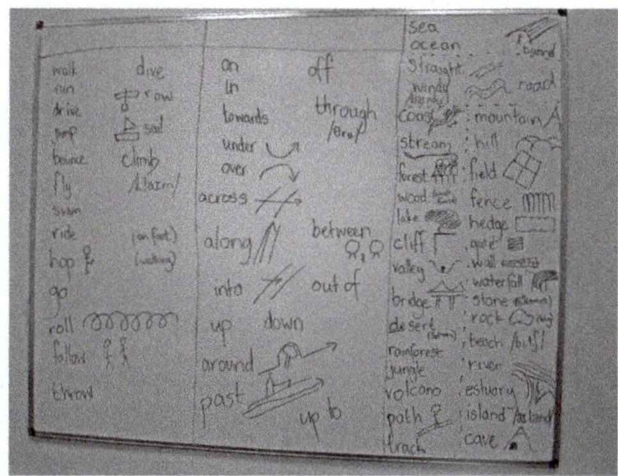

Figure 3.3: An example of boardwork for discussion

Metaphors are rather like images painted by (or revealed by) words, so they work very similarly as discussion prompts. Thornbury argues that 'to teachers in their classrooms . . . it is the *image* of teaching that has potency, not the *theory* of teaching' (Thornbury, 1991, p. 196), and highlights that when trainees' images of teaching clash with those underlying the practices they are expected to adopt, the result is likely to be frustration (and ineffective teaching – recall the study we described on page 17). Working with metaphors can help to bring trainees' mental images of teaching to the fore so that they can examine them and consider what practices align with them.

2 In your opinion, the teaching of language is most
  similar to the teaching of which of the following?
  (Choose one only.)

  maths   history   swimming   the piano
  chemistry   carpentry   typing   law
  Why?

3 In your opinion, which of the following jobs would
  best prepare a person for language teaching?
  (Choose one only.)

  sports coach   actor   social worker
  tour group leader   lecturer   sales person
  driving instructor   nurse
  Why?

Figure 3.4: Examples of awareness-raising tasks using metaphors (Thornbury, 1991)

Critical incidents work by using events from teachers' professional lives as prompts for discussion. The idea, outlined as a teacher education tool by David Tripp, is to consider a small snippet of school activity in detail, a situation chosen by a teacher either because it stood out in some way for them at the time, or because it is indicative of something more meaningful despite appearing to be quite mundane. As we saw in Chapter 1, classroom practice can often be guided by instinct rather than conscious reasoning, so the aim of thinking critically and systematically about routine events is to uncover the relationship between teaching beliefs and teaching practice, and between specific biographical incidents and broader pedagogical principles. In this way, trainees become more aware of how their beliefs and assumptions affect their practice and become more able to make lasting changes to them, turning 'an incident that was not particularly important at the time it occurred into one which is important to [trainees] for all time' (Tripp, 1994, p. 71).

This process begins with a simple description. Tripp gives an example of an incident in which a student, Mary, raises her hand and asks to sharpen her pencil. Turning this into a critical incident involves first explaining Mary's actions within the immediate context (she is following a class rule that students must ask the teacher before they can get up from their desks), and then 'zooming out' from that context to find what the incident means more generally. In this case the incident is an example of how student decision making is limited in many schools, and we can then decide if we agree with this position or not, and how our teaching might change as a result.

As you can see, the incident itself – Mary asking to sharpen her pencil – is fairly unremarkable. Nevertheless, it can be challenging for trainees to identify events like this. Tripp suggests a range of strategies for helping teachers notice incidents, such as using a particular adjective (*interesting, funny, trivial,* etc.) to 'prime' teachers before they enter the classroom, or selecting from events that are either quintessentially typical and routine, or the opposite: those which are atypical. They then need to be described, and although there's no particular format that should be used, the critical incident should go beyond description of the event itself and include an element of explanation of the values it reveals, both about the immediate context, as well as about the broader educational context.

When it comes to analysing critical incidents, Tripp (1993) suggests several thinking strategies to get students started, including:

- Plus, minus, interesting – what was positive, negative, or interesting (not necessarily good or bad, but perhaps raising further questions or sparking new ideas) about the situation? This strategy involves thinking about the incident as described; thinking about what *did* happen. (This strategy alone can prompt extensive discussion if trainees disagree about what is good and bad!)

- Alternatives, possibilities, choices – what other courses of action were open to the teacher? This strategy involves somewhat more imagination and creativity, because it's an analysis of what *didn't* happen, but could have.

- The Why? Challenge – encourages trainees to delve into the choices made during the incident, but also the reasons the incident stood out in the first place. Trainees start with the question 'why does this matter?' and give their answer, which is then followed by a further 'why?' again and again until an unavoidable conclusion is reached. This usually ends with one of two answers: either 'because that's the way it is' or 'because that's the way it should be'. Both of these can be explored further. 'The way it is' may be more malleable than trainees believe, or it may reveal an aspect of the teaching context that is fundamental to practice in that context. 'The way it should be' suggests a deep-seated belief about the nature and purpose of teaching and learning. Once out in the open, it can be explored, discussed and challenged.

The critical incident analysis can be done 'live' in the training room, but once the process has been explained to trainees, they can be asked to select their own incidents in advance of sessions and bring their analyses to the training room for subsequent discussion, which tends to be more fruitful. One reason for that is that preparing critical incidents for other people requires them to be described fully and with consideration of other perspectives, which means that trainees do plenty of thinking even before they come to the training room and discuss their incidents with others.

Coursebook material is a useful basis for Personal discussions because comparison and analysis of coursebooks can help to reveal not only trainees' beliefs and assumptions, but also those of the coursebook producers. Coursebooks also provide a clear link between beliefs and practice, and are readily available in most training contexts (trainees can always be asked to bring their course materials to the training room).

Professional

Professional session content aims to present information: theories, frameworks, research insights and the language to talk about them all. For many of the techniques below it is worth remembering that teaching practices can still be modelled, so there are opportunities to include a Practical element while conveying Professional content (Sofia, for example, models the stages of a reading lesson and includes Professional content within the reading text). More often, though, you will introduce teaching practice with Practical content, and use Professional activities to provide the rationale for that practice and the terminology to talk about it.

Quizzes are a useful way of introducing input to a group that may already have some knowledge of the subject, or to groups that include trainees of varying experience. Here is the example from Emad's session, which he has based on a research paper (Chandler, 2003):

1. Students like it when teachers provide corrections on their writing	True / False
2. Students believe they learn better when they have to correct their own mistakes	True / False
3. Underlining errors is more effective than using a correction code	True / False
4. Students prefer underlining to correction codes	True / False

CASE STUDY 3.7: EMAD, THE TRAINING CO-ORDINATOR

We don't have a lot of time so I will introduce the teachers to some principles with a quiz, which is fast and engaging. They have to choose true or false (the answers are all true!). I would like to use an online quiz tool to make this more dynamic, but I have also prepared the quiz on my presentation in case there are problems with the internet connection, which can occasionally happen here. After the quiz I will allow a few minutes for the teachers to discuss anything that was surprising or new to them, and I will answer any questions they might have.

The quiz is based on a research paper that I used to prepare the session, so I have included a reference to the paper and I will send it to the teachers afterwards.

Card sorting / matching activities can be a good way of contrasting ideas with those that trainees are already familiar with. Marie does this in order to highlight the differences between teaching adults and young learners:

CASE STUDY 3.8: MARIE, THE CELTA TRAINER

I want to keep the session light on theory because it's already quite a lot to take in. So I've created my own card sorting activity to introduce some of the main ideas: basically the trainees have to compare and contrast teaching adults and kids by putting cards that describe various aspects of teaching into one category or the other. There's a range of sources for this, and some of it is simply my own teaching experience. Once the trainees have matched the cards, I'll give them a handout with the answers on so they have a record of this part of the session, and some links to further reading where they can learn more.

Card sorting is also very effective for helping students to make sense of classroom practices they have been presented with in Practical stages. For example, after taking part in a demonstration the trainees might be asked to work out the stages of the lesson by sorting cards into the right order.

Key terms lend themselves to modelling techniques for teaching vocabulary, such as matching terms to definitions (an example of an adapted activity, mentioned above). If you're introducing terms that you expect trainees to know already, simple techniques for eliciting them, such as showing only the first letter, or introducing them as anagrams, can help trainees to stay engaged.

CASE STUDY 3.9: SOFIA, THE ONLINE TUTOR

In this case, including some theory was easy for me because I needed a text to model the stages of a reading lesson with, and what better text than one about the stages of a reading lesson! It was an easy choice because the book I took the extract from is quite new, the text is a good length, and it's written in an accessible way. There have been times in the past where I've have had to edit some articles to make them more readable, but this one was perfect. All I had to do after that was create some comprehension questions around it.

Articles or **book extracts** are an obvious source of unfiltered Professional content, but as Sofia suggests, some texts are more appropriate than others for an audience of trainees. Shorter is usually better, and that might mean extracting quotes or key paragraphs and presenting them separately. The register of the text is also important: texts written in dense academic prose can be confusing or intimidating, especially if the trainees' English language level is not high. Good sources of texts are *English Teaching Professional, Modern English Teacher, the ELT Journal*, or the Cambridge University Press ELT blog (www.cambridge.org/elt/blog/).

One clear advantage of using articles or extracts from books is that they can be presented to trainees using the same activity frames used in the language classroom, such as jigsaw reading, gap fills, dictation, gallery walks, etc. If you have the time and resources, you can even adapt written texts for **audio presentation** – conveying the findings of an otherwise dry research article by recording a dialogue between a teacher and researcher, for instance.

TASK 3.5

...To trainer

Go to page 221 to see the text that Sofia plans to use in her session (Case study 3.9). What comprehension questions would you write if you were Sofia?

Is there anything that she could do to make the text more accessible?

For notes see page 221

Flipped learning in the context of teacher training involves providing trainees with Professional content before they come to the session. Melissa Lamb (2019) describes this approach on an intensive preservice training course, in which Professional input in the form of 'bitesize' texts was provided through a dedicated website. Trainees were responsible for accessing relevant content online before attending face-to-face sessions focusing on guided planning, teaching skills workshops and teaching practice.

Although you may not be able to create your own website, the principle of providing trainees with material in advance of a session is easily applied. You might provide trainees with an article or extract from a book, or a link to an online resource such as a blog post or video. The key to making this approach work is in allowing trainees to discover the relevance of the input to their own teaching through practical experimentation (e.g., microteaching), when they come to the session, so the role of the trainer is much less prominent. Lamb argues that flipping training in this way 'moves the trainees away from trying to master teaching skills simply because they are a requirement of the course, towards having the confidence to use those skills in practice' (Lamb, 2019, p. 48).

Lecturing trainees in order to convey Professional content tends to be considered bad practice, probably because it presents a model of education that communicative language teachers are advised to steer clear of in their classrooms – many of us will have been trained to keep our 'teacher talking time' to a minimum. But as Tessa Woodward points out, lectures can be a useful part of a trainer's toolkit if used judiciously:

> Trainers nowadays seem to favour discovery group work
> and are often slightly embarrassed when caught lecturing.
> I feel that discovery group work is simply another tool,

equally varied in type, underutilised in practice and just as
inappropriate in some contexts as the lecture is in others.
(Woodward, 1991, p. 10)

There's no doubt that lecturing can be a time-efficient way of conveying
ideas, that it probably requires less preparation than other forms of
Professional input (for trainers familiar with their subject matter), and
that many trainees appreciate an opportunity to learn directly from the
trainer (without the mediation of peers, as in jigsaw reading or discussion,
for example). But to promote active learning a traditional 'chalk and talk'
approach will be insufficient. Gabriel Diaz Maggioli (2012, p. 47) suggests a
number of ways to both make lectures more engaging and provide trainers
with a better sense of how well trainees are following than traditional
lecturing:

- Provide trainees with a handout with gaps to fill in as they listen.

- Trainees discuss questions on the topic, then listen to the lecture to
  check their ideas.

- Trainees summarise the lecture after hearing it, adding examples from
  their own teaching.

- Individual trainees are asked for examples in advance and they are
  asked to contribute them during the lecture.

These techniques help to ensure that trainees are engaged throughout
the lecture, provide them with a framework for understanding and
absorbing what they hear, and help the trainer check that ideas have been
communicated as intended. Ideally all lectures should end with a brief
discussion of trainees' thoughts, comments and questions – again, one of
the aims of these is for you to evaluate how successfully the content of the
lecture has been conveyed.

A central principle of Professional input, and one modelled by Emad and
Marie in their sessions, is that participants should be able to take away some
kind of **record of the main ideas**, or have access to them after the session,
and that this resource should include suggestions for further learning
opportunities. This is an important way of helping teachers to develop
more agency over their professional development and provides a valuable
connection to the knowledge base of the language teaching profession.

Reflection and planning next steps

The final stage of the session allows teachers to (1) look back at the
session and consider what they have learned from it, and (2) look ahead
to forthcoming lessons and plan how to apply their learning to teaching
practice (what we described as 'preflection' in Chapter 2). Providing
support for this kind of thinking is key: when teachers are supported in

experimenting with new ideas in the classroom they are more likely to make lasting, meaningful changes to their teaching practice (Ingvarson, Meiers, & Beavis, 2005, p. 15).

Sentence stems are a useful way of guiding teacher reflection. For example, teachers might be encouraged to think about what they learned from a session by completing the following:

- *Today's session covered the topic(s) of . . .*

- *The most useful thing I learned today was . . .*

- *What surprised me was . . .*

- *I would like to learn more about . . .*

- *I realised that my teaching . . .*

- *A question I (still) have is . . .*

When it comes to making plans for applying new learning in the classroom, trainees can usually benefit from taking a collaborative approach. Discussing future plans with other trainees generates a sense of accountability, encourages trainees to look for solutions to potential barriers, and enables sharing of creative strategies for classroom experimentation. Trainees could begin this kind of collaborative dialogue with questions like:

- What are you planning to do differently in your next lesson?

- How do you think it will affect your students' learning?

- What will you need to do to make it work?

- How will you know if it has worked?

Summary

The tasks and materials suggested in this chapter represent only some of the possibilities open to trainers. As you become more familiar with them, be creative: mix and match activity frames, the materials you use as prompts, and the tasks you ask trainees to complete with them to create new ways of exploring Practical, Personal and Professional content.

How do you choose between one training activity and another?

- Use your session outline (Chapter 2), particularly the learning outcome and the details of the training habitat, to decide what is most appropriate.

- Consider the teachers' level of experience: expert teachers are better able to take on board new activities and put them into practice without experiencing them; novice teachers need to see how they work.

- How much time is there? It may be worth demonstrating practice of more activities and not providing time to try them out if time is short.

- How similar is the training room to the teachers' contexts? If it is very different then there may be limited value in something like peer teaching.

- How much do you expect the trainees to know about the topic already? If they have some prior knowledge then Professional activities that allow them to share it will be most fruitful.

These and other questions will help to guide your decisions about the activities that you slot into your outline, and you will find that your experience of planning lessons helps you to reach those decisions. Emad's completed session plan (Figure 3.5) gives a sense of the level of detail you might aim for when you prepare your own session plans:

Session title	Giving feedback on academic writing		
Profile of trainees	Multiple groups of up to 20 in-service teachers of English for academic purposes in a university context		
Time available	60 minutes		
Resources needed	Student texts on handouts, projector		
What trainees will know	As a result of the session, trainees will know a range of evidence-based techniques for giving feedback on academic writing and the principles behind them.		
What trainees will do	Following the session, trainees will use a range of contextually appropriate evidence-based techniques in their teaching for giving feedback to students on writing.		
Session outline			
Stage aim	**Procedure**	**Interaction**	**Time**
To set the context for the session, to introduce the idea that feedback is teaching too	Ts work in pairs to examine a piece of student writing and feedback on it, to decide how effective the feedback is. They have a profile of the student and the task.	T–T	10
	Plenary discussion to share ideas. TR to elicit the idea that the main aim of feedback is writing skill development.	Plenary	5
To find out how Ts approach feedback on writing and why	Ask Ts *Do you give feedback in the same way? Why / why not?* Ts think, pair, share.	T>T–T>plenary	5

To introduce some principles of giving feedback on writing	True/false quiz on principles of feedback on writing, based on research paper by Chandler. Ts have the chance to ask questions after each answer is revealed.	Plenary	10
To practise applying the principles just learned	Ts are given a piece of student writing to mark, individually. TR monitors in preparation for plenary discussion.	T	10
	Ts discuss their feedback in groups.	T–T	5
	Plenary discussion of the task, questions.	Plenary	5
For Ts to reflect on what they can take away, and to plan how	Ts reflect individually, completing sentence stems.	T	5
	Ts share plans for future action, collaborating where possible.	T–T	5

Figure 3.5: Emad's completed session plan (TR = trainer; T = trainee; T–T = trainees work with each other)

When you have a plan like this, all that remains is to put it into action! How to do that is the focus of Chapter 4.

TRAINER VOICES

Scan the QR Code and watch the videos 'Effective modelling' and 'Changing beliefs' to hear how trainers put the principles we've looked at into practice. Do you recognise any of their techniques from training sessions you've attended?

TO FIND OUT MORE

Ellis, R. (1990). Activities and procedures for teacher education. In J. C. Richards, & D. Nunan, *Second language teacher education* (pp. 26–36). Cambridge: Cambridge University Press. (A useful chapter on how to generate workshop tasks from different types of input.)

Thaine, C. (2010). *Teacher Training Essentials: Workshops for Professional Development*. Cambridge: Cambridge University Press. (This is a collection of materials – session plans and handouts – ready for trainers to deliver, so it's a useful set of examples to take inspiration from as you start designing your own sessions.)

4 Training sessions: Delivering your session

Here we consider:
- How to prepare yourself
- Dealing with practicalities
- Managing resources in the training room
- Trainer talk in the training room
- How to follow up on your sessions with trainees
- How to evaluate your sessions

It's about sharing what you know, not setting yourself above the people that you're working with.

Olha, teacher trainer, UK

You may have planned your own session, or you may be starting off with a session design prepared by someone else. Either way, it's now time to deliver it! In this chapter we look at how to take your session from design to delivery, thinking about how to best manage the resources and the people in the training room to maximise teacher learning. Finally, we think about how to follow up with the trainees, as well as why and how to evaluate your training session.

It sounds obvious, but it's worth remembering that the session design is not the session itself. Having spent so much time preparing, it would be understandable to feel that the only thing left to do is work through the stages you've put together, or take the session design you've been provided with and head straight for the training room. But of course, the reality is not so simple, just as teaching a good lesson involves more than purely realising the plan. Trainers must be as alert to the 'planning paradox' (Harmer, 2007, p. 364) as teachers: we have a professional responsibility to prepare for training sessions, but we must also remember that sticking rigidly to the session design might mean that we miss impromptu opportunities for teacher learning. Bringing the session to life means being flexible and alert to the possibilities in the training room and recognising that the lightbulb moments in the session may not be obvious from the session design.

Besides being alive to learning and opportunities for learning during the session, we need to consider how to manage what is available in the training room – resources and people – to achieve our goals. And since our ultimate goal is improved teaching and learning in the classroom, ensuring that the session really does translate into better learning outcomes for students will mean looking ahead to what will happen after the session has ended, both for the trainees and for ourselves.

To exemplify the ideas in this chapter let's use a session plan (Figure 4.2) designed by a trainer named Lydia, that she's delivering on a preservice course. She begins by teaching a short demo lesson using the coursebook page in Figure 4.1.

4.3 LOOK AWAY!

LESSON OBJECTIVE
- discuss problems caused by staring at screens

1 LISTENING

A **PAIR WORK** What types of screens do you look at for work or For pleasure? About how many hours a day do you spend a screen? What effect might this be having on your eyes?

B 🔊 **1.33** **LISTEN FOR MAIN IDEA** Listen to an ophthalmologist (eye doctor) discussing the effect of screens on our eyes. Which statement best summarizes her position?

  a Screen viewing causes serious and lasting damage to our eyes.

  b There is no need to cut back on the amount of time we spend looking at screens.

  c We can take a number of practical steps to help protect our eyesight.

C 🔊 **1.33** **LISTEN FOR DETAILS** Listen again and pay attention to the structure of the presentation. Use the chart to take notes.

	How and why this affects eyesight	Proposed solution(s)
Blinking		
Glare and reflections		
Blue light		

D **PAIR WORK** Compare your notes. Did you capture all the same information? Was it presented in an organized way? Do you think the ophthalmologist offers good advice? Do you do any of these things? Will you do any of them now?

> **INSIDER** ENGLISH
>
> *Easier said than done.* = It's not as easy as it seems.

2 PRONUNCIATION: Listening for /t/ between vowels

A 🔊 **1.34** Listen to the two sets of phrases. In which set are the <u>underlined</u> /t/ sounds pronounced more like /d/?

  a But the truth of the matter is …   **b** … there are lots of practical things …

    It's a vital function for healthy eyes …   … special yellow-tinted glasses …

B 🔊 **1.35** **PAIR WORK** <u>Underline</u> the /t/ sounds that might sound more like /d/ sounds. Listen and check. Then practice saying the sentences with a partner.

  1 We've invited ophthalmologist Kit Bradley to the studio today …

  2 This constant fatigue leads to eyestrain with all its related problems.

  3 Blue light is emitted by digital screens.

C Circle the correct words to complete the sentence.

  The /t/ sound is often pronounced more like /d/ when it comes after ¹*a stressed / an unstressed* vowel and before ²*a stressed / an unstressed* vowel.

38

Figure 4.1: B. Goldstein and C. Jones, Evolve Student's Book 6 (Cambridge University Press, 2020), p. 38

Session title	Introduction to teaching listening
Profile of trainees	12 trainees on an intensive preservice teaching course.
Time available	60 minutes
Resources used	Projector and computer Handout — Coursebook: *Evolve Student's Book 6* (see Figure 4.1)
What teachers will know	Following this session, trainees will have a better understanding of how listening lessons are structured, and how to teach listening using published materials
What teachers will do	Plan an appropriately staged listening lesson from a coursebook Use appropriate techniques to support student listening comprehension (e.g., peer checking, pre-teaching vocabulary)

Session outline			
Stage aim	**Procedure**	**Interaction**	**Time**
1. Demo lesson *To introduce the teaching practices for a listening lesson*	Tell CPs [course participants] that they will take part in a demo lesson from *Evolve 6*. They are a C1 (advanced) class. ○ Discussion (1A) in pairs. Plenary feedback. ○ Pre-teach *blink, eyesight, eyestrain, ophthalmologist* with example sentences on board. Use CCQs [concept checking questions] to check understanding. Drill pronunciation and elicit word stress. ○ CPs read task 1B. Which position do they think the ophthalmologist will promote? ○ CPs listen and peer check their answers. ○ Point out task 1C. Explain that in a lesson we'd listen again to complete this. ○ Discussion 1D in pairs for 2 mins. Plenary feedback. Explain that in a lesson the ss would have more time to talk. ○ Elicit CPs' reactions to the lesson – what did they enjoy? Was anything surprising? Do they have any questions?	Plenary	25'
2. Understanding listening lesson stages *To highlight the structure of a listening lesson, the rationale for each stage, and how they look in coursebooks*	○ Give groups cards with stages of the lesson and cards with the stage aims. Groups work to order the stages and match the correct aims to each one. ○ Give handout with correct order when each group has finished. ○ Early finishers can turn to a different listening lesson in the coursebook and identify the stages. ○ Answer any questions in plenary	Group work	15'

3. Reviewing key terms *To ensure that trainees can recall and understand key concepts*	○ Give CPs one minute to review their handouts then ask them to put them away. ○ Play 'backs to the board' in two teams with these terms: *gist, pre-teach, detail, peer check, context, prediction, transcript*	Plenary	10'
4. Closing reflection	○ Opportunity for questions/comments ○ Teachers reflect and write key takeaways from the session in their journals.	Plenary Individual	10'

Figure 4.2: Lydia's session plan

TASK 4.1

...To trainer

Where do you see Professional, Personal and Practical elements in Lydia's session design? Can you guess the rationale for her choices?

For notes see page 223

Preparing yourself

Let's begin by thinking about how you might prepare *yourself*, particularly if you have never delivered a training session before.

CASE STUDY 4.1: PETER

My first 'formal' teacher training session took place during the early 1990s in Muscat, Oman, at a language school where I was working. The school offered Cambridge CELTA, which in those days was called CTEFLA. One of the school's full-time trainers was off work and I had to step in to deliver a language awareness session. The regulations were far less strict and there was no check on my suitability or my ability to talk to trainee teachers about different types of conditionals. I remember worrying about the session the night before, without very much guidance from anyone, and not really knowing where to start. Also, as I had never met the CTEFLA group, I had no idea about their knowledge and experience, nor their backgrounds.

My experience as a trainer was also extremely limited, and I had never been involved in anything as high-stakes as the situation I found myself in. But I decided that if I had a detailed plan with plenty of activities, and drew on my own classroom experience, I would survive. Furthermore, I had taken the CTEFLA course myself some seven years previously,

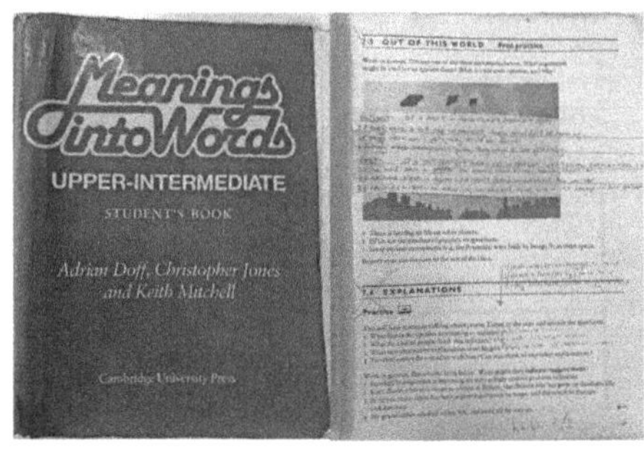

and I would be able to review the notes and materials I had collected from that experience.

The trainees were using a book called *Meanings into Words* (Doff, Jones, & Mitchell, 1984) for their teaching practice (I still have my copy), which I had taught from in a previous job. Luckily for me, Unit 7, *Deductions and explanations*, included some exercises using conditionals. That book and the materials from my own CTEFLA course saved my life!

You can see how the book has survived with plenty of sticky tape, as well as the notes I made and which I fixed to the page as a reminder.

Just like Peter (Case study 4.1) every teacher trainer had to deliver their first session; we were all beginners once. Inevitably, it can be a nerve-wracking experience, especially if you've designed it on your own. (If you have someone to support your transition to teacher training, you might be asked to deliver a session that has been designed by a more experienced trainer, which can be helpful – if it has been well designed!) As the time to deliver your session approaches, you might feel a twinge of impostor syndrome, asking yourself questions like: *What if there are teachers in the room who have been teaching longer than me? What if they already know everything that I've planned to show them? What if someone asks me a tricky question? What if one of the teachers used to teach me?!*

These questions aren't unique to first-time trainers. It's perfectly normal to feel nervous, especially if you are training your own colleagues. And nerves may well be a sign that you simply want the session to be successful, for the trainees and for yourself, which of course is what everyone wants. If you recognise yourself as an adaptive expert (see Chapter 1) in the area covered by the session, then you will almost certainly have something to offer the trainees. Ultimately, the key to managing any doubts is to prepare thoroughly, so that during the session you are able to focus on what you do best: helping people learn.

One idea that you might find useful in dealing with nerves is the concept of 'vision' (Dörnyei & Kubanyiova, 2014). The motivating power of vision lies in picturing yourself in the future after achieving, or at the moment of achieving, a personal goal. The more vivid and multifaceted the vision, the more effective it is likely to be in spurring you to do what's necessary to achieve it, so the aim is not just to evoke mental images, but also sounds, smells, sensations, and emotions, so that you can really feel yourself in the imagined moment. It's a technique commonly used by sportspeople, but it translates well to teaching and training. Expert teachers, for example, describe a similar process in relation to lesson planning that you may recognise: 'I have a vision. I sort of know exactly how it's going to go. I've imagined what will happen', and 'when I plan a new activity, I can picture it in my mind and predict how it will go, and I plan for that' (Westerman, 1991, p. 298).

In Chapter 1 we discussed how teacher beliefs, attitudes and experience all influence the way that trainees respond to trainer interventions. Vision is part of the same family of teacher cognition, and it too can have a profound impact on the effectiveness of training activities. Dörnyei and Kubanyiova explain that 'teachers' vision of themselves in the future plays a central role in how they engage with new ideas and, consequently, how they grow as professionals' (Dörnyei & Kubanyiova, 2014, p. 24). So if trainees are asked to apply practices that do not mesh with their visions of themselves as teachers, whether because (1) they see themselves as a different kind of teacher, (2) they feel they have already mastered those practices, or (3) their visions feel threatened by the imposition of those practices, they will not embed those practices into their everyday teaching.

On the other hand, if trainees are encouraged to articulate a vision of their future selves that resonates with the practices and ideas they are being trained to apply, there is a good chance that those visions may prove to be valuable sources of inspiration and motivation when professional learning becomes more challenging.

You can practise this technique for yourself, either in relation to the session you are about to deliver, or to your journey towards becoming a teacher trainer more generally. For example, you might choose to:

- Visualise yourself delivering the session in the training room, taking note of what you and the trainees are doing, and what you notice – see, hear, smell, etc.

- Picture yourself successfully demonstrating target teaching practices in your classroom so that you know what trainees should be aiming to do as a result of the session.

- Write a letter from your future self – an experienced, confident teacher trainer – to your present self, describing the journey you took to mastering second language teacher education, and your challenges and successes along the way.

Creating these mental images is not always easy, and it is a skill that needs practice and time to develop (Dörnyei & Kubanyiova, 2014). Once you have created your vision, take time to check in on it every now and again, and enjoy a confidence boost!

Logistics

In addition to preparing yourself mentally, there's a good chance that you will need to navigate some practicalities on the way to delivering your session. These tasks aren't flashy or glamorous but they are, nonetheless, essential.

Organising the session

Obviously the session needs a venue, which may or may not be
determined in advance. If you're delivering a session to your colleagues
you might need to book a classroom in which to hold the session. If you're
delivering it online, you'll need to set up an event on your chosen web
conferencing platform and distribute joining instructions to participants. In
both cases, you will need to choose a date and time, and of course you'll
have to make sure that it suits your target audience. If someone else is
organising the session then be clear when it will take place, and gather as
much information as you can about the participants, the venue itself and
what resources will be available (see below).

Getting people to come

There's nothing worse than delivering a training session to an empty room!
So don't neglect the task of publicising your training session and letting
people know where and when it will take place. Whether the trainees are
your colleagues, course participants, or conference attendees, they will
want to know what they can expect in return for giving up their time, so
provide a clear title and short abstract that summarises what you hope
to achieve through the session. Our experience is that session titles that
are both catchy and specific attract a good audience; a good example is
Alan Marsh's 'Making your toenails twinkle: Creativity in the language
classroom', whereas something like 'Teaching Reading' is not likely to
draw much of a crowd if your potential audience has other options to
choose from.

The other thing to consider here is your target audience. What level of
expertise is the session aimed at, and what is the level of knowledge that
participants can hope to leave with? It can be very frustrating to attend a
session that has been misleadingly promoted and find that your time could
have been better spent elsewhere, so define the target audience clearly in
describing the session, and your attendees will thank you.

Even if your trainees are attending as part of a longer programme of training,
clear titles are important because they will help trainees to make sense of
the session in the context of the rest of their learning on the course. One
important difference from delivering standalone sessions may be that you
choose to be more explicit about the links to other sessions, or to preparatory
work that you expect the trainees to have done before they attend.

Being ready when the session starts

As a teacher you will know that your materials need to be prepared and
any printing, photocopying or cutting (or creating polls and quizzes, if
online) needs to be done in good time ahead of your lesson. The same is
true of delivering training sessions, with the potential added complication
of using an unfamiliar space – be prepared to spend extra time setting up

any digital resources and rearranging furniture to suit your needs. For her session plan (Figure 4.2) on page 69, Lydia will have to bring her handouts to the training room, as well as copies of the coursebook that she'll be using. She may also want to cue up the listening text or just test that the audio system in her classroom is working so that she can arrange a plan B if necessary.

Being organised is always a good thing, but it is particularly important if you plan to go on to deliver sessions as part of an intensive course such as CELTA – you will find that the unforgiving pace of the course demands it. On such courses, being ready for the session may not simply mean having your materials and resources prepared, but also having an awareness of other sessions the trainees have attended or will attend that day, which trainees will be teaching next and need to hand in lesson plans or other assignments, and so on (see Chapter 9). The more organised you can be, the easier you will make it on your trainees, and on yourself.

Managing the training room

Managing the classroom and the physical resources within it should be part of your skillset as an experienced teacher, but it merits attention here because in many cases you are likely to find yourself 'borrowing' a room in which to deliver your training, rather than having the benefit of a dedicated training room. Both of us delivered our first training sessions to colleagues in the schools where we worked, and those sessions took place in a classroom ordinarily used for language teaching. There are some clear advantages to delivering your session in a classroom: the physical context is an accurate representation of where your trainees will be applying whatever they've learned, and that makes the process of mentally translating practices from the session to teachers' own classrooms much easier. Classrooms are also spaces that are set up for learning, which means that you shouldn't have to bring too many resources with you from outside, as you might if you have to train in more makeshift surroundings. When we refer here to resources, we mean items that make up the physical 'landscape' of the classroom or training room, such as the space available, a board and other furniture, as well as consumable classroom items in that landscape, like pens, paper, and so on.

Of course, classrooms have their downsides too. They can be small and cramped, and in primary teaching contexts the furniture may not be designed for adults. So you will probably be aware from your training experiences as a teacher that it is reasonably common for training sessions to be held in school auditoriums or in entirely non-academic environments. The obvious example is sessions at teachers' conferences, which usually take place in conference centres, but in our years training we have had to give sessions in all sorts of locations: in bookshops, in an outdoor play area, online through a range of different platforms, in office

meeting rooms, and even in a cinema! These different training contexts all
have their own idiosyncrasies, and while the training rooms you work in
will hopefully be more conventional, it's a good idea to be ready to adapt
to whatever situation you find yourself training in, while still keeping
your trainees and their learning at the front of your mind. We suggest that
there are four key considerations that can help guide the use of physical
resources in any training room:

1. **Modelling good practice**
   This is as important in relation to the use of physical resources as it is
   in regard to other teaching techniques.

2. **Engaging trainees**
   Skilful resource management is part of the trainer's toolkit when it
   comes to engaging teachers in the session.

3. **Communicating the message clearly**
   This may be a message making up the content of a Professional stage in
   the session, or it may simply be about making task requirements clear
   and signposting the session effectively. Trainees should be clear about
   what's happening in the session and why.

4. **Staying in control**
   A useful rule of thumb for using any training room resource is to keep
   an eye on the bigger picture of the intended learning outcomes for the
   session, so that the resource doesn't become the focus.

The first of these considerations requires some additional explanation.
Classrooms vary in the resources they offer, and so do training rooms. In
an ideal world we would ensure two things: that trainees are well prepared
for the teaching contexts they are, or will be, working in, and also that
they are able to adapt to contextual changes and teach well in alternative
contexts too. But training time is often limited, and that can create tension
between the desire to model teaching in the trainees' target context, and
the goal of preparing trainees to be adaptable and resourceful in a range
of classroom environments. Case study 4.2 offers an example of how
trainers might adopt contrasting perspectives on the use of resources when
the teaching context and training context differ, and in this case it is very
difficult to say who is right without going on to ask the trainees some
months after the course (judging the value of such decisions is part of
session evaluation; see below). Encouraging the trainees to notice features
of the training context, and to reflect on how and why you choose to
exploit them, is therefore a good idea.

CASE STUDY 4.2: MARTHA, TEACHER TRAINER

I once worked alongside a senior trainer who insisted that our trainees on a preservice course should not be allowed to use the interactive whiteboard (IWB) in the classroom when teaching, nor any other form of digital technology. His rationale for this was that trainees would probably go on to teach in poorly-resourced schools, since well-resourced schools rarely employ newly-certified teachers. They should therefore use only the wipe-clean whiteboard and marker pens. He encouraged me not to use the IWB when training for the same reason, and instead there was a single session on the course that covered the topic of teaching with technology as a sort of concession to the presence of this 'machine' that we had staring out at us from the front of the class.

I did not agree with this approach. I really felt that the trainees would have gained more if we had modelled a range of approaches, and encouraged the trainees to reflect on the merits of each one. What I really wanted them to take away from the course was the ability to think critically about the resources that would be available wherever they ended up working (without seeing digital resources as somehow separate or special), and the ability to use resources creatively and flexibly. I still tried to achieve that by prompting reflection, but it was frustrating to have to work with an artificially restricted set of resources for the whole course, and I think the trainees felt that too. But that was a little while ago and I'm now the senior trainer, so things have changed!

Let's take a look at four types of resources that are common to nearly every training room.

Training room space and furniture

Find out what furniture there will be in the training room, how it will be arranged, and whether you can move it. Make conscious decisions about the layout of the room, don't just go with what's already there. Do you want to replicate the trainees' classroom environments? Perhaps there is a way of rearranging the furniture to maximise opportunities for interaction, or perhaps you expect the trainees to be working on paper for a large part of the session and table space will therefore be important. Allow time for moving furniture before and after the session so that it doesn't eat into your session time. Consider also what opportunities there will be to invite the trainees to stand up and move, and where in the room that standing work should happen.

If furniture in the room is not moveable, and space for standing up and moving is limited, then try to provide a variety of opportunities for interaction by asking trainees to work with peers sitting in front or behind them as well as those to either side.

Presentation apparatus

Most training rooms will include some form of presentation apparatus, such as a chalkboard or whiteboard, a screen and projector or an interactive whiteboard (IWB). Boardwork is an important component of good teaching, so if you are modelling teaching practices take the opportunity to model effective use of the board by dividing it into sections and ensuring that you write clearly, using colours systematically. If you are using a projector or IWB and have the option of preparing presentation slides, consider your reasons for doing so – it's a good idea to make these the last element of the session that you prepare, so that you already have a clear vision for the session that is driven by teacher learning rather than by presenting information, and so that the slides are fulfilling a purpose that other resources cannot. Ensure that if you quote texts or use images on your slides, you pay attention to how they are sourced and attributed, as attention to copyright requirements is an assessment criterion for trainees on courses such as CELTA.

If you do use an IWB or projector, turn it off whenever it is not needed (e.g., when trainees are engaged in discussion). Be prepared with adapters if you need to connect to presentation hardware and keep backups of your slides both on your device and in the cloud so that you have a plan B when technical issues arise – as one day they inevitably will!

> ## TASK 4.2
>
> **From teacher ...**
>
> Think about a training session you have attended that used PowerPoint or similar. What (if anything) did the PowerPoint presentation add to the session, and how?
>
> *For notes see page 223*

Paper

Paper, whether blank (e.g., participants' notepads, flipchart paper) or pre-printed (your handouts, coursebooks), usually appears in some form during training sessions. It can be extremely helpful, particularly as a means of varying training room tasks, but as the number of trainees increases it becomes harder to manage in terms of preparation, distribution and task set-up. The key consideration is time: in Lydia's session on page 69 she has only one handout, and a small number of trainees, so she has kept things simple. Allow time for trainees to write and make notes where necessary, and think about how you (or others) will prepare and distribute paper resources. A neat but time-intensive solution to distributing a session handout is to stick it on the underside of each participant's chair. This takes a long time before the session starts but saves time during the session, while ensuring that trainees aren't distracted by handouts before they are needed. Similarly, if you want to put things on the wall, be sure to allow time for doing that in advance of the session. For sessions that form part of a course, the most elegant solution may be to print and bind the handouts for all sessions in a single booklet, but obviously this requires preparation even further in advance of the session date. Whether you opt to do that or distribute handouts in each session, add the session title to the bottom of each page and number each sheet. This will help both you and your trainees to stay organised during the session and when reviewing handouts afterwards.

The other thing to consider is what paper resources really are necessary: perhaps there are reasonable substitutes, such as resources the trainees may have brought with them, or that they could create for themselves during the session. In the past, one of the principal benefits of paper resources was that they provided trainees with a record that they could take away from the session and refer to later. Providing that kind of record is as important as it ever was, but there are other options available now, such as emailing a summary of the session to participants afterwards, or allowing trainees to take photos of slides as the session progresses.

You might find that the techniques and activities you model (in other words, *how* you run the session) are what trainees are frantically scribbling down. One of the most helpful paper-based takeaways from a session is often a list of the activities you presented and how to run them, and of course this can be made available electronically very easily. Alternatively, you could give trainees a standard template to use for this in each session: Tessa Woodward calls this a 'record and review' sheet, explaining that 'it can be used for review purposes later, for reminding trainees of administrative details, or simply as a way of making overt and conscious the processes of the session' (Woodward, 1991, p. 55).

RECORD AND REVIEW SHEET

Session name   Date   Term   Session no.

1. Warm-up idea

2. One-minute break idea

3. New vocabulary

Word in original context	*Meaning in EFL*	*Own sentence*

New meetings of the words in fresh context (from reading, etc.)
Usual collocation

4. Pair work organisation
   How split up
   How started
   How finished
   Point of pair work

5. Group work organisation

Activity	*Criteria for grouping*	*Size*	*Role of group members*	*Tutor's role*

Reason for splitting into groups

Integration of group work and individual work	*Evaluation of work done in groups*	*Own comments / reactions*

6. Reading associated with session
7. Homework
8. Quotes of the week
9. Other things

Figure 4.3: Tessa Woodward's record and review sheet

Participants' devices

It is now almost unheard of for teachers attending training sessions to be without a mobile phone. Many will use these as part of their training without being prompted, to take photos of the board or of other materials, or to look up unfamiliar terms. But you may wish to make explicit use of them in certain circumstances. Perhaps the most obvious use is as a way of modelling how trainees could use their students' devices for language learning in their own classrooms. One of the most productive purposes of mobile devices in the training room is to use polling tools such as Mentimeter to better understand your audience: their teaching contexts, their needs and interests and their understanding of the material presented in the session. Such tools involve trainees using their devices to answer mini questionnaires, with collated responses appearing on the trainer's screen at the front of the training room in real time. This can be a neat way of gaining a general picture of the beliefs and practices of a large audience, as long as the trainees have internet access.

Trainees can make good use of their devices in a session in two other ways. The first is by video recording their microteaching efforts, and if teachers agree to do this you can provide them with criteria (or elicit suitable criteria) for evaluating their technique. The second trainee-driven use of mobile devices is in producing digital content that allows them to capture their understandings of ideas and practices in text, photos, audio or video form. For example, lesson plans or materials that are produced as part of a session could be photographed or presented, acting as a record that trainees can share. Such activities also provide a good opportunity to model how to effectively manage digital resources in the classroom, and to discuss issues of digital citizenship and digital welfare so that your trainees are able to have similar discussions with their students.

Managing trainees

A lot of the work that happens in the training room is invisible, in the sense that it can't really be seen in the session design (at least, not in proportion to the time it takes or the impact it has) or on session materials such as handouts and presentation slides. That's because it is spoken. A great deal of teacher learning during your session will be prompted through dialogue or will involve dialogue, so it is worth thinking about how this particular resource – the trainees' voices and our own teacher trainer voices – is used during the session. To be valuable to teacher learning, interaction in the training room needs to be skilfully managed by the trainer, so let's look at how you might create the right atmosphere in the training room, how to signpost and manage collaborative learning activity, how to respond to trainee contributions and how to follow up on the session.

TASK 4.3

...To trainer

In the language classroom, encouraging spoken interaction between the students is very important. What do you think the benefits of interaction in the training room might be?

For notes see page 224

Opening the session

According to Jim Scrivener, a teacher's most important task 'is perhaps to create the conditions in which learning can take place' (Scrivener, 2011, p. 54). Similarly, as a trainer, one of your main goals when you begin the session will be to establish the right atmosphere in the training room. This can feel like a challenge, because your teacher 'persona' won't translate directly into training – you are facing your peers, not students, and the relationship is different. The type of learning environment is very similar, however. For the best chance of teacher learning the training room should be a welcoming, supportive place, trainees will be clear about what they should be doing at each stage in the session, and there will be agreed expectations about how to participate (Williams & Burden, 1997).

The following techniques are tried-and-tested ways of kicking off a session when you begin to speak, and are a first step towards creating the right environment. They allow you to demonstrate some authority as an experienced educator, reassure the trainees that they're in safe hands, prepare them for what the session will entail, and rely on a familiar routine while any nerves settle down. The order below flows well, but not all the techniques will be relevant to every session so treat it flexibly and make it your own, depending on your individual training context:

Greet the teachers	○ Say hello, thank teachers for attending and introduce yourself. Smile!
Get a general picture of the audience	○ If the group is unfamiliar to you, it can be useful to get a sense of the teachers' contexts: who has been teaching a long time vs who is less experienced, who teaches children vs who teaches adults, who teaches large classes vs who works with smaller groups, and so on. You can do this by show of hands, or through polls if online.
Explain the intended outcome of the session	○ In general terms, explain what the session is about and what teachers should leave with (e.g., 'I hope that by the end of the session you'll have a clearer idea of what differentiation is, why it's important, and a range of strategies for differentiating your classes.')

Explain that teachers will need to consider their own context	○ It can sometimes be useful to highlight that teachers are the experts when it comes to their own classrooms and their own students, and to encourage them to think about how the ideas they encounter during the session could be applied in their own contexts. Not everything will fit perfectly, so what adaptations or adjustments might they need to make?
Explain that teachers will be involved	○ Prepare teachers for discussions and other tasks by explaining that you will call on them during the session to speak to those around them and actively participate. This can be a particularly helpful primer when the participants don't know each other.
Ask teachers to move if necessary	○ If the training room is larger than necessary, invite teachers to move so that they are not so spread out that they can't engage in discussion. ○ Allow some time for people to move. ○ When teachers have found new seats, ask the whole group to introduce themselves to the people around them.
Learn trainee names	○ If you have 20 trainees or less, jot down names on a seating plan if you can so that you can use them during the session.
Introduce some basic expectations	○ If the group is larger than ten or so, it's usually helpful to show trainees a gesture that you will use to indicate that you want them to stop talking. ○ You might explain that trainees can say 'pass' if they are called upon to say something to the group and would prefer not to answer (they can use this only once). ○ It's a good idea to ask trainees to keep devices on silent and out of sight unless they are being used as part of the session.

In the case of Lydia and her session on teaching listening, many of these stages wouldn't be necessary because she's working on a course and will be familiar with the trainees after delivering several sessions to them. But all of these steps would be appropriate on the first day of a course, when you first meet the trainees.

Signposting the session and managing tasks

Most trainees will arrive at your session without a real sense of how the session time will be divided up; all they know is that it will occupy them for a given time. So it is important to signpost transitions between one stage of the session and another, and to ensure that trainees are following the developments and connections between concepts and practices as the session progresses. Managing interaction during the session is largely a question of setting up tasks clearly, and monitoring those tasks as they take place, to make sure that the trainees are working in the intended way. Many of these techniques will be familiar to you from your language teaching experience.

TASK 4.4

...To trainer

In the list below are some of the ways in which a trainer may need to signpost a session or manage learning in the training room. What would you say to a group of trainees to accomplish each one?

- Introduce or explain the aims of a session.
- Say why the topic might be useful to this group of teachers.
- Link the session to other sessions on the course / at the event.
- Signpost a transition between group work and plenary work.
- Summarise and close the session.
- Break down instructions, and set a time limit for the next task.
- Speak to a pair or group who are off task.
- Set an extra task for fast finishers.
- Give a reminder about time.
- Prepare for next stage (e.g., prepare group for next task, by allocating tasks to different groups before the plenary begins).
- Prepare participants for plenary work, by giving them a time limit within which to finish their task.

For notes see page 225

These are all familiar teaching skills, but it is precisely for that reason that they should be modelled effectively and, if you're working with preservice teachers, made explicit to trainees from time to time. Highlighting these aspects of training room management is important because one of the problems faced by novice teachers trying to learn from observing others is that the better a teacher is at managing the classroom, the less they actually say (Johnson, 1990)! Having to repeat instructions, for example, suggests that they weren't given very effectively the first time, so if you're watching a teacher manage the classroom very effectively (e.g., giving instructions only once and seeing them successfully carried out) it's easy to miss subtle but powerful classroom management cues.

It's also worth noting here that modelling teacher behaviour is as important in the 'in between' moments of the session as it is when you are working through the tasks you've designed: arriving and finishing on time, using people's names, paying attention to where you stand – practices like these are all things you want your trainees to develop so you need to model them too.

Pay attention to this type of talk in your session, particularly if your trainees are experienced teachers. Are you managing the learning, or are the teachers managing the learning for you because they know what to expect?

Responding to trainees

Feedback to teachers is crucial to their professional learning, as we'll see in Chapter 8. The interventions most valuable to teacher learning are often in the form of feedback to what trainees have said or done in the training room, or in their classrooms.

In a training session, you might find yourself responding to trainee contributions in any of the following ways, amongst others:

- providing feedback on teachers' work as part of a task (either individually, to a small group, or to the whole group)

- responding to trainees who have answered a question you posed

- summarising the main points of a discussion

- answering a question from a trainee

- dealing with trainees whose actions or comments threaten to derail the session

Many of these situations will take place in plenary interactions, so there is a need to respond sensitively and, where possible, to use such moments as opportunities for further input and as opportunities to model the management of interaction in classrooms. Of course, a prerequisite for responding to trainees is the ability to listen, and we trust that as an experienced teacher you will be able to do this well.

We have found that there are three things that help when responding to trainees: firstly, to acknowledge the question or comment in a positive way; secondly, to invite a response from other trainees who might be able to give an answer; and thirdly, to add some brief insights of your own. If the group is relatively inexperienced you might first give your own answer before checking whether anyone else has something to add.

For disruptive trainees, it's been our experience that they tend to want acknowledgement of their skills and experience more than anything, and fall largely into the category of routine experts (see Chapter 1). Sometimes questions are well-meaning but not relevant to the whole group, in which case it is fine to say that you can come back to it at the end of the session or answer it privately.

Following up

When your session is over, take a moment to congratulate yourself – you just took a step towards being a more effective teacher trainer! Bear in mind, though, that for the teachers the session was only a small step towards better student learning. There is still plenty of work to be done to translate the content and activity of the session into routine teaching practice. Thomas Guskey advises that 'training sessions must . . . be extended, appropriately spaced, or supplemented with additional follow-up activities to provide the feedback and coaching necessary for the successful implementation of new ideas' (Guskey, 2000, p. 23). A trainer like Lydia, working on a course, will be able to review session content later on and refer back to sessions in teaching practice feedback, for example.

Your training context will determine what you can do to provide additional follow-up activities, but at the very least aim to provide a summary handout or follow-up email that trainees can use as a reference to guide their next steps. If you're helping to deliver a training course, the next step for trainees might be preparing a lesson for teaching practice and aiming to incorporate some of the ideas and techniques you presented. Options in other contexts might be a discussion group that meets once the trainees have had a chance to try out new practices in their classrooms, perhaps based around critical incidents, video snippets, or samples of student work. Remember that, for the most part, trainees will be applying what they've learned in your absence, so resources that will support them through that potentially rather lonely endeavour will be very useful. Encourage trainees to work together in the period following a session to provide support and peer feedback as they try to implement new teaching practices – perhaps through an instant messaging group or online platform. Collaborative teacher development can be a very powerful way of extending the learning that begins in a training session.

Evaluating your session

What evaluation is and why it matters

Evaluation is the process of working out how effective your session (or your training course or programme – see Chapter 9) was, and why. When you teach a lesson, you probably leave the classroom with an intuitive sense of how well it went, perhaps picked up from students' contributions, their body language or work they handed in. It is possible to develop a similar sense of how successful your training sessions have been, but effective evaluation should be carried out in a systematic way, and be based on the analysis of specific evidence (Guskey, 2000).

If you are new to training, or aiming to develop your skills as a trainer, this is an essential part of your development. Successfully evaluating sessions will show you what you are doing well and where you might want to focus your development efforts (see Chapter 10), as well as providing clear evidence that you are helping teachers to improve what they do. Evaluation also proves useful if the session is part of a course, when it can help to inform the planning of future sessions in order to make them as supportive of trainee learning as possible. But the main reason for getting evaluation right is that it is exactly the same process that we want our trainees to adopt as part of their everyday teaching practice. You may remember from Chapter 1 that our ultimate goal is for our trainees to be *evaluative practitioners* who can establish which aspects of their teaching are working well, as well as what they need to work on to improve those aspects that aren't. As with the other aspects of professional practice that we deal with in the training room, modelling good practice when it comes to evaluation is important. If we can't be evaluative practitioners as trainers, how will trainees learn to evaluate their teaching?

We are introducing it now at the tail end of our discussion of training sessions, but evaluation really begins at the very start of the session design process. That's because in order to know if the session had any impact, we need to know what the starting point for the trainees was, and, on that basis, what the session aimed to achieve. Weston and Clay talk about a 'golden thread' (2018, p. 18) connecting three things: the session design process, what happens in the session itself and what happens in teachers' classrooms to improve student learning. The aims determined at the very beginning should form the basis for action at each point on the thread.

Principles of evaluation

Session evaluation often tends to take the form of feedback questionnaires completed by the trainees once the session is over, and is often an afterthought, 'left until the last minute and done rather hastily' (Woodward, 1991, p. 211). There are two problems with this sort of evaluation: firstly, that it is a relatively shallow estimation of the impact the session had, telling us more about how much the participants enjoyed themselves than about what they learned; and secondly, that it ends too soon – the questionnaires handed out at the end of the session usually mark the end of the evaluation process, even though teachers won't yet have been able to apply any new learning to their teaching practice. This is a bit like rating a film after only seeing the opening scene.

Guskey warns that evaluation 'cannot be something we simply tack on at the end [of teacher training], hoping for good results. Systematically gathering and analysing evidence to inform our actions must become a central component in professional development' (Guskey, 2000, p. 92). So here are three principles that can help you to make evaluation a core component of your training practice:

1. **Attend to evaluation at various points on the golden thread**

   In Chapter 2 we recommended setting the aim(s) for your session by having a clear picture of what teaching practices you want the trainees to change as a result of attending, and of what knowledge they will gain in order to support that change. This is the start of the golden thread, and it's here that the foundations for successful evaluation are laid, because those aims will form some of the criteria by which you judge the success of your session. The next checkpoint is the session itself, after which you should review whether trainees found it useful and if they left with the intended professional knowledge, and a further check is needed some time after that, when trainees will hopefully be applying what they have learned in their classrooms.

2. **Use a range of evaluation tools**

There's no denying that gathering evidence to show your session has had the intended impact is a very tricky business. Classrooms are such complex places that you really ought to gather several different types of evidence, at different times, to be able to 'prove' that your training had an effect on student learning. The tools you use will depend on what sort of impact you are evaluating, but could include:

- things participants said or did during the session
- products of participants' work in the session (e.g., posters, lesson plans)
- a trainer journal that you keep, including 'hot' (written immediately after the session) and 'cold' (written sometime later) entries
- comments from session participants
- comments from a co-trainer (formal or informal)
- questionnaires
- assessments of trainees (e.g., portfolios of work or assignments)
- trainees' reflections on their own teaching after the session
- structured interviews with trainees
- focus groups with trainees
- observation of trainees

3. **Understand what it is you are evaluating**

We've mentioned that evaluation traditionally focuses mainly on whether trainees enjoyed the session, and that can be a useful thing to find out – people seldom learn very efficiently if they are uncomfortable or unhappy. But in addition to the reactions of trainees, there are four further levels of evaluation, outlined by Guskey (2000):

- Trainee reactions – *did they enjoy the session, was it useful?*
- Trainee learning – *did they learn what they were meant to learn?*
- Organisation support and change – *did the conditions in trainees' teaching contexts develop to support changes to their practice?*

- Trainees' use of new knowledge and skills – *did trainees go on to apply new skills and knowledge in their professional practice?*

- Student learning outcomes – *did the changes to teaching have an impact on student learning? Was there any other impact on students?*

TASK 4.5

...To trainer

Looking at the evaluation tools listed under principle 2 'Use a range of evaluation tools' above and Guskey's five levels of evaluation listed under principle 3, what tools do you think might be most appropriate at each level, and why?

For notes see page 226

Getting started

In reality, you will probably have limited opportunities to evaluate your session in great depth, but you should aim to gather data on trainee reactions and on your intended learning outcomes: the 'what teachers will know' and 'what teachers will do' sections of your session design. In most cases, a short questionnaire is the best option for the first two of these – if it is administered digitally (an online search will show many free survey tools), the results are easily collated and shared or saved. We suggest three questions to gauge trainee reactions: first, a simple 'would you recommend this session to your colleagues?' with responses on a five-point scale, and then two additional open questions: 'what was done well?' and 'what could have been done better?' The first question is a familiar idea and produces a numerical value which is a crude but easily comparable measure of success. Questions two and three allow respondents to elaborate on their answer to question one and add some detail to the numerical data. To evaluate trainee learning, the fourth and final question is 'What new knowledge do you feel you will take away from this session?' This allows for reporting of unintended outcomes as well as those specified in the session design. These four questions make for a survey that is easy for you to administer and for trainees to complete.

Trainees' use of new knowledge can't be evaluated until much later, when they've had a chance to implement new ideas and techniques in their classrooms. That's a process that should involve experimentation over many lessons in order to find out what works in the trainee's particular context. It's also a very personal process and teachers are unlikely to adopt new practices in the same way. If you can observe trainees, which may be possible on intensive courses or if your trainees are also your colleagues, that is likely to be the most accurate measure of how they are putting new knowledge into practice. If observation is not possible then interviews with trainees or trainees' reflections (written or spoken) on new practices they have developed can also be helpful.

When you've gathered all these questionnaires or other data, you will need to analyse them, but this doesn't need to be a complex process. Remember that you are simply trying to find out the extent to which you achieved your aims, and what, if anything, you could do better next time. The only time this is ever really problematic is when you embark on the session design process without a clear idea of what you are trying to achieve, so the value of clear learning outcomes – specifically what you expect teachers to know and to do as a result of the session – cannot be overstated.

More important than producing flashy charts or statistics as a result of your analysis is keeping a record of the overall messages coming from your session evaluations, and using those to guide your development. We will look in more detail at how you can do that in Chapter 10, and the topic of evaluation will arise again in Chapter 9, in the context of evaluating whole programmes of training.

Summary

It should be reasonably clear that running a successful session will involve a lot of the skills you already have as a teacher. In this chapter we've tried to highlight those elements that are different as a result of having trainees in front of you rather than students. When you deliver a training session you will need to manage the room and the people in it, just as you do when you teach. But you will be doing so in different ways and to achieve different outcomes. In addition, we've seen that there is often some logistical planning to be done before delivering a session, and an evaluation process to follow once it is over.

Chapters 2, 3 and 4 have focused on working with groups of teachers to improve their practice. This is a very common training format, but as we saw in Chapter 1, group training sessions are more suited to developing awareness – *Knowing about* – rather than adaptive expertise. So developing teaching skills to the point where they can be performed automatically or effortlessly requires working with teachers individually, or in very small groups. It is this kind of training that we now turn to in Chapter 5.

 **TRAINER VOICES**

 Scan the QR Code and watch the videos 'Delivering my first training session' and 'Dealing with challenges'. Do you feel more confident after hearing some of the trainers' stories?

TO FIND OUT MORE

Dörnyei, Z., & Kubanyiova, M. (2014). *Motivating learners, motivating teachers.* Cambridge: Cambridge University Press. (Includes tasks to help trainees develop vision.)

Guskey, T. R. (2000). *Evaluating professional development.* Thousand Oaks, CA: Corwin Press. (This is the most comprehensive text on evaluating training, but Weston and Clay (2018, Chapter 3) and Malderez and Wedell (2007, Chapter 12) also give useful overviews.)

5 Mentoring practices

Here we consider:
- What mentors and mentoring practices are
- How mentoring practices fit alongside other training skills
- How to implement mentoring practices
- Mentoring practices on training courses
- Mentoring practices in schools

Of course there is a formal part [of working individually with trainees] . . . but there's also a part which is informal and is as simple as conversations with trainees and checking in about how they feel during the course.

Zhenya, teacher trainer, Ukraine

In Chapters 2–4 we looked in detail at how teacher trainers can work with groups of teachers. Now we turn to the skills needed to work with individuals or very small groups of trainees. This chapter looks at how we can adopt mentoring practices to give ourselves options when working with individual trainees, whether that's in a formal mentoring situation or as part of other training.

Defining mentors and mentoring practices

Hollywood loves mentors. The very best stories are stories of learning: of characters who go on a journey and change their beliefs, behaviours and perhaps also the circles in which they can belong as a result of what they learn. On film, the main character on that journey is often helped along by a mentor, like Obi Wan Kenobi in *Star Wars*, or Professor Dumbledore in *Harry Potter*. A particularly good example appears in the 1996 comedy film *Happy Gilmore*, in which the eponymous protagonist is a failed ice hockey player in need of cash to pay his grandma's sky-high tax bill. Gilmore discovers that his hockey swing translates well to the golf course, and embarks on a career as a golfer in order to earn the money his grandma needs. But he needs to overcome multiple hurdles along the way. To begin with, Gilmore knows nothing about golf other than how to hit the ball hard. He's also an outsider from a completely different sport, unaware of the traditions and etiquette that govern the game of golf. And he needs emotional support in the face of provocation from his bitter rival, superstar golfer Shooter McGavin.

Gilmore's mentor figure in the film is Chubbs Peterson, a former golf star who was forced to retire when an alligator bit off his right hand. Peterson helps Gilmore improve his golfing technique, but he also inducts him into the golf 'scene' while allowing Gilmore to retain elements of his identity as a hockey player. He provides an outlet for Gilmore's frustration as he struggles to adapt to golf, and crucially, asks questions that force Gilmore to evaluate his approach to the game and to his rivals, thereby prompting him to confront his weaknesses as a golfer and find solutions to them.

The film may be far-fetched, and it certainly portrays a world that is very different to the lived experience of most teachers and learners. The typical mentor in education is an experienced teacher who provides one-to-one support to a less experienced teacher (or 'mentee'), usually in the teaching environment where they both work. But in fact, one-handed Chubbs Peterson exemplifies many of the ways in which trainers might need to support individual trainees as part of their work, in that he:

- **develops trainees' practical skills** through demonstration, focused practice and feedback

- **provides emotional support and motivation** when things aren't going well

- **leads trainees towards autonomy** and towards their own professional identity

- **acts as a guide** in the unfamiliar world of a new profession (for beginning teachers) or new teaching environment

We can see these traits in the following stories of three trainers providing individual support.

CASE STUDY 5.1: JASON, MENTOR

The school where I work has a mentoring programme for new teachers, and I'm one of the mentors. We run initial training courses here, and sometimes the best trainees are taken on once their course has ended. Even though they've done well on the course, they still need a lot of support, and that's where I come in!

Generally, the mentoring period lasts for three months, but it can be reduced or extended if myself and the teacher agree that that's ok. The way it works is that we meet once a week and talk through any issues that came up in lessons over the past seven days. We also spend some time talking through plans for lessons coming up, but some teachers need more support with planning than others so it really just depends on the teachers themselves. Right now, I'm mentoring a fairly young teacher who did well on the course but is struggling to manage her classes – I suspect it's more an issue with her confidence than anything else so I'm going to observe a lesson to get a better idea of how I can help her, and we might also arrange for her to observe me.

CASE STUDY 5.2: KAVITHA, MENTOR

At the moment I'm mentoring a colleague, and that is because she asked to be mentored so that she can prepare to take a diploma course next year. I think she felt that she needed some guidance about what her strengths and weaknesses were and what to work on, but actually she's been quite proactive in her professional development and I think she's shown that she's quite a good judge of her own teaching.

The format we've settled on (I've been mentoring her almost three months) is that Anita (that's the teacher) reads a key text from the diploma reading list, plans how she is going to incorporate what she's learned into her teaching, and then teaches those lessons and discusses it with me. We meet every week and she spends 4–5 weeks working through each book, so we have several opportunities to talk about what she's read, discuss her plans, and then also to talk about how the lessons have gone. My role is to make her accountable for doing the reading but also to explain some of the parts that she finds difficult to understand, and I think I have helped her to reflect more thoroughly on her lessons, too. Because we work together we have plenty of chances to talk about her teaching outside of our weekly meetings, but it's good to have them as a focal point, I think.

It's been very interesting for me, and Anita is very happy with how her teaching has improved too, so I would say that we have been successful! I think we will continue this right up to the end of the year, and who knows, maybe next year when she starts the diploma as well.

CASE STUDY 5.3: PETER

I remember one particular trainer during my Cambridge CTEFLA (now CELTA) course whose particular techniques were and continue to be an inspiration for me. As part of her tutor role she welcomed me and made the first steps in introducing me to the world of the teaching profession (which was quite scary for a novice like me). While she was never officially my mentor, and we never actually worked together, as my course tutor she encouraged me at every step by being there for me and by listening to my concerns about my abilities. This capacity to listen without immediately offering solutions encouraged me to self-reflect and to develop my own thoughts about teaching.

To this day, nearly 40 years on, I can still picture her demonstrating a vocabulary elicitation technique while kneeling on the classroom floor in front of me and my fellow CTEFLA trainees, sitting in a semi-circle. After the CTEFLA course we kept in touch for some years, and initially she was able to provide me with some important contacts and employment possibilities, but in those days communication was by handwritten letter and I'm sorry to say that neither of us was very good at it. I lost my role model, my mentor, but what I learned from her will always be with me.

In each of the three case studies above, a teacher is learning from a more experienced peer, and referring to that person as a mentor. That's only a formal role title in Jason's case, though – Kavitha's situation is an informal mentoring arrangement, and Peter's mentor was the trainer on his preservice course. So mentoring is defined more by the relationship between an inexperienced teacher and an experienced one than it is by the institution where it takes place.

The emphasis in each case is slightly different, but in all the case studies the teachers in the role of mentee need a combination of help with their training skills and support on a more personal level, whether that's to overcome a lack of confidence or to help provide continuing motivation. Nevertheless, the arrangements between the mentor and mentee look different in each case (frequency of meetings, the duration of the relationship, whether the mentor observes the mentee's lessons), depending on the mentee's level of experience and their needs, and on the practical restrictions of each context. Two of the three mentees in the case studies are inexperienced teachers, and that is usually the case where mentoring is concerned, but not always, as Kavitha proves.

Peter highlights how his mentor enabled him to develop his own thinking and way of being a teacher. Rather than aiming to create teachers in their own image, mentors will offer support in a way that allows teachers to develop their own unique professional identities in their own unique teaching contexts. In the words of Angi Malderez, mentoring 'deals with the realities of the particular – the particular school, class, child, and teacher, within particular contexts' (Malderez, 2009, p. 260). There's a clear contrast there to training sessions, which have to deal with issues at a more general level because they are aimed at a larger number of teachers.

Despite the importance of mentoring to teacher learning, relatively few people in the world of teacher education have the title of mentor. So we find it more helpful to separate mentoring skills from the role title itself and refer to *mentoring practices* – the roles, functions, techniques and overall orientation of mentoring – which can be learned and adopted as part of a teacher trainer's toolkit. There are many times in the life of a trainer when these practices are needed, and they are often required from teachers, too.

Most experienced teachers will have provided support to a colleague in some form – sharing materials, giving advice on a challenging class, recommending a useful resource or answering a grammar question. In thinking about the times that you have taken on one or more of the roles of mentor, hopefully you felt that your interventions had positive results for the teacher(s) in the role of mentee. But you might also be able to identify ways in which you benefitted as part of the process too. Mentoring relationships are now recognised as reciprocal and collaborative, with both parties benefitting, not just the mentee. For mentors, the advantages include improved professional competency and reflective skills, enhanced self-esteem and a feeling of being re-energised professionally (Hobson, Ashby, Malderez, & Tomlinson, 2009; Huling & Resta, 2001). For us personally, mentoring has provided chances to examine individual teachers' practice and its development in detail, which is vital for trainers.

Because mentoring practices are part of the broader trainer toolkit, the same conditions for success that we saw in Chapter 1 need to be in place (Hobson, Ashby, Malderez, & Tomlinson, 2009; Malderez, 2009). The institution, or the course provider, needs to allow time for mentoring to take place, both for the trainer and the teacher. All parties involved need to be clear about the objectives and roles of the relationship, especially the teacher whose learning and development is the main objective, and in school-based mentoring, teacher managers. And both trainer and trainee will benefit from a supportive environment in which colleagues are encouraging (e.g., willing to be observed by the trainee) and in which resources for self-directed trainee learning are available.

Mentoring practices and the trainer toolkit

Delivering training sessions to groups and training one-to-one are both teacher education processes. What that means is that mentoring conversations will retain the same basic elements that training sessions include; they still need to deal with the Practical, the Personal and the Professional (see Chapter 3) because the underlying principles of teacher learning are the same. But mentoring conversations will deal with those elements with respect to the individual characteristics of the person acting as mentee, because that person can be the sole focus of the trainer's attention.

Mentoring practices, then, sit alongside the practices we have already looked at for designing, delivering and evaluating training sessions; they are part of the same 'trainer toolkit' and based on the same principles of teacher learning. Working with individual teachers in the classroom inevitably makes it easier to focus on developing the Practical domain of their work – improving the way that individual teaching techniques, such as questioning, or monitoring, are carried out. But the real advantage of mentoring practices is in the development of skills that are less easily observed, but crucial to the development of adaptive expertise: noticing what is happening in the classroom in terms of student learning, reflecting on teaching and linking theory to practice.

Mentors also play an important part in helping teachers to develop the Personal – their beliefs, assumptions and professional identity – particularly newly qualified teachers who may still be learning their craft. In these cases, mentors help not just with practical teaching skills but by 'showing the ropes'. Mentors help new teachers to talk and act like teachers amongst their peers and in front of students. For all these reasons, there is good evidence that mentoring leads to enhanced confidence in mentees, greater teacher retention, better teaching and better learning (Hobson, Ashby, Malderez, & Tomlinson, 2009; Ingersoll & Strong, 2011).

Heron's six categories of intervention

Mentoring interactions are too diverse to be able to offer a one-size-fits-all model for approaching them. But a useful way of thinking about possible routes to take in a one-to-one conversation with a teacher is John Heron's six categories of intervention, defined in Table 5.1 (Randall & Thornton, 2001, p. 78).

Table 5.1: Heron's six categories of intervention

Authoritative	Prescriptive	The mentor gives specific instructions about what to do or what to change.
	Informative	The mentor provides the teacher with information or demonstrates a technique.
	Confronting	The mentor challenges the teacher on areas felt to be problematic.
Facilitative	Cathartic	The mentor creates opportunities for the teacher to express their feelings.
	Catalytic	The mentor prompts the teacher to reflect or to recall previous learning.
	Supportive	The mentor offers positive affirmation of what the teacher is doing.

Heron's six categories offer a very basic menu of options for trainers who find themselves in a mentoring situation. No conversation will be simple enough for the trainer to stick to one category throughout the conversation, so they will always need to be combined. There's also no given 'recipe' for combing the categories in any particular situation; it's a question of careful listening, sensitivity and tact on the part of the trainer. But despite these limitations, Heron's categories can help us to reflect on how we might respond to trainees in one-to-one interactions, and to explore what kinds of interventions will prove most effective in the training contexts we find ourselves in.

CASE STUDY 5.4: KAVITHA, MENTOR

I start every mentoring meeting with Anita by asking about the action point from the previous meeting, which is either to have read part of the book she's currently working through, or to have tried something in the classroom. When she's done some reading, she'll often have questions for me about things that she hasn't fully understood, and then we talk about what she could take from the reading and experiment with in her teaching. If she's coming to the meeting after trying something in the classroom then she'll talk me through what happened and we discuss anything that was problematic and might need to be tweaked, as well as what she has learned from the experiment.

On just a couple of occasions we've had our meeting and Anita hasn't done what she was meant to do. In these situations I just try to be supportive and encourage her – I know that on the whole she's really trying hard to make progress, and that there will be some weeks when work or life gets in the way. But she's quite self-motivated in general, so I know I can rely on her to maintain the momentum, and that's not been the case with all the teachers I've mentored. Some need a more rigid approach, which is fine; I find that it's helpful to discuss these things explicitly at the beginning so that we can find a way of working together that works for both of us.

CASE STUDY 5.5: JASON, MENTOR

There are three factors that influence my approach to mentoring. Firstly, the teachers often find it a shock to go from their preservice course, where they've always been observed teaching, to working in the classroom alone. They're really not used to having to work out for themselves if lessons are going well or not. Secondly, they tend to be very focused on themselves and whether the students like them, and thirdly, they are often just completely overwhelmed – the lessons are so much longer than the teaching practice they did on their course, they're spending hours and hours planning so they're tired, and sometimes they're beginning to wonder if teaching is for them.

So I try and start every meeting by asking how they're doing, and try to go beyond the 'fine thanks' that usually comes back and probe a bit deeper as to whether they really are coping or not. Then we talk about their recent lessons and they get a chance to ask me any questions they've got. I try and prompt them to think about whether they're achieving their lesson aims and what the students are taking away from the lessons. Finally, we run through some of their plans for upcoming lessons and I'll often point to resources they can use to supplement the coursebook – obviously as they're new to teaching there's a lot they're not aware of yet.

This is how I structure the meetings but to be honest any of these things could also happen more informally in the staffroom – we're colleagues so we're also interacting in and around the school.

TASK 5.3

...To trainer

Which of Heron's categories are being used by Kavitha and Jason in their mentoring meetings, and for what purpose?

For notes see page 226

It should be reasonably clear by now that mentoring practices have less in common with teaching than training sessions do. Of course, there will be times as a teacher when you offer more tailored support to individual students, but the examples we've seen represent quite a departure from conversations with students, or even from the times when you may have supported teaching colleagues. So for most new trainers mentoring practices will involve a steeper learning curve and will take longer to master. The good news is that there is some overlap between mentoring practices and giving feedback on teaching, and some of the ideas covered in this chapter, such as Heron's categories, are also relevant to what we discuss in Chapter 8.

Let's now look at specific examples of the situations in which you might turn to mentoring practices as a trainer. Some of these will arise as part of longer training courses; others are more likely to arise within your institution. You may come across other opportunities for mentoring, but we hope that the examples here will give you a sense of how to dig into your trainer toolkit and turn to mentoring practices as and when they can bring something to a teacher learning situation.

Mentoring practices on training courses

Training courses combine a mixture of teacher learning activity: there are usually training sessions, but there may also be practice teaching, observation, guided lesson planning or assignments to write. This combination of different course content means that, as a trainer, you will perform various roles, and some of them will involve mentoring practices.

Lesson planning

Planning lessons often seems to become an all-consuming task for teachers on training courses, particularly at preservice level. Most of the planning that trainees will do will happen outside scheduled course hours, but many courses include timetabled sessions for supervised lesson planning, and if you are a course tutor you will need to support trainees during this time, individually or in groups. Depending on how the course is set up they may be teaching the same day, or the following day, but trainees are likely to be a little anxious either way.

Preservice trainees find lesson planning difficult for three reasons. The first is that the possibilities open to them – in terms of aims, materials, activities and resources – often feel overwhelming, and selecting what to do can seem impossible. In the words of John Hughes, 'it can feel like someone has asked them to cook a three-course meal in a giant kitchen with every ingredient imaginable' (Hughes, 2015, p. 81). The second reason that planning is difficult for novice teachers is that they have no mental frameworks to draw upon for the sequencing of techniques and activities, so everything has to be imagined from scratch. Experienced teachers don't need to do this because they can assemble their lessons from larger 'chunks', which are reusable routines of techniques or activities that are familiar from repeated use. Tessa Woodward, explaining this idea, describes how

> teachers have to think about individual small units of content, steps, activities and material before being able to work at a broader level. But I believe that as soon as possible we need to start thinking about putting steps together, subsuming them into larger units and thinking about shaping lessons and sets of lessons. (Woodward, 2001, p. 7)

The third reason that novices often find planning difficult is that they have no experience of how students will react to lesson content, so estimating timings and anticipating problems and solutions are extremely difficult. It is our job as trainers, then, to help trainees overcome these limitations when they first start planning, by familiarising them with appropriate resources, and to highlight lesson planning chunks by referring back to course input. In addition, guided lesson planning has the objectives of:

- fostering an effective thought process for lesson planning, encouraging trainees to take the lesson aim as the starting point for planning decisions and to think of the lesson in terms of what students will learn, not just what they will do

- helping trainees to put into practice the techniques and concepts they've learned in input sessions

- helping trainees prepare plans that will actually support them when they go into the classroom, for example by scripting some of the questions they will ask, or the instructions they will give

- ensuring that any documentation required as part of the course is being prepared in the right way

Here are some suggestions for managing these conversations. Take them as a point of departure – you may well find that in your training contexts there are other ways of achieving the goals above. What you will need, though, is for trainees to bring draft lesson plans to these discussions. If they haven't done any thinking about the lesson already it is difficult to help them develop their thinking further!

Ask the trainee to begin by giving the lesson aim. This reinforces the aim as the starting point for the lesson planning process, and means that you can refer back to it during discussion of lesson stages. It also means that if the lesson is built on a flimsy aim (i.e., one which doesn't express how the students will be better able to communicate in the target language as a result of the lesson), or no aim at all, you can deal with that from the beginning.

As trainees talk through their plans, **ask them to relate each lesson stage to the lesson aim**. If a lesson structure such as Test-Teach-Test has been used, this is the time to talk through it, as well as what techniques and materials will be used at each stage. If you are with a small group of trainees, you could ask those listening to help identify the links between the overall lesson aim and each stage of the plan.

In your feedback on aims and lesson stages, **link planning to input**. This is a key mentoring skill, particularly in terms of highlighting chunks of lesson steps (activities, techniques) that have been presented. Elicit ideas from trainees before providing them with these connections.

Nudge trainees towards autonomy in planning by asking them to justify their choices. The key to making this manageable is to narrow the choices that trainees need to make. At the very earliest stages, this might mean providing a complete lesson plan with two options for certain stages. The teacher then needs only to choose the option they feel is most appropriate and the conversation will be about the reasons for their choice. Later in the course you might provide the lesson aim and the material to be used, so that the teacher needs to make more choices about how the lesson will unfold – encourage them to link these choices to the aim and to the characteristics of the learners.

Preservice trainees do not have enough experience with learners to be able to accurately **predict how long activities will take or to anticipate potential problems**. Encourage trainees to talk through their plans stage by stage and others in the group to guess how long each stage will need, and what problems students might have.

Start by scaffolding the planning process, and reduce the amount of support given as the course progresses. This may mean that at the start of the course the trainees are provided with lesson materials, aims and a skeleton lesson plan, which is then reduced to just materials and aims later in the course, and finally just aims as the course nears its end. This is a form of modelling – the trainees begin by working from examples of good practice and eventually have to emulate those models by creating their own lesson plans.

Pastoral support

The word *pastoral* comes from the Latin term for shepherd, and besides attending to the trainees' learning, there is usually a certain amount of shepherding to do to help trainees get to the end of a teacher training course! It is here that the support role of the mentor comes into play: there are times when you will need to 'be there' and act as a sounding board for trainees who are finding things difficult.

If you are someone who has, as a teacher, always enjoyed training sessions and courses, it may seem odd that so many trainees need this kind of support. So it is worth considering why training courses might be experienced as 'intense, emotional and stressful' (Davies & Northall, 2019a, p. 49), because understanding these feelings from the trainees' point of view is essential to our ability to provide the support they need.

First of all, intensive courses are exactly that: intensive. There may be very little time outside the course for routine activities like exercise or socialising, and that in itself can be stressful. The effect is arguably greater for preservice trainees, who are grappling with entirely new concepts and a completely new identity as a teacher. Teaching practice can be a particular source of anxiety, because it is uniquely challenging to that new teacher identity, and because it often takes place off the back of late nights spent planning – it is very easy to forget how long it takes novice teachers to plan a lesson once you have developed a certain level of planning expertise.

Secondly, professional learning involves change, and several writers have turned to the literature on change management to throw some light on what teachers experience as part of the process of changing their teaching practice. What emerges is a roughly 'u-shaped' sequence of emotions that gets worse before it gets better: the lowest point for teachers comes shortly after trying new practices when the significance of a proposed/needed change has sunk in – termed 'informed pessimism' (Malderez & Wedell, 2007, p. 130) or 'awareness of incompetence' (Waters, 2005, p. 221). This is when teachers need encouragement, motivation and emotional support, because the only route to subsequent integration of the new practices is to continue working on them, to '"trust the process" and keep going' (Malderez & Wedell, 2007, p. 131). This may all seem unduly negative, and it does contrast with the collaborative energy of the training room, but it is when it comes to applying new ideas in the classroom that the real challenge begins – there is suddenly much more at stake than there was in the training room. There is the risk of losing face in front of the students and in front of peers, and there is a risk to the teacher's own professional identity. That's when the scale of the challenge ahead starts to become clear, and there will be times for all trainees when it just gets a bit too much.

The other time when emotions can run high is in response to feedback, particularly when it involves delivering bad news to trainees. This might be a 'below standard' mark for a practice lesson or an assignment that needs to be resubmitted, or it could simply be an area for development in an otherwise well-delivered lesson – sometimes it is more difficult to take negative feedback on board when the lesson in general has been a success; poor feedback on a lesson that was truly disastrous, on the other hand, comes as no surprise.

Providing pastoral support to trainees, then, requires some sensitivity to the pressures that might be causing emotional strain in the first place. Nevertheless, there are some general actions you can take to mitigate the chances of trainee anxiety, and to facilitate helpful conversations if and when you are needed to talk to:

> Put effort into building a **trusting relationship** with trainees. Your getting-to-know-you phase at the beginning of the course is important for this, but ensure also that you learn trainees' names quickly, emphasise that they can approach you, and demonstrate openness in your interactions with them. This is something that needs to happen throughout your time with the trainees, not just at the beginning.

> **Make yourself available at certain times** and communicate those times clearly. Obviously, trainees can't come to you for help if you're not available. This is very difficult on intensive courses but try to make yourself available during break times by scheduling your own breaks while trainees are doing something else, perhaps in a session with a co-trainer. Clarifying times that you are available also means clarifying when you are not available, and that's important – trainers need a break too.

> **Deal with feedback tactfully and sensitively** – we will discuss feedback in more detail in Chapter 8, but try to remain empathetic throughout, and allow space for emotional reactions.

> Davies and Northall (2019a) suggest giving trainees a '**candidate agreement**' to sign that outlines clear policies for absence, deadlines, and so on. This ensures that trainees know what is expected of them and can plan ahead to avoid work bottlenecks.

It is also important to be aware of how emotional strain can manifest itself in trainees. The following are all possible signs of a trainee struggling to cope:

- absence from the course, perhaps without warning (e.g., not turning up for teaching practice)

- irritability, or a reluctance to participate in group work / plenary discussion

- being overly critical of their own teaching and seemingly unable to identify the positives in their lessons

- being overly critical of other trainees' teaching

- an unwillingness to engage with feedback, particularly after being receptive initially

You may need to be proactive about supporting trainees exhibiting these signs, rather than waiting for them to come to you for help. Encourage them to share how they are feeling by asking 'How are you coping with the course?' rather than closed questions such as 'Are you OK?'

TASK 5.4

...To trainer

You are observing teaching practice with a group of five trainees. It is the first teaching practice session and three of the five trainees are each teaching part of the lesson. When trainees are not teaching, they are observing the lesson.

The lesson has begun and the first trainee is teaching, but the trainee due to teach next has not turned up. What will you do?

For notes see page 227

Managing workload and deadlines

An expectation on most training courses is a certain level of professionalism from the trainees. This means attending on time, meeting deadlines for the submission of work, working effectively with other trainees, and so on. It's important to be clear with trainees about what these expectations are, especially in relation to group work. Working collaboratively can be a relatively new experience for some trainees, but it is an important professional skill to develop, and many aspects of a course can be hampered if trainees are not aware of how they should conduct themselves in, for example, group feedback sessions or group planning time.

This area involves a combination of implicit and explicit mentoring. You can support trainees implicitly by acting as a role model – not in the sense of modelling teaching practices, but in the sense of modelling what it means to be a language teaching professional, someone who works in an educational environment. In addition, these are some ways that you can clarify expectations of your trainees more explicitly:

Provide a course timetable with all deadlines clearly marked.

Ensure trainees understand how they are being assessed – you might want to devote some time in a session to this at the beginning of the course.

Draw up a class contract at the beginning of the course – you can use this as an opportunity to model the same process that teachers might use with their own (probably young learner) students.

Communicate the policies for illness/absence, late submission of work and plagiarism.

Smile! Teaching is fun, and teachers need to convey enthusiasm for their subject, so trainers need to convey enthusiasm for theirs. Show trainees you enjoy what you do!

Many training centres combine the documents in this list into a course handbook that is distributed before the course, or on the first day.

Mentoring practices in schools

Mentoring practices in schools can look rather different, because there isn't a course timetable governing the frequency of meetings or the period of professional learning for the trainee involved. This can be a positive thing, because it generally means a more long-term mentoring relationship between trainer and teacher, but it also means that mentoring practices need to be organised around the teaching timetable. In addition, the teacher and the trainer acting as a mentor will probably need to be proactive about building the relationship, keeping it going and scheduling reasonably regular meetings in order to stop it fizzling out.

In most school-based mentoring situations the relationship between the mentor and mentee will be just one relationship in a broader programme of mentoring. Often such programmes are set up within the school for one of the following reasons:

- to help a newly qualified teacher make the transition from training into day-to-day life as a teacher (possibly during a placement as part of a preservice training course)

- to induct new teachers to the school, who may arrive with teaching experience gained elsewhere

- to cater to teachers who require support with a particular need, usually in response to a change in their teaching life (such as teaching children for the first time, or dealing with a difficult class)

- to support teachers who have been deemed to be underperforming

The mentor is therefore assigned to the mentee by the administrator of the school mentoring programme, and there will be certain guidelines for when and how frequently meetings should take place, as well as what outcomes are expected from the institution's point of view. Ideally, there should be some preparation or training for mentors as part of the programme too, but that kind of support is often sadly lacking.

CASE STUDY 5.6: CAROLINA, MENTOR

I remember, when I was still 'just' a teacher, being asked to act as a mentor for a new teacher who was joining my school straight from her initial training course (the school was also a training centre so she had been recommended by training colleagues). I didn't really know anything about mentoring at that time, and I had never been mentored myself, but I was considered a good teacher and I thought I would be able to help her. My main point of reference was my own experience – I really just tried to remember how I had felt as a new teacher and what would have been helpful to me at that time.

TASK 5.5

...To trainer

If you were Carolina in Case study 5.6, how would you approach your first meeting with the new teacher? What would you want to find out, and how would you want to structure the meeting?

When you are first assigned to a teacher as a mentor, there are tasks that will need to be done in order to get the ball rolling, regardless of the situation the teacher is in. You will want to plan for your first meeting with the teacher so that you can start off on the right foot. There are various different aims to that first meeting: you want to get to know each other a little and build trust, establish how the mentoring relationship will work in terms of when you will meet and the nature of support that the teacher can expect from you, what your expectations of the teacher will be and the goals that each of you will have for the relationship. Before that can happen, you will need to be clear what the school's set-up is for mentoring. Table 5.2 outlines the type of questions to think about for these initial steps.

Table 5.2: Planning for mentoring

Stage	Questions/tasks
Clarifying the school's policies	◦ Is there a place where you can meet? ◦ Will the school make room in your respective timetables for the meetings or are you expected to schedule meetings around your normal teaching timetables? ◦ What payment is there for mentors? Are mentees also paid to take part? ◦ What paperwork are you each required to complete and submit as part of the programme, and when? ◦ Who needs to be aware that the mentoring relationship is in place in order to support it?
First meeting	◦ Break the ice and build trust. ◦ How often will you meet? When? Where? ◦ What should happen in between meetings? ◦ What shape are meetings likely to take? ◦ What kind of support can the teacher expect from you? ◦ What channels of communication will you use? ◦ What are the goals that you are each trying to achieve?

This is by no means an exhaustive list – depending on your mentees' situations, it might be appropriate to show them around the building, introduce them to colleagues and point out where they can get a cup of coffee! Every mentee is different and you will need to think carefully about how they might be feeling and what kinds of support will help them to flourish. You may also find yourself in a situation where you need to advocate for a mentee in the face of unforgiving or inflexible school decision making. One of us, for example, was assigned a newly qualified teacher as a mentee at a school that was severely understaffed. Because of the pressure to keep classes running, she was assigned seven different classes, encompassing adult and young learners, and a wide range of levels. That was far too much; a newly qualified teacher really needed support from the school in the form of a reduced teaching load and the opportunity to teach the same lessons to different groups. So in such situations be prepared to 'stick up' for your mentees, who may not feel in a position to know what is reasonable or to speak out themselves.

CASE STUDY 5.7: CAROLINA, MENTOR

I was so relieved that I had planned that first meeting because it quickly became apparent that the teacher had expected us to have a similar type of relationship to what she'd had on her course. I explained that this was a different kind of support, that I wasn't an observer or assessor, and that our meetings would be directed much more by her. I also explained the rationale for this, but she seemed uneasy and wanted clear feedback on what she was doing. We eventually agreed to meet halfway. This turned out to be very important: as we went on we both knew what to expect and I think she was clear about why I was taking the approach I was taking (not observing, not saying 'do it this way') as she felt her own reflective skills developing.

CASE STUDY 5.8: JOHANNA, MENTOR

The school where I teach actively supports a mentorship scheme. The way it works is that there are three or four teachers in different groups, each with a different focus, and the members of the group all share the same mentor. It's possible to be a member of more than one group, and therefore to have the benefit of more than one mentor. Each member of a group has different amounts of experience, knowledge and skills (as do the mentors), so we all feel that we can contribute something when we get together. I belong to two groups and the mentors meet us as a group, usually once a week. Their role is not to train us, but to provide a sympathetic ear, to listen to us and sometimes to make suggestions. Also, we sometimes take part in role plays, taking on different roles each time, and talking through various situations from our classrooms. We can also meet the mentors individually if we want to, and for one in particular I value this, but for the other one, it rarely happens. However, both are extremely supportive in different ways for someone like me, even with nearly 10 years' teaching experience.

Summary

Just about all trainers will, at various points in their careers, have to open up their trainer toolkit and wield some mentoring practices. Some trainers will do that more than others, perhaps even taking on the role of mentor in a formal capacity, but for most of us mentoring practices will be a resource that we turn to as the training situation demands.

We've already seen that mentoring practices are a bigger step from teaching than delivering sessions, but learning to perform mentor roles also tends to be more challenging because many of us may not have had much or any experience of being mentees in the past. The private nature of mentoring relationships also makes it hard to observe mentoring conversations in order to learn how to carry them out – those who are lucky enough to attend mentor training programmes will spend a significant portion of time on those programmes role-playing mentoring conversations. So most trainers develop their mentoring skills on the job, finding their way as they go, and reflection therefore becomes extremely important. Keeping a journal of mentoring conversations can be especially useful, because it is almost certain that you will be able to reflect on it as you gain confidence as a mentor and identify areas for your own development.

Observing lessons is not necessarily something that mentors need to do – there are good reasons for not observing, such as providing the mentee with more autonomy, lowering anxiety and making discussions of lessons more authentic (Malderez & Wedell, 2007). Nevertheless, the role of mentor in many contexts might include observing teachers and then discussing what went on in the classroom, and we will deal with pre- and post-lesson discussions, and lesson observation itself, in Chapters 6–8.

 **TRAINER VOICES**

 Scan the QR Code and watch the videos 'Training individuals' and 'Offering pastoral support' to hear how trainers put the principles we've looked at into practice. Is there anything that surprises you in what they describe?

 **TO FIND OUT MORE**

Malderez, A., & Bodóczky, C. (1999). *Mentor courses*. Cambridge: Cambridge University Press. (Includes lots of excellent tasks for developing mentoring skills.)

Randall, M., & Thornton, B. (2001). *Advising and supporting teachers*. Cambridge: Cambridge University Press. (Ostensibly focused on observation feedback, but also provides an excellent overview of the counselling approaches and techniques that underpin much mentoring, including Heron's Six Categories.)

6 Observing teaching and learning

Here we consider:
- The purposes of observation
- What to do before observing
- What to do during the observation
- Challenges of observation and how to deal with them
- How to prepare for feedback

The trick to doing observations, I think, is to make sure the observees know that it's coming from a place of caring, a place that says I'm here because I want to help you.

Allen, teacher trainer, Thailand

Teachers can only learn so much in the training room. Eventually, the ideas and practices encountered in training sessions, books, staffroom discussions or mentoring conversations need to be unleashed on real students in real lessons. That's where observation comes in.

A recurring theme in twentieth century writing on schools in the US is the idea of the school as an 'egg crate' (e.g., Lortie, 1975), where teachers are kept separate in their classrooms like eggs in a box. It's a very compelling metaphor because there's a lot of truth to it – teachers do their most important work in isolation from one another, and this puts great pressure on teachers to decide for themselves how successful their lessons are and what should be done to improve their teaching. Observations, at their best, are a chance to break down the divides between teaching professionals and to allow someone else to come into the classroom to take on the burden of evaluating what takes place: they are opportunities for collaboration and sharing of expertise. When it works well, lesson observation can be transformative for teachers: we have both benefitted enormously in our careers from observations that provided us with crucial insights, improving our teaching markedly and permanently.

But not all observations work well. It is almost certain that, as you read this, hundreds of teachers around the world are being observed teaching. And unfortunately, it is equally likely that only a tiny proportion of those observations will have the professional learning of the teacher as their main aim. Instead, they are largely used to check that teachers are meeting the expectations of school management. Some of them will be live observations, with a staff member sitting in the classroom; one of only a handful of times that the teacher will be observed in the year (perhaps the only time). Others will be observations via video camera, with CCTV in schools on the rise globally.[1] In these scenarios there is often no formal process, and the teacher will not know when they are being observed and when they aren't. The first indication that someone has been watching would be a summons to the principal's office.

For most teachers, these observations offer little. If teachers do well, they are considered to have met expectations, a box has been ticked, and they can put the thought of observation aside until the next time it is imposed upon them. If, on the other hand, a teacher's performance in the observation is deemed unsatisfactory, that teacher may well lose their job.

Many observers dread these observations, too. They are required to conduct observations by institutional policies, but rarely have the necessary time in their schedules and are often untrained in how to observe or how to manage the process from start to finish, particularly the delivery of feedback. As a result, observations seem to take on the form of a kind of scheduled confrontation with teachers, which both parties would prefer to avoid.

This bleak picture isn't true for everyone – we are both fortunate to have been part of observations in which professional learning was the goal (although not in every case!), and we now welcome observations as some of the richest opportunities for professional learning available to us. But for many of the teachers that we work with, the situation outlined above forms the backdrop for discussions about observation, drawing all the bad experiences and ill feeling of teachers into those discussions. So we need to be very clear how and why we are using it as a tool for teacher learning.

Why observation matters

TASK 6.1

From teacher ...

Think about the times you have been observed as a teacher. What was the purpose of each observation? Who benefitted more each time, the teacher, the observer, or someone else?

It may seem strange to question the purpose of observation. For both of us, and most probably for you too, it is a fact of professional life, one that has been there since our earliest experiences in front of a class. And when we learn any new skill, seeing others do it is often the very first step, while being seen and getting feedback are important to further

---

1 For example, in the state of Delhi, India (https://timesofindia.indiatimes.com/city/delhi/no-sc-stay-on-cctv-in-govt-schools/articleshow/70198849.cms) and in the UK (www.independent.co.uk/news/education/education-news/spying-teacher-cctv-classrooms-rise-9271501.html)

improvement. Observation, however, 'does not just mean "seeing"' (Malderez, 2003, p. 179). In fact it is probably more useful to think of it as a process of data gathering (Bailey, 2001; Randall & Thornton, 2001), because the information that an observation yields will probably be used for a specific purpose. Those different purposes naturally lead to different ways of collecting data, so understanding exactly why we are observing is key to knowing how to do it well. But if we think of observation as data gathering, we can also come to a clearer understanding of what information it *can't* yield, and how it might therefore be complemented by other forms of data collection. What an observer sees is just a snapshot of teaching and learning at a particular time, and it should rarely be the sole basis for further decision making.

To begin to understand why observation takes place, let's consider some real-life examples:

CASE STUDY 6.1: MARIE, THE CELTA TRAINER

I work with trainees who are just starting out in teaching, so when I observe I hope to see them taking new concepts from our input sessions and applying them, and learning from that what works and what doesn't. I find that really satisfying because they can make dramatic progress very quickly, even with short lessons, and because it makes me feel like my training sessions are useful! What I am looking at is guided by the assessment criteria for the course, which is helpful, but it took me a long time to remember all the criteria and pay attention to all the different areas they cover. It also took me time to learn how to balance the competing need to assess trainees – my decisions will affect whether they pass or fail – and the need to develop their skills. In fact, I still find that difficult.

An added dimension to CELTA observations is that I'm not the only observer – I'm joined by the non-teaching trainees in the group at the back of the room, and they need to learn something from the observation. For that I provide an observation task, but there is *always* something in the lesson that is worth drawing their attention to in its own right, too. I've started using an online group chat tool for doing that with them, and this can be a really nice starting point for discussions after the lesson.

CASE STUDY 6.2: MOSES, THE TEACHER

My first lessons as a teacher were on my initial teacher training course, and they were all observed. It was completely normal for someone to sit at the back of my lessons, and I actually felt strange when I started my first teaching job and had to face the students completely alone. I had also been watching my fellow trainees teach during the course, and I wanted to keep doing that. So I developed a habit of inviting my colleagues to observe my lessons to point out things that I didn't see and to help me build my confidence, and now we visit each other's classes once every two weeks. We found that the best way to do it is to ask whoever is observing for feedback on a very specific area, such as pronunciation drills, whatever we have been working on improving. That usually means the observation can be quite short, and it helps to make each observation meaningful. I have learned a huge amount from being observed but also from observing. The only downside is that we have to do the observations in our own time, so there are some colleagues whose classes I can't see because they teach at the same time as me.

CASE STUDY 6.3: CARMEN, THE MANAGER

I regularly observe lessons in my role as Director of Studies, and I have two 'modes' of observing. There are times when I'm looking at what teachers are doing from a perspective of 'what's happening in my classrooms?' and for that I do learning walks: literally walking round the school and stopping in classrooms for around ten minutes at a time. From these walks I get a sense of whether teaching meets the standard we expect here, a sense of professional development needs, and a feel for each classroom. But I'm really careful to look at other evidence of what's happening too – I can't use the learning walks as my only basis for judgement because they're just too brief, and if I stay longer than ten minutes it's not a learning walk anymore, it's a surprise observation, which I don't do because it's not fair.

The other mode of observing is what I would call formal observation: I go and watch a significant portion of a lesson and I discuss the plan with the teacher before, and feed back after. The aim with those is to get a much more detailed picture of where each teacher is at, not just in the classroom but in planning and reflecting too, and to really support their development on an individual level. I'm always aware that my presence in the room can create a different atmosphere, and visiting the same class several times on the learning walks helps teachers and students get used to me being there, which helps me to see more natural lessons when I do the formal observations.

In all of the case studies above, observation is being used as a tool for teacher learning (although not exclusively), and it has a uniquely significant role in that process. We saw in Chapter 1 that teacher learning begins with *Knowing about*, often in the training room. But after that initial encounter with a technique or concept, each teacher really needs to apply it to their own teaching context for it to become embedded in practice, evaluating the results and adapting as necessary. Most of the time teachers are left to do that on their own, but it is arguably the point during the learning journey at which expert guidance is most valuable, because translating theory into successfully contextualised practice is difficult. Observation offers the opportunity for that kind of guidance. It is an essential component of learning at the levels of *Knowing how* and *Knowing to* because it promotes the vital connection between the teacher's teaching and the teacher's professional learning, leading to the improvements in student learning that are our ultimate goal. The case studies in this chapter illustrate how observation can be used at different stages in a teacher's professional learning journey, taking the teacher from novice to adaptive expert. But they also illustrate that teacher learning isn't always the only consideration when observation takes place.

Purposes of observation

For Marie (Case study 6.1), observing teachers on a CELTA course, there are multiple purposes to observation. Her main goals are to help the trainees develop their teaching skills, and assess them against the CELTA criteria. The need to assess each lesson that she observes means Marie has to direct her attention to the areas highlighted by the assessment criteria, and this has its advantages and disadvantages, as she describes. There's an additional purpose to observation for Marie to bear in mind, too: the non-teaching trainees in the group are also observing, and she needs to manage their learning in addition to assessing and developing whoever is teaching. Part of that final objective is inducting trainees into the practice of observation itself – how to behave as an observer in a classroom – although that may not be made explicit.

From her trainees' point of view, these observations as part of their CELTA course help to 'level up' their learning in several ways:

- The assessment criteria map out the skills they are expected to demonstrate and provide a consistent framework for thinking about what takes place in their lessons.

- Marie's presence in the classroom provides some reassurance as the trainees face their first classes (in the way that Moses also describes).

- Marie's observations and feedback help to link the trainees' developing practice to what they have learned in their input sessions.

- Feedback (from both Marie and co-trainees) steers trainees towards effective practice and away from misunderstandings of key concepts or unhelpful beliefs and assumptions.

The peer observations Moses describes are developmental in nature – there is no assessment taking place, and no trainer involved. Peer observations may be the only way for teachers who are not participating in formal training to see others teaching, and to have their lessons observed. To some extent, the learning process is similar to that of Marie's trainees: Moses and his colleagues are developing *Knowing how* and *Knowing to* by applying ideas in the classroom, reflecting on them, and making adjustments to their practice. But as Moses describes, this kind of arrangement works best when there is a clear focus for the observations, which is usually chosen by the teacher (although a peer observation task could also provide that focus). Knowing what to look for helps the observer look beyond all the other classroom activity that is not of immediate interest, aids in giving clear feedback (which is important, since peer observers may not have been trained in giving feedback), and helps the teacher to effectively direct their efforts at improvement. In developmental peer observations, it also means that the observer has opportunities to focus on something that they want to learn from the observation, so both parties are able to benefit.

Carmen's observations are driven by slightly different goals. While she wants to help her teachers develop wherever possible, she is observing to gain knowledge that she can use in running her school: she wants to know what is happening in classrooms, and she wants to build a profile of each teacher's skills so that she can appraise their effectiveness and meet their training and development needs. Carmen has adopted different observation routines for each of her goals, which shows that she has carefully considered what she wants to learn and how best to collect the classroom data she needs.

Table 6.1 lists the main purposes for observation, based on similar taxonomies from Kathleen Bailey (2001), Angi Malderez (2003) and Jim Scrivener (2011). In reality these purposes are often found together in a single observed lesson – a typical CELTA observation, for example, combines a training observation, assessment of the candidates' teaching and peer observation by the non-teaching trainees in the group. Similarly, what Carmen describes as a 'formal observation' is a combination of performance appraisal and training observation, and when aggregated with other observations across an institution may also serve as school audit.

Table 6.1: Types of observation

Overarching goal	Observation type	Observer	Description/purpose
Teacher learning	Training: observation	Trainer	Helps the trainer to determine the strengths and weaknesses of the trainee with a view to giving feedback. If part of a course, it may be diagnostic (early in the course) or formative (mid-course) in nature.
	Training: assessment	Trainer	Takes place as part of a course, with reference to detailed criteria laid out in course documentation. Results in a grade.
	Training: apprenticeship observation	Trainee	Trainee(s) in the role of observer attend the class of an experienced 'master' teacher in order to learn from them. Trainees may be given a task to guide the observation.
	Developmental observation	Trainer	Set up and led not by a trainer but by the teacher, who, in order to develop teaching skills, requests feedback on a specific area from the observer.
	Peer observation	Colleague / co-trainee	Usually set up between colleagues for their mutual benefit, with a relatively informal approach to post-lesson discussions. May be required, or facilitated, by some institutions (e.g., by providing tasks).

Academic management	Performance appraisal	Manager	Usually takes place one to three times a year, or following a student complaint. Aims to judge whether the teacher meets the institution's standards for professional competence. The main beneficiary is the manager/institution.
	School audit / inspection	Manager / inspector	Undertaken in order to get a general sense of the quality of teaching and learning in the institution, either for internal purposes, or as part of regulatory requirements. Inspectors will work with detailed standardised criteria; managers may work with school-wide criteria or none at all.
Research	Classroom research	Researcher	Observation in order to gather data with a view to answering a specific research question.

It is important to be clear about the different goals in each situation so that the observation can be set up and managed in such a way that it fulfills the objectives of everyone involved. Lack of clarity about the purposes of observation can reinforce negative feelings about it: for example, it's not uncommon for management goals to overshadow the teacher learning side of observation, creating a sense of 'box-ticking' and reinforcing the antipathy that many teachers already feel towards the process of being observed. In some cases it may even be preferable to limit the use of observation to a single purpose to avoid conflicting objectives: 'there is a good case to be made for removing teacher observations from the performance appraisal system altogether, including them as a clearly developmental tool' (White, Hockley, van der Horst Jansen, & Laughner, 2008, p. 69).

With the exception of research, all of the purposes for observation in Table 6.1 are exemplified in the case studies of Marie, Moses and Carmen, underlining how most observations encompass a range of objectives. That's not surprising when you consider how much time and effort is required to organise and conduct an observation well.

Before observing

To a large extent, what takes place before the observation itself will depend on the purpose of the observation. However, there are decisions to make that don't, and these relate to your personal preferences as an observer, such as:

- When do you want the teacher to provide any relevant paperwork for the lesson? At minimum, you will need to see the materials being used, if there are any. You may also wish to see a lesson plan, seating plan and/or register. Do you want printouts or will soft copies suffice?

- How will you record your observations? Handwrite, type, draw? Diagrams? On the materials/plan provided or on separate paper?

- How will you structure your notes? See the While observing section below (p. 122) for some suggestions.

- Where do you prefer to sit in the classroom? Often the classroom layout or the teacher's plans for the lesson dictate this, but if you do have a choice you may want to consider who you will be looking at more, the teacher or the students, and which point in the room will enable the least disruptive entrance and exit.

- What will your involvement in the lesson be? In most lessons you will wish to stand, walk around and see student work, monitor speaking activities or even sit with groups of students during the lesson to observe how much they are understanding. It is very difficult to evaluate learning (and by extension, teaching) without leaving your chair. That expectation should be clarified with the teacher in advance of the lesson, though.

- When will you conduct your feedback meeting? This may be scheduled in advance if you are delivering a training course. If not, you should consider when you and the teacher are able to meet to discuss the lesson, and schedule that meeting in advance of the observation itself, making it clear what will be involved and how long it will take.

- What paperwork do you want the teacher to complete ahead of the feedback meeting? Give the necessary templates to the teacher before the lesson so they know what to expect, and explain it if necessary so that it's not a source of additional stress.

For most of these questions, you will work out your preferred way of working as you gain experience of observing, and you'll develop routines that you fall back on whenever a new observation comes up. As long as these are working well for you and the teachers you observe, there's no need to change them.

To consider what else ought to happen ahead of an observation let's now consider the three different scenarios in our case studies: the CELTA (preservice course) observations described by Marie, Moses' peer observations and Carmen's formal observations of her teaching staff. We'll consider what administrative tasks are required ahead of the observation, and what should happen if the goals of the observation are to be achieved. As you read, try to notice the different ways in which the observer handles the preparation stage for each of these, and make your own decisions about how best to proceed in your own context, bearing in mind the purpose of the observations you are conducting or organising.

Before preservice course observations

As we've seen from Case study 6.1, on a course like the CELTA there are generally three purposes to observation: training, assessment and peer observation. Each of these necessitates its own preparation.

As with all observations there is an administrative element, although for a course like CELTA there is significantly more, partly because it is an assessed qualification but also because many (most, in some contexts) trainees will have no prior experience of teaching or being observed. Certain aspects of the process that could be taken for granted with more experienced teachers must therefore be made explicit. On the other hand, there are so many observations in quick succession that once expectations are established they shouldn't need to be repeated for every observed lesson. Trainees should be informed early on:

- when they will be expected to teach

- which of those lessons will be observed by the trainer (probably nearly all of them)

- when they will be expected to observe their peers teaching

- what to teach, at least for the early part of the course, and how to coordinate their lessons with other trainees who are teaching on the same day

- when and where they should provide lesson plans and any materials they plan to use for each observed lesson

Since many or all the trainees will also be new to classroom observation, we have found that it is a good idea to clarify 'observation etiquette' with trainees, so that peer observation is productive for all concerned, since all trainees will be observing their co-trainees. One option is to include this in a course handbook and draw trainees' attention to it before their first teaching practice session. Your own course may have its own expectations, but it is likely that they will include the following, or similar:

- As a general rule, observe as you would like to be observed.

- Pay attention to the class – using a mobile, eating, chatting to other trainees, planning your own lesson or leaving the room is not appropriate.

- Complete whatever task has been set.

- Be ready to discuss the lesson afterwards.

- Do not distract the tutor.

- Do not get involved in lessons when observing, even if students ask you for help.

CASE STUDY 6.4: MARIE, THE CELTA TRAINER

A lot of the organising that you would do with a typical school-based observation is done in the first day or two of the course – we run a dedicated input session on teaching practice – so it's not necessary to do much of it later on for each and every observation. One thing that we build into the course schedule is guided lesson planning, when trainees can discuss their lesson plans with myself and the other trainees in their teaching practice group, and I suppose that takes the place of a pre-observation discussion that might happen in other contexts. For me those sessions are about guiding the trainees and helping them to develop the right thought process when they plan a lesson, as well as helping them to feel comfortable with the whole observation process. I make sure the trainees know that they need to hand in their lesson plans first thing on the day that they're teaching – that ensures that I get time to take a look at them before the lesson itself, but I think it's also good that they're not tinkering with them right up to the last minute, because they just wouldn't pay any attention to anything else on teaching days.

Trainees should have access to a lesson planning template that they can use for each observed lesson, and any expectations of how much to write, layout, font size, and so on should be made clear. It is well worth talking the group through a completed example to reduce the possibility of questions or misunderstandings later on, and you may wish to incorporate this into an input session on lesson planning if time allows. As a general rule, providing plenty of support is a good idea: trainees are likely to be nervous, at least for the first few observations they have, and the aim of using the observation as an opportunity to develop their nascent teaching skills is probably best served by offering lots of reassurance and encouragement, and framing the observation as an opportunity to learn, rather than as a test.

Nevertheless, there is an assessment angle to observations on a preservice course, and from your point of view as the observer it requires organisation and preparation. We deal more fully with assessment of teaching in Chapter 7, but when it comes to being prepared for preservice course observations the key is to be organised. Observing and assessing two to three teachers, providing feedback and supporting the peer observations of non-teaching trainees is demanding, and you will need to have various documents at your fingertips (bear in mind that you will go into the classroom with lesson plans, materials, reflection templates, observation task sheets, etc.). Remember, too, that although you may be seated in the corner of the room for two hours, you will be working intensely – be sure to have a proper break beforehand, eat lunch and take a bottle of water with you!

Before peer and apprenticeship observations

Peer observations between colleagues, like the ones Moses takes part in, generally don't require a great deal of preparation by the observer. As Moses describes, he and his peers have discarded pre-observation meetings, often seen as an integral part of the observation process:

CASE STUDY 6.5: MOSES, THE TEACHER

For me and my colleagues, we observe each other to improve our teaching and if I want to improve my lesson planning I will plan a lesson with them, I will not ask them to observe. So we do not meet to discuss the observed lesson before it takes place, we only tell each other what to look for. I can give you two examples: the last time I was observed I asked my colleagues to pay attention to the clarity and effectiveness of my instructions. And the last time I was the observer, my colleague who was teaching asked me to look at how she dealt with students' pronunciation, and whether there were opportunities for teaching pronunciation that she was not exploiting. We have learned to make these requests very specific. Initially we were not precise enough and it was difficult for the observer to provide insights that really gave us the information that we wanted.

The approach that Moses describes is a pragmatic one. He and his colleagues have limited time to meet outside their teaching schedule, and they see no real benefit in discussing a lesson plan or describing a group of students when their professional learning goals are not planning-related, and when they are already familiar with each other's class groups.

Apprenticeship observations, which are when peer observations are arranged with the goal of the observer benefitting from observing a more experienced colleague, are a common part of certificate and diploma teaching qualifications. They are an important option for trainers because it is only the trainee who must commit significant time to them (in most cases, the teacher being observed is simply teaching their regular classes). Even then, like Moses, trainees probably won't meet the teacher before the observed lesson, and pre-observation preparation for the trainer may simply be to make sure the observing trainee has a task to focus their attention during the lesson. As Ruth Wajnryb highlights (her book on the subject offers a comprehensive selection of observation tasks), the advantage of such tasks isn't just that they limit the scope of what trainees need to look for, but that they also ease the burden of forming an opinion of what is seen until later: observation tasks are about collecting data during the lesson itself, and analysing it afterwards (Wajnryb, 1992). Nevertheless, the value of apprenticeship observations can be much enhanced by discussions between the teacher and the trainee at the end of the lesson, if the teacher is willing and available to answer questions and explain some of the choices made during the observed lesson.

Before management observations

Carmen described different purposes for her observations: her learning walks are carried out to audit teaching and learning at whole-school level, while her formal observations have a performance appraisal and training function. Unsurprisingly then, in Case study 6.6, she explains that her preparation for these different kinds of observation is not the same.

CASE STUDY 6.6: CARMEN, THE MANAGER

If I'm planning to do one of my learning walks, there isn't much that can be done before observing, other than to look at the timetable to check who's teaching, and when and where. I notify the teachers that I will be visiting classes during the week, but apart from that they don't know if or when I will come in. Of course, I may check who hasn't recently been observed, and anyone who is new, or who is teaching a new class, as they will need to have priority. I'm quite strict with myself about the timing of them though – by keeping them to no more than ten minutes I don't intrude on each lesson for long, and I can see more classes in the time I have available. Sometimes that means leaving when I would like to see more, but I accept that as inevitable.

If my observation is going to be more formal, then the questions of when and for how long need to have been discussed and agreed in advance with the teacher, so there is more preparatory work involved. I also make sure to find time to look through the lesson plan together with the teacher so that I can see and understand things from their perspective, and build a level of trust with them. I try not to impose myself with suggestions and changes as I believe it is very important for the teacher to follow through with their plan and to reflect on its success (or lack of success!) themselves. Finally, I always try to agree with the teacher on a focus for the observation, for example if the teacher asks for support in a particular aspect of their teaching, or if there is a certain student who needs attention.

You will probably know from the times you've been observed that the process for formal observations within institutions will usually be laid out by the institution itself, so questions of how frequent observations should be, and how long each one is, are predetermined. However, formal observation should:

- involve agreed and clear criteria

- be carried out by trained staff

- include preparation and follow-up

- have provision for mentoring and support for teachers needing help

- involve agreed records which are part of a teacher's personal file and professional portfolio

(White et al., 2008, p. 226)

These details should all be made clear to the teacher at the very outset, and any questions answered. Giving the teacher some choices about how the observation is carried out means that they have some agency in the process and may be more likely to view it positively. Such choices might include:

- which class/lesson will be observed (within the limits of the observer's schedule)

- at which point in the lesson the observer should arrive and leave

- what areas of development should be the focus of feedback

- where the observer should sit

Pre-observation meetings

Both Marie and Carmen mention pre-observation meetings in their case studies above. It's highly likely that if you are conducting observations of teachers you will also conduct some of these meetings, and understanding how they fit into the observation cycle (the total process of pre-observation meeting, observed lesson, and post-observation feedback) is important for ensuring that they are effective.

Pre-observation meetings in both Marie's context (preservice) and Carmen's context (in-service) have several goals, as Table 6.2 shows:

Table 6.2: Pre-observation meeting goals

Observer's goals in pre-observation meeting	Teacher's goals in pre-observation meeting
◦ To clarify the purpose of the observation ◦ To learn about the teaching context and the learners in the class in order to understand the teacher's perspective ◦ To understand what the teacher aims to achieve in the lesson and the rationale for their choices ◦ To identify areas of teaching that are of particular concern to the teacher ◦ To establish a trusting relationship with the teacher	◦ To clarify the aims, content and structure of the lesson so that the observer will understand what they observe ◦ To specify what they would like the observer to look for and provide help with

TASK 6.2

...To trainer

Scan the QR code and watch the pre-observation meeting between Peter (the trainer) and Theresa (the teacher). What questions does Peter ask, and why?

For notes see page 228

The pre-observation meeting is a necessary preliminary step to ensure that the observation itself and the subsequent feedback meeting are successful. As Randall and Thornton point out, 'the benefits of effective observation can be lost if the teacher is unclear about the purposes of the observation or if the observer misunderstands key aspects of the lesson' (Randall & Thornton, 2001, p. 195). So in general, it shouldn't be seen as an opportunity for training teachers by intervening and offering advice – the post-observation feedback meeting is a more appropriate setting for that. Instead, it's a chance to listen and understand how the teacher perceives and thinks about their learners and their lessons. Trainers will rarely agree with everything they see in a lesson plan, but the goal is not to 'correct' the teacher's plans for the lesson. The goal is to understand how the teacher approaches planning and teaching, and use the post-observation feedback meeting to help them to do that more effectively.

The exception to this general principle is preservice observations, because in these situations trainees are still developing their skills and need more support. As Marie reveals, and as we saw in Chapter 5, pre-observation meetings on preservice courses often take place in groups, so that trainees can learn from the conversations they hear between the trainer and their peers. It is quite common for the scaffolded support for lesson planning that trainees receive to be reduced as the course progresses (for instance, by reducing the number of questions trainees can ask, requiring them to plan and deliver longer lessons, or reducing the detail of outline plans that they receive as a starting point), so that trainees get more support at the beginning of the course than at the end, when they are expected to be able to plan lessons more autonomously. But the nature of the supportive interventions is often quite predictable, with formulating aims, understanding the goals and structure of coursebook materials and predicting student reactions (such as how long students will take to complete a task, or what problems they will have) all recurring themes.

While observing

If you think back to the people who have observed your lessons, you may be able to remember a few of them sitting in your classroom, but for most you may have no recollection at all of the observer's presence in the lesson itself. That's probably a good thing because it suggests that the observer's main task is to gather data on teaching and learning that is relevant to the purpose of the observation, rather than to participate in what is happening in the classroom.

CASE STUDY 6.7: MATTHEW

I worked for a year at a fairly small school of around six teachers where all observations were carried out by the academic manager, and I remember one of my colleagues telling me about her observed lesson, in which her aim had been to teach students how to use the present continuous tense to talk about actions in progress now. While she was presenting the grammar point, the manager observing interrupted to say, 'but you can use present continuous to talk about actions in the future, too.' My colleague was furious because she had been undermined in front of her students, but on top of that, the manager's intervention had only served to confuse the students!

TASK 6.3

...To trainer

Put the following observer actions into three categories according to your own opinions: *do, don't* and *maybe*:

- Walk around the room.
- Speak to students.
- Take over the lesson.
- Make faces to indicate approval or disapproval.
- Take photos of the classroom during the observation.
- Stay longer than you previously agreed with the teacher.
- Give a thumbs up when you leave.
- Discuss what's taking place with other trainee observers.

For notes see page 228

General principles

Objective vs. subjective observations – one of the most crucial skills in observing is to be able to describe what you see taking place in the classroom without applying assumptions or values to those observations. Values and assumptions may have a place later on, in assessing or giving feedback on the lesson, but it is vital to be able to distinguish between those and more objective description of the lesson. So we need to delineate description (what you see), interpretation (what you assume to be the reasons for, or connections between events) and evaluation (how successful you believe those events or actions to be) in our accounts of what goes on in class (Malderez, 2003). This model of looking at the classroom (describe, interpret, evaluate) gives us the morbid but memorable acronym DIE! Elaborating on this, Jon Wendt (1984, p. 397) gives the following example:

<table>
<tr><td>Description:</td><td>Maxine is leaning forward in her chair with her elbows on her knees.</td></tr>
<tr><td>Interpretation:</td><td>Maxine is listening intently.
Or:
Maxine has a stomach ache.</td></tr>
<tr><td>Evaluation:</td><td>I'm impressed with her interest in our discussion; I like that.
Or:
Serves her right for eating up all the chocolate ice cream.</td></tr>
</table>

We can see how this might translate into classroom observation:

<table>
<tr><td>Description:</td><td>Two students are yawning.</td></tr>
<tr><td>Interpretation:</td><td>They are bored.
Or:
They are tired.</td></tr>
<tr><td>Evaluation:</td><td>This teacher needs to work on making his lessons more engaging.
Or:
It's the afternoon and the students have probably been sitting all day – maybe opening the windows and having the students move around would help them stay alert. I wonder if the teacher has tried this . . .</td></tr>
</table>

Evidently, jumping to interpretations and evaluation too soon can lead to wrongful conclusions being drawn about what's taking place in the classroom and about the teacher's practice more generally. It is appropriate to interpret and evaluate, but not during the observed lesson itself – it is far better to develop our descriptions first with input from the teacher, and then jointly interpret and evaluate the lesson in the feedback discussion (see Chapter 8).

Note-taking formats – In keeping with our view of observation as a process of data collection, it is very important that you record effective descriptions of what takes place during the observed lesson. There are various ways of doing this, including making audio or video recordings of the lesson, or taking photographs, but in practice your main form of data collection will be the written notes that you take while you're observing. Your notes should:

- Provide objective descriptions of what you observe during the lesson, which can later be used as the basis for interpretation or evaluation if necessary.

- Help you to make initial decisions about what is worth focusing on (you can't write down everything that happens in the classroom, so you will have to make these decisions as you write).

- Form the basis of your written and spoken feedback to the teacher after the lesson.

Broadly speaking, there are two possible ways to set out your notes. The first is as a running commentary on what takes place. Figure 6.1 indicates how this might look.

Lesson stage	Time	Description	Thoughts, questions, and comments

Figure 6.1: Running commentary observation template

Lesson stage – the observer might use the stages outlined in the lesson plan here, their own labels for the stages (based on what they would expect to see), or perhaps the task numbers in the lesson materials the teacher is using.

Time – this might be recorded as the actual time, or as how much time has elapsed since the beginning of the lesson, depending on observer preference.

Description – this should include descriptions both of what the teacher is doing and of what the students are doing.

Thoughts, questions and comments – this is a space to note down interpretive or evaluative thoughts or questions for further consideration later on, after the lesson.

The running commentary is probably the most logical way of taking notes because it is linear and closely reflects the format used for lesson plans. Some institutions even include columns for observer feedback in lesson planning templates, so that the planned lesson and the description of the actual lesson are directly comparable.

The other possible format for taking notes involves grouping your observations into themes. Figure 6.2 provides an example of this format, but the themes that are selected will vary depending on the training context. The advantage of this format is that the themes encourage the observer to keep paying attention to various aspects of the classroom, and, if necessary, to consider what is *not* happening as well as what is taking place. It may also help with preparing written feedback, if the themes that are used are required on the feedback form. The drawbacks are that it involves a little more jumping around (whether on paper or on screen), allows less room for distinguishing between description and interpretation, and doesn't correspond so closely to the format that lesson plans tend to take. For these reasons it is helpful to add the time to each new comment that you write, so that you can read your notes chronologically later, if you need to.

Time	Lesson planning	Time	Classroom management
Time	Use of learning resources	Time	Subject knowledge
Time	Supporting learners	Time	Thoughts, questions, comments

Figure 6.2: Theme-based observation template

Regardless of the format you decide to use for your notes (and many institutions will provide their own template), notes are very much a first draft of your observations, written for your own use. So they will be written quickly, they may include abbreviations or your own shorthand, and will need editing and refining before they reach trainees as feedback (see Chapter 8).

Handwriting vs typing – the volume of notes in some observations, particularly CELTA-style teaching practice where there are two or three teachers being observed, can make handwriting notes challenging. Chia Suan Chong explains that when she's observing CELTA lessons 'after two hours of nonstop frantic scribbling, my hand starts to hurt' (Chong, 2012, p. 54), and that's certainly true for us too. So we prefer to type notes – if you can touch type then it is faster, if the lesson plan has been submitted digitally you can annotate that, and typed notes are usually easier for your trainees and co-trainers to read. Nevertheless, there's nothing wrong with writing by hand if that's what you prefer, and some trainees may be happier not to hear the sound of your fingers on a keyboard while they teach.

Moving around – it is useful to be able to stand up and move so as to get a better sense of what students are doing and how much they have understood, for example during a speaking activity or a written exercise. Many students are adept at appearing to be on task and/or appearing to be keeping up with the lesson, even when they are not, and it is often only by actually looking at their work that the true extent of their understanding (or misunderstanding) can be assessed. The teacher should be monitoring in this way too, of course, and you can only evaluate the effectiveness of a teacher's monitoring skills if you are also able to monitor student work (teachers may be as adept as their students when it comes to *appearing* to monitor – we've seen plenty of 'pseudo-monitoring', or 'cocktail monitoring' as one colleague described it!). Try to be as discreet as possible when moving around the room so as not to distract students or undermine the teacher's role as 'the boss'.

Preservice course observations

You will be assessing trainees according to the course assessment criteria, so you will need to have a good grasp of those before the observation itself, and some will be more relevant than others depending on which stage of the course the observation takes place at. Your training centre may have a template for recording feedback that incorporates the criteria, which can be helpful. We tend to find, however, that we just glance at these during the lesson and only make decisions about the achievement of each criterion once the lesson is over – more on this in Chapter 7.

The trainees observing the lesson alongside you should be completing an observation task, but there may be times when you want to focus their attention towards something in the lesson that isn't related to the task. Post-it notes, which you can pass to one trainee to pass to the others are one way of doing this. If your trainees are using laptops you can use instant messaging software to do this, and they may be able to share ideas related to their observation tasks, too.

Finally, on rare occasions you may need to intervene to end a lesson so that the next teacher(s) gets their full-time allocation. On even rarer occasions you may need to step into the role of teacher yourself if a trainee doesn't show up!

CASE STUDY 6.8: MARIE, THE CELTA TRAINER

I do think that you have to be ready for anything when you're observing! Our trainees team teach their classes, so in most observed lessons there will be three trainees teaching, one after the other. I remember once, when I hadn't been a trainer very long, the first teacher was coming to the end of her slot, and the trainee due to teach next still hadn't appeared. So I had to borrow a copy of the coursebook from another of the trainees, and step in to teach that part of the lesson, before returning to my chair to observe the third part! It has happened again since then; I think that some trainees find the idea of teaching overwhelming at first and just panic.

During peer and apprenticeship observations

For observations of this kind it may be more difficult to structure an account of the lesson, or events that seem notable. If a task has been provided (and it should be if the observation has been organised as part of a course) it should provide a structured way of recording responses. Figure 6.3 shows a simple example of an observation task that does this.

Observation task 9: error and correction

Note down any instances of learner error, the teacher's response (if any) and the learner's response, e.g., self-correction.

Learner's error	Teacher's response	Learner's response

Figure 6.3: An observation task (from Thornbury & Watkins, 2007)

If the observation has been arranged more informally, such as in Moses' case, then the following four-column table works well:

Time (mins)	What's happening	[Observation focus]	Standout thoughts / questions

Figure 6.4: An informal observation task

During management observations

In order for teachers to be judged fairly and transparently there should probably be a standard observation template that clarifies which areas are being scrutinised. The role of the observer is then to look for evidence of achievement in each area and complete the template with that evidence, which ought to be relayed to the teacher as part of the post-observation feedback process. This is not unlike the assessment that Marie carries out in her role as a CELTA tutor. As a manager, Carmen will need to justify her decisions to the teacher very carefully because there is a lot riding on the observation for the staff members she observes. What she must avoid is any sense that her evaluations of teaching and learning are based on her personal preferences. Instead, they must be clearly linked to the effectiveness of the teaching she sees.

Besides the decisions and actions taken by the teacher during the observed lesson, managers may notice things in the classroom that are of interest to them in relation to institutional decision making, such as how students react to course materials. These insights can be valuable, but it is important that they are kept separate from the notes relating to the teacher's performance. A separate document should be used to jot down points that can be explored later.

As in other forms of observation, managers should be a discreet presence in the classroom so as not to undermine teachers. They should also model the kind of behaviour they would expect from their staff when observing. On occasions, we have seen managers send text messages and emails during lessons, and even answer phone calls. Needless to say, this is an unacceptable distraction – observing effectively requires your full attention.

Managing observation challenges

Observing lessons is fascinating and immensely enjoyable, but it is also surprisingly hard work and presents a number of challenges. Let's look at some of the main ones.

Looking for learning

In television cooking competitions, the contestants are often observed as they cook, not just by the cameras but by the judges who decide who wins and who goes home empty-handed. You'll often see the judges speak to the contestants about what they're making and why, and then give their thoughts to us, the viewers, as we watch the dishes being created – in fact, that's usually what makes up most of the show. But the real test for the contestants, and the point at which the judges make up their minds, is when the finished dishes are tasted. It is what ends up on the plate – the food itself – that is the key determinant of success or failure, not what the judges see in the kitchen. Nevertheless, the judges observe the contestants at work in order to understand why the food turns out the way it does, and that means they can recognise mistakes when they happen, as well as high levels of cooking ability.

In a similar way, there should be an outcome or 'end product' to teaching: better student learning. So an observer is not only looking at the teacher in the classroom, but at the students and whether or not they are learning anything. The proof of the pudding, as they say, is in the eating – any judgement on the effectiveness of the teacher's practice rests primarily on the learning outcomes that are observed. Hence the title of this chapter: it is not enough to observe teaching, we need to observe learning too.

The first problem for observers, then, is that learning, and language learning in particular, is not easily observed because it is a tacit, complex, non-linear process – we can't see what is going on inside the learners' heads. The solution is to look for more visible signs that learning might be happening, such as whether learners are:

- engaged and actively participating in the lesson

- completing activities and tasks as instructed by the teacher

- making meaningful, relevant contributions when called upon

- asking questions to clarify their understanding of lesson content

- attempting to use target language

- getting feedback and acting on it to improve their performance

Of course, looking for these means observing learners more than observing the teacher.

Filtering out classroom 'noise'

The second challenge for observers is the difficulty of gathering useful, objective observations from the enormous number of interactions and micro-events taking place at any given moment in a classroom. Focusing on the teacher alone could easily lead to pages of notes from an observed lesson, but when you begin to focus on students as well it is impossible to pay attention to everything or everyone. Classroom events are as much social and emotional as they are technical or pedagogic. John MacBeath describes classrooms as 'a living laboratory of human behaviour . . . rivalries, collusion, power struggles, strategic task avoidance, subversive ploys as well as learning moments, flashes of insight, congratulation and reward' (MacBeath, 2013, p. 3). And as we saw in our discussion of critical incidents in Chapter 3, even the least notable classroom events can reveal profound insights about the dynamics of teaching and learning. As an observer, trying to make sense of all this in an unfamiliar classroom can be a bit like trying to pick up the threads of a soap opera you've never watched before, while also being tasked with evaluating teaching and learning!

This is one reason why observation tasks are so important for the success of peer observations. One strategy for trainers (who don't get to work from observation tasks!) is to select a handful of students to focus on when you first enter the room, and try to track their progress through the lesson. It's easy to notice the most able students, and the most disruptive ones, but try also to pay attention to students who seem to be struggling or not participating and those who are somewhere in the middle. What is important is to be able to balance your view of the class as a whole with your observations of individuals, whose performance during the lesson may or may not be representative of the whole group.

The Hawthorne effect

One of the upsides for teachers of being observed (beyond the professional learning benefits) can be the reaction from students who, wanting to ensure the process is as positive as possible for you, are on their 'best behaviour' throughout. Endearing though this is, it doesn't represent the way the classroom normally works, which is what observers tend to be interested in. Similarly, it is sometimes obvious when observing that a teacher has made changes to their usual way of doing things, again meaning that the observer isn't seeing a representative sample of teaching and learning in that class. These are both examples of the Hawthorne effect – the idea that people modify their behaviour when they are being observed (or when they think they are).

This phenomenon makes life particularly difficult for observers because classroom observation is often high-stakes, with conclusions about a teacher's general practice (dozens of hours of teaching week after week) made on the basis of relatively little data (one hour of teaching or less). If what observers see doesn't correspond to the reality of the day-to-day classroom, then those conclusions will be inaccurate, and may lead to the wrong interventions being made. It's also frustrating as an observer to see a lesson that you feel has been 'staged'.

The more you are able to observe a class, therefore, the better, because the Hawthorne effect should diminish as your presence becomes less novel. Another way of modifying the effect is to complement in-person observations with video recordings of lessons, although the presence of a camera can also have an effect. The most important consequence of the Hawthorne effect is in your feedback, when you should attempt to find out how representative the observed lesson was of the teacher's practice in general (see Chapter 8).

Staying objective

Teachers aren't the only ones who are susceptible to traps set by the mind when it finds itself in the observation room. There are various cognitive biases that can distort an observer's perception of what's happening too. These include:

- The **halo effect** – when the observer evaluates a teacher favourably because they made a positive impression in ways not pertinent to the observation, for example in how they dress, how they speak, what they look like, and so on. It can work the other way round, too: an observer under the influence of a negative halo effect will unfairly evaluate a lesson because they had a negative impression of one or more traits not relevant to the lesson itself. A similar effect may result from observing a string of poor (in terms of assessment criteria) lessons in a single sitting, so that a subsequent lesson in the same sitting appears much better than it really was (or the other way round).

- **Anchoring** – the over-dependence of an evaluation or decision on evidence presented early on. For example, an observer may form a negative judgement of a teacher's overall competence very quickly as the result of an altercation with a student early in the lesson, even though most other aspects of the lesson are carried out effectively.

- **Confirmation bias** – the inclination to look for data that confirms what you already believe. For an observer, this might lead to a skewed evaluation of a lesson as certain classroom events are highlighted at the expense of others because they confirm pre-existing ideas about the teacher, perhaps based on previous observations, or reports from other observers of previous observations.

Another cognitive phenomenon – though not necessarily a bias – that can affect classroom observation is **inattentional blindness**, in which significant events aren't perceived because the observer's attention is directed elsewhere. This was famously illustrated by an experiment in which half the participants failed to notice a person in a gorilla costume walk across the screen in a short video they were asked to watch (Simons & Chabris, 1999).

The lesson to be drawn from these potential pitfalls is that all observers are fallible and the best way to mitigate against observational errors is to focus on describing classroom events as thoroughly and objectively as possible, leaving interpretation and evaluation for after the lesson. As we've mentioned above, a good rule of thumb is to focus most of your attention on what learners are doing in the lesson, and how they're reacting to teaching, rather than focusing on the teacher.

Teacher resistance

As we've already described, it is sadly the case that many teachers view observation very negatively. That may be because the observation is part of an assessed course and therefore high-stakes, or simply because the observer is an unfamiliar presence in the classroom, both of which are understandable sources of anxiety. But a lot of the negativity felt by teachers towards observation arises because it has been badly conducted. We have found that for many teachers who feel this way they:

- are often denied a voice in the observation process, e.g., they have no say over when the observation takes place

- associate observation with being judged (Malderez, 2003), often quite arbitrarily and without reference to specific criteria

- often get told little, if anything, about the purpose and focus of the observations they undergo

The result of these shortcomings is that teachers stop engaging in the observation process. Not to the extent that they refuse to be observed, but rather by 'playing safe' and doing no more than is necessary to complete the process and emerge unscathed. Clearly, under such circumstances there is little hope of any professional learning taking place. So it is essential that observers aim to engender trust in their relations with teachers. They can do this by being open and transparent about the observation process, and by giving teachers a meaningful say in how it operates and in the conclusions that result from it (see Chapter 8). Unfortunately, institutional requirements of observers (e.g., to rate teachers as part of appraisal) can severely undermine trust.

Being aware of all these challenges is the first step towards tackling them, but subsequent steps are really a question of practice. Observation is a training skill and it can be learned, but that learning process will benefit from reflection, both alone and with other observers.

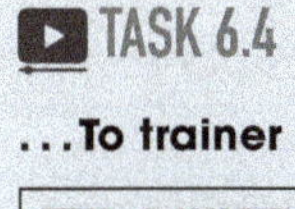

TASK 6.4

...To trainer

Theresa is going to teach an online lesson and has asked Peter to observe her for development purposes (see Task 6.2 for the pre-observation discussion).

Spend some time reading through Theresa's lesson plan on page 239. Then, scan the QR Code and watch the video of the lesson. Make notes on what you observe. When you have finished, compare your notes with Peter's in the Notes on tasks section.

For notes see page 229

Preparing for feedback

Having collected your observation data from the classroom, it's time to put it to use. You will need to shape your notes and any other data you have gathered into useful feedback for the teacher, both written and spoken. That process is detailed in Chapter 8, but one of the most helpful things you can do for yourself is to try and schedule some free time after any observations that you conduct. You will need a short break – observing is tiring – but you can also use that time to go over your notes, recap the lesson, and begin to decide on the key points for feedback. You may be unable to make that time (your course timetable may not allow for it, and sometimes there's no option but to go and teach a lesson immediately after observing), but it is much more difficult to remember details from a lesson you've observed even an hour after doing something else.

Observations, as a form of teacher education, can and should be evaluated. So as you gain experience of observing teachers do reflect on your practices before, during and after the observed lesson. You should be able to find ways to improve the speed and efficiency of the notes you make, to help teachers feel more informed and confident about the process, and to manage the set-up of observed lessons more effectively.

Summary

In this chapter we've seen that observations take place for a range of different purposes, and that those purposes influence what the observer will look for, and how the observation cycle will play out. Nevertheless, there are some principles that hold regardless of the purpose of the observation. First of all, the onus is on the observer to collect objective data from the lesson in order to support feedback or teacher reflection. Secondly, in most cases, that data will relate to student learning, and so the observer's attention will tend to be on what students are doing, rather than on the teacher. Finally, it is essential to conduct the whole observation cycle on the basis of a trusting relationship between teacher and observer, acknowledging how difficult it can be to have an observer in the room while teaching.

TRAINER VOICES

Scan the QR Code and watch the videos 'Observation habits' and 'Structuring observation notes' to hear how trainers put the principles we've looked at into practice in their own observations. Which trainer's practices do you think would suit you best?

TO FIND OUT MORE

Eken, D. K., Çeltek, S., & Bosson, A. (2015). Observation-related professional development. *ET Professional, 98*, 53–56. (Offers practical advice on how to run various types of developmental observation.)

Wajnryb, R. (1992). *Classroom observation tasks.* Cambridge: Cambridge University Press. (Provides numerous observation tasks for peer or apprenticeship observations.)

7 Assessing teaching

Here we consider:

- What we mean by assessment in teacher training
- The different reasons for assessing teachers
- The assessment process
- Assessing the Professional, the Practical and the Personal
- Challenges posed by assessment for trainers and how to overcome them

Every teacher is different and so in a sense you're assessing the teacher to see if they're the best teacher that they can be.

Scott, teacher trainer, Spain

Very often the main way of discovering what teachers know and can do is through classroom observation, which is why we are discussing assessment alongside chapters on observation and feedback. However, there are other ways of assessing teaching beyond lesson observation, and it's important to understand when to use them.

Defining assessment in teacher training

The word *assessment* tends to conjure up images of tests, but teachers are usually the ones marking test papers, not sitting them. Nevertheless, there was a time when assessment of teachers looked very similar to the tests you will have given the students in your classes: for example, the original Certificate of Proficiency in English (CPE) exam that appeared in 1913 (now C2 Proficiency, the highest of the Cambridge English Qualifications) was intended for those who planned to go on to teach English (Weir & Saville, 2015). In many countries to this day, the main qualification for becoming an English teacher is a degree in philology, so in language teaching the idea of content knowledge as a proxy for teaching ability has been hard to shake. It is not entirely without merit – assessment of teachers can be test-based (as in TKT or the Delta Module One exam) – but there are other ways of assessing teaching, too. Let's begin exploring them by considering how one trainer assesses her trainees.

CASE STUDY 7.1: WENDY, CELTA TRAINER

On the CELTA course that I help to deliver, we assess the trainees throughout, and on the basis of those assessments they are awarded a grade at the end of the course. When I first started as a CELTA tutor I very much thought of 'assessment' as observing lessons, but I now see that aspect as one part of a bigger picture of assessment. On CELTA, that bigger picture is represented by the portfolio that trainees have to put together, which includes things like the record of attendance, all the trainee's lesson plans and handouts, TP ('teaching practice', in other words, observed lessons) feedback, and all their assignments and feedback comments on those. So there's a range of different kinds of evidence being collected and assessed all through the course – it is a big job! But it needs to be so that we can get an accurate picture of each trainee's teaching ability.

Assessment of teaching takes place in many ways and in many different contexts, but the situation that Wendy describes in relation to her CELTA courses is a useful example because it embodies many of the main issues that you will need to consider when you come to assess teachers and trainees.

The aim of teacher assessment is neatly encapsulated in Wendy's stated goal: to get an accurate picture of each trainee's teaching ability at a point in time. This is not as straightforward as it sounds, for two reasons. First of all, because that picture will always have to be built up from limited evidence – a handful of observations, some lesson plans, lesson reflections, and so on. It simply isn't practical to collect and examine data of that kind in significant quantities. And secondly, teaching ability is a combination of knowing and doing, as we saw in Chapter 1. Wendy has to assess what trainees understand and demonstrate at the levels of *Knowing about*, *Knowing how* and *Knowing to*. As Jo-Ann Delaney explains, 'in a sense, we are looking at teachers' knowing and doing and attempting to assess both and, as assessors, make decisions about what this tells us in a more holistic way about the teacher's ability to teach effectively' (Delaney, 2019, p. 386).

Purposes of assessment

TASK 7.1

From teacher . . .

Think about the times that you have been assessed in your teaching career. What was the purpose of each assessment?

There is a small number of very common purposes for assessing teachers. The first, exemplified by Wendy's case study, is to decide whether they have met the standard required to be awarded a particular qualification, such as CELTA, a Master's degree, or a teaching licence. Qualifications like these play a gatekeeping role in the teaching world, in that a successful assessment means you are 'let in' to the teaching profession. Even for teachers who are already practising, qualifications might act as a way in to more senior roles. So this kind of assessment is very common.

A similar kind of assessment is often carried out by institutions who want to reassure themselves that teachers are meeting certain standards of classroom practice – a form of quality assurance. This is very common, as we saw in Chapter 6. It's similar because it serves to answer a question posed by the institution, not the teacher. In the case of the gatekeeping qualifications mentioned above, the question is 'Does this person meet the minimum requirements to work as a teacher?', while in a quality assurance setting it becomes 'Does this person continue to meet the minimum requirements to work as a teacher *here*?' These two purposes intersect when a teacher applies for a job – to answer the second question before hiring a teacher, the institution has to rely on the answer to the first one.

Assessment should also be able to answer questions posed by teachers themselves, however. Those questions are most likely to be 'What am I doing well in my teaching?' and 'What can I do better?', both of which can be used to inform future professional learning. But we also get personal and professional satisfaction when assessments of our teaching are positive, whether that's in the form of encouraging feedback after a lesson observation, or a certificate that demonstrates we've reached a certain level of professional expertise.

Students make assessments of teaching when they ask questions such as 'Do I want to continue paying for this course?' or 'Would I be better off in that afternoon class that my friend is in?' They may also be invited to assess teaching once their course has ended, with a feedback questionnaire from the institution – we've found that this is particularly common in the tertiary-level institutions we have worked with.

Finally, we have our own questions as trainers: 'What impact did my training have on my trainees' teaching?' or 'What impact did my training have on student learning?' and like teachers, we want to know what teaching practices to focus on with our trainees in the future. We've already considered these questions to some extent when discussing evaluation in Chapter 4, and there is significant overlap in the processes of evaluation and assessment. Very often the assessments undertaken for the purposes above are the only form of evaluation on a programme or course (Malderez & Wedell, 2007), so these questions that trainers have about the impact of their work are answered using the results of the other forms of assessment mentioned above.

The assessment process

An accurate picture of each teacher's ability is therefore very important, because it may be used as the basis of very significant decisions by various parties. Accordingly, 'the assessment of teaching needs to be done with care, and must be valid, transparent and fair' (Rossner, 2013, p. 121). A good way of achieving that benchmark is to assess teachers from multiple viewpoints, using evidence gathered at different times, in different ways, by different people. One form of evidence might be a paper-based test, as we've already mentioned, but in itself that would give us a very narrow perspective of a teacher's abilities. The solution is to build up a more complete picture of a teacher's abilities by combining that test result with evidence gathered in other ways, such as observation, or lesson planning.

In Chapter 6 we presented a view of observation as a process of data gathering, and assessment, whether through observation or through other means, is a similar process. There are some important differences, though. Two definitions of assessment help to highlight how it goes beyond simply data gathering:

> Assessment is a process which involves gathering evidence of some kind on which to base judgements (Malderez & Wedell, 2007, p. 146).

> Our definition of assessment . . . refers to a process of inquiry that integrates multiple sources of evidence, whether or not test based, to support an interpretation, decision or action (Moss, Girard, & Haniford, 2006, p. 152).

So while observation alone might be a process of data gathering, a single observation is unlikely to provide enough evidence for an assessment. Even several observations will still leave gaps in our view of what the teacher is capable of that only other forms of evidence (such as tests or written assignments) can fill. Lee Shulman described this collection of different kinds of evidence that we can use for assessment as 'a union of insufficiencies' (Shulman, 1988) because they only provide adequate coverage of teaching ability when considered jointly. Each piece of the puzzle reveals something different about the teacher's abilities, but no piece gives us the full picture.

The other theme to draw from our two definitions of assessment is the idea of making a judgement or an interpretation. To make judgements consistently and fairly, data gathering alone is not enough. We need to collect the same data for each trainee, and measure or compare our data against a benchmark in order to make a judgement. For that purpose, we use assessment criteria, which for a qualification such as CELTA are produced by the exam board, Cambridge Assessment English. Other criteria frameworks are publicly available, such as The European Profiling Grid (https://egrid.epg-project.eu), which describes language teaching competences at six different levels of expertise. Assessing each teacher is therefore a process of comparing the evidence that has been collected with each criterion and deciding if it has been fulfilled. In discussing assessment, we are referring to *evidence* instead of *data* because it is evidence *of a particular skill or area of knowledge* that has been deemed relevant and important by the assessment criteria.

CASE STUDY 7.2: MARIE, THE CELTA TRAINER

I would say that it took me a little while to see the bigger picture when it comes to assessment on the CELTA. When I started as a trainer I looked at observation of teaching practice as one thing I had to do, marking assignments as a separate thing, tutorials as another, and so on. But they are all part of how each trainee is assessed, and each one contributes something different to the overall assessment of a trainee. The problem, I think, is that each element can be quite challenging to get to grips with initially, and I certainly found that things got a lot easier once I was familiar with the criteria – I don't have to think about them so much now because I have been through them so often. So I think my advice would be to familiarise yourself with the assessment criteria as soon as you can, and remember that they all contribute to the overall goal of assessing each trainee.

What remains relevant to teacher assessment is the distinction we made in earlier chapters between the Personal, the Professional and the Practical. The evidence that we draw on to assess what teachers are able to do needs to have a certain level of completeness to be valid, transparent and fair in the way that Rossner demands. We need to make sure our 'union of insufficiencies' covers everything that it needs to cover to form the basis of a valid assessment. We can use the three Ps to do that. When assessing teachers we want to gather evidence of:

- the Practical – what the teacher does, both in the classroom, and in planning or assessing students

- the Professional – the concepts, terms and research insights that the teacher knows and is able to put into practice

- the Personal – the teacher's ability to self-reflect on their teaching and on their learning in order to make future improvements

TASK 7.2

...To trainer

What methods can you think of to gather evidence of teaching ability? (Some have already been mentioned, such as observation, written test, written assignment).

Categorise your list according to whether each method of assessment relates principally to the Personal, the Professional or the Practical.

For notes see page 230

Assessing the Professional

We've previously outlined the Professional as the body of concepts, research insights and terminology that inform effective practice and that we would expect well-qualified professionals to be familiar with. The

Professional is related to the understanding of terms and concepts, so it can be assessed outside the classroom, which can be helpful in practical terms because it means that observations don't need to be arranged, and assessment methods can be applied to large numbers of teachers at once. Very broadly the kind of knowledge that is of relevance here involves two main areas: language awareness and pedagogy.

Language awareness, or knowledge about language (Bartels, 2009) is knowledge of language skills and systems, such as grammar and writing, how languages are acquired, and how they are used. This is not the same as being proficient in the language (although that is a prevalent misconception). Knowledge about language might be described as the content of language teaching (Freeman, McBee Orzulak, & Morrissey, 2009) or knowing *what* to teach. Pedagogy, on the other hand, is knowledge of techniques, methods, approaches – knowing *how* to teach.

The way that teachers demonstrate this knowledge in their professional lives is in the act of teaching: in the lessons they design, the decisions and interactions they have in the classroom, and the feedback they give their students. Assessment of this knowledge necessarily overlaps with assessment of the Practical, therefore – 'the practice elements [in the assessment of teaching] should evidence an underpinning knowledge of both language and language pedagogy' (Delaney, 2019, p. 389). So the distinction we are making here, between knowledge of language and methodology as the Professional, and the ability to implement that knowledge in the classroom as the Practical, does not fully represent what teachers know about teaching. This is because successfully enacting knowledge of content and methodology takes place in context, and so further knowledge is needed:

> If L2 teachers are to successfully use knowledge of the perfect aspect [for example] for giving students feedback, they need to possess knowledge of more relevant factors than universal grammar, acquisition orders, and other linguistic related factors. In addition, they must also understand how social, emotional, technical, and local factors *in their particular classrooms* [emphasis added] aid or hinder students' use of such feedback.
>
> (Bartels, 2009, p. 127)

The practical reality, however, is that while a lot of what teachers know can be observed in the classroom, much teaching knowledge cannot be observed (Rossner, 2013) and it would be impractical to assess the full breadth of trainees' language awareness by observing them, since most lessons deal with only a limited area of target language.

Certificate and diploma qualifications therefore tend to incorporate assessment of the Professional in various forms, which include purely theoretical assessments alongside more practically-oriented tasks. The

Delta Module One exam paper, for example, begins with a task in which trainees have to provide terms for given definitions – testing pure content knowledge (Figure 7.1).

Task One   (6 marks)

Provide the term for each definition.

Write your answers in your answer booklet. Provide only **one** answer per question.

a   the verbal signals given by the listener to indicate interest, attention, surprise etc.
e.g. *really, uh-huh, yeah*

b   a test employing tasks which replicate real-life activities e.g. role-playing a job interview, writing a letter of complaint, or reading and completing an application form

c   using the medium of English to teach a subject such as geography, natural science or history, to learners whose first language is not English

d   a verb which does not take an object e.g. *He <u>arrived</u> early*

e   a consonant sound in which the air flow is initially stopped, but is then released slowly with friction e.g. /tʃ/

f   a word which has the same pronunciation as another word but a different spelling and meaning e.g. *see* and *sea*

Figure 7.1: From the Delta Handbook for Tutors and Candidates (answers to the task are a backchannelling, b direct test, c content and language integrated learning, d intransitive verb, e affricate, f homophone)

But later in the same exam, trainees are required to complete tasks that are much more clearly pedagogical, such as evaluating a piece of learner writing or analysing a piece of teaching material. The CELTA also assesses aspects of the Professional on a spectrum from theoretical to practical. For example, there is an assignment focusing specifically on language awareness, again assessing content knowledge, but trainees are also expected to demonstrate their grasp of language in the lesson plans they prepare and in the lessons they subsequently teach.

Assessing the Practical

The Practical, for the purposes of assessment, is concerned with what teachers do as part of their professional lives, mostly teaching lessons. It tends to be more heavily weighted than the Professional and the Personal, and Delaney (2019) points out that to earn a grade beyond pass in CELTA, trainees need to meet criteria that relate solely to planning and teaching. In accordance with what we have said above, however, assessing the Practical isn't just about assessing *doing*, it's also a question of seeing what teachers' actions reveal about the things they *know* (and don't know) in terms of content and methodology. For example, in order to 'focus on language items in the classroom by clarifying relevant aspects of meaning and form (including phonology) for learners to an appropriate degree of depth', which is a CELTA criterion, trainees need knowledge of language and knowledge of how it can be presented in order to successfully practise this teaching skill. So although assessment of that criterion is practical in nature (observation), it is assessment of knowledge as well as practice.

Observation is the main tool for assessing the Practical, and the process of observation usually encompasses lesson planning as well as teaching, so planning is assessed at the same time. Some practical skills can be assessed in other ways, in the way that the Delta exam requires teachers to evaluate student output, but the main principle is of validity – to assess what teachers do, you need to see them doing it – so observation is by far the most desirable method of assessing the Practical. It is the way that the following CELTA criteria are assessed, for example (Table 7.1).

Table 7.1: CELTA criteria that are assessed through lesson observation

Demonstrate professional competence as teachers by:

1. a teaching a class with an awareness of the needs and interests of the learner group

    b teaching a class with an awareness of learning styles and cultural factors that may affect learning

    c acknowledging, when necessary, learners' backgrounds and previous learning experiences

    d establishing good rapport with learners and ensuring they are fully involved in learning activities

These criteria are phrased in such a way that they would be very difficult to assess without seeing a trainee teaching, and a skill such as establishing rapport with learners really can't be demonstrated in any other way.

The drawback of observation as an assessment tool is that it is time-consuming and labour-intensive. As a result, there is usually quite limited assessment of practical teaching skills in most courses – in the CELTA it is six teaching hours per trainee, and in Delta only around four teaching hours. The same might be said of other practical skills that are, by their nature, more elaborate: curriculum development is one example. The principle of assessing the performance of the skill is still important, but developing a course curriculum takes a long time, so in Delta Module Three, in which this skill is assessed, trainees produce only one curriculum for assessment.

Because there isn't a great deal of assessed practice on most courses, what little there is becomes high-stakes, and trainees often become very nervous. Demystifying the assessment of teaching by explaining to trainees how they will be assessed is an important way of mitigating nerves – this is discussed further below.

Assessing the Personal

In Chapters 2 and 3 we described the Personal as a teacher's beliefs, assumptions, knowledge and experience. These are relevant to teacher learning because they influence the decisions that teachers make in the classroom and when planning or assessing learners, but they also influence the way in which trainees understand and absorb new ideas. That's true of completely new ideas, presented in a training session (*Knowing about*), but it's also true of insights that might arise during teaching, as a teacher works out how to put prior learning into practice (*Knowing how / Knowing to*). So assessing the Personal is a question of assessing teachers' ability to understand and evaluate their own decision making and learning processes – it's not about assessing their experience or beliefs per se, since these are unique to each teacher and only indirectly relevant to their effectiveness as practitioners.

Generally, we refer to this ability as 'reflection', or 'reflective practice', and we alluded to it in Chapter 1 when we discussed the unending curiosity that teachers need to have if they are to reach adaptive expertise. Reflection is the principal way in which teachers make sense of *Knowing about* and translate it into more practical knowledge, so it is a prerequisite for professional learning (Mann, 2005) and an important skill to assess. In assessing the Personal we are trying to assess 'the heart of teaching, the capacity for intelligent and adaptive action' (Shulman & Shulman, 2004, p. 263).

The relevant assessment criteria from CELTA and Delta, shown in Table 7.2, reflect this and show how reflective practice can be split into component skills. Typically, some of these component skills focus on evaluating past actions, while others are centred on the developmental measures needed to improve teaching outcomes in the future.

Table 7.2: Assessment of the Personal on CELTA and Delta

CELTA	Planning and teaching	Trainees should show convincingly that they can:
		○ prepare and plan for the effective teaching of adult ESOL learners by reflecting on and evaluating their plans in light of the learning process and suggesting improvements for future plans
		○ demonstrate professional competence as teachers by noting their own teaching strengths and weaknesses in different teaching situations in light of feedback from learners, teachers and teacher educators
		○ demonstrate professional competence as teachers by participating in and responding to feedback

	Classroom-related written assignments	Trainees can demonstrate their learning by: ○ noting their own teaching strengths and weaknesses in different situations in light of feedback from learners, teachers and teacher educators ○ identifying which ELT areas of knowledge and skills they need further development in ○ describing in a specific way how they might develop their ELT knowledge and skills beyond the course
Delta (Module Two)	5a Language Systems and Skills Assignments	Trainees demonstrate that they can effectively: ○ reflect on and evaluate their own planning, teaching and the learners' progress as evidenced in this lesson ○ identify key strengths and weaknesses in planning and execution ○ explain how they will consolidate/follow on from the learning achieved in the lesson
	5b Professional Development Assignment: Reflection and Action	Successful trainees can focus on their professional development by: ○ selecting some key strengths and weaknesses in their teaching practices and providing a rationale for their selection (2a) ○ selecting approaches/procedures/techniques/materials to use to address the issues identified in 2a above (2b) ○ critically evaluating the effectiveness of the selected approaches/procedures/techniques/materials (2c) ○ critically evaluating the effectiveness of methods and/or documents they have selected to gather data to allow them to focus on their teaching practices (2d) ○ providing an appropriate action plan to promote their professional development (2e) ○ critically reflecting on their teaching practices and beliefs during the course of this assignment (2f)
	5b Professional Development Assignment: Experimental Practice	Successful trainees can focus on the topic by: ○ justifying the selected approaches/procedures/techniques/materials with reference to the teaching context, the specific group of learners and their own professional development ○ evaluating the success or otherwise of the experiment with reference to the planned aims and outcomes for both the learners and the teacher

Teachers tend to demonstrate this kind of professional self-awareness in their day-to-day work in fairly informal ways. We may think about what happened in our lessons during the journey home from school, or discuss events from the classroom with colleagues or friends in the staffroom or at home. And although these are informal ways of demonstrating an understanding of our own teaching and professional development, they can have profound consequences for future practice and the development of teaching knowledge.

An informal understanding of how to reflect is a necessary precursor to more structured, systematic approaches to reflection (Farrell, 2013), and in order to actually assess the Personal a more formal approach is needed. That usually means some form of written task, designed to allow trainees to demonstrate an ability to self-reflect. Almost all the CELTA and Delta criteria in Table 7.2 have to be met in writing (the exception is 'participating and responding to feedback' which is assessed orally), so even though teachers can and do reflect on their decisions and their learning during lessons (what Donald Schön (1983) called 'reflection-*in*-action'), it is 'reflection-*on*-action' that is assessed, for practical reasons.

The assessment criteria in Table 7.2 relate to the following three examples of how teachers might be able to demonstrate their reflection skills in order for the Personal to be assessed. These are taken from the CELTA and Delta syllabuses, but similar tasks are often set as part of other courses and qualifications.

1. **CELTA and Delta post-lesson reflection** – trainees on both courses are asked to complete written reflections, guided by a template, after each of their observed lessons. In CELTA (and occasionally on Delta) these are complemented by group feedback discussions involving the observed teacher(s), the tutor and other trainees.

2. **CELTA assignment 4 and Delta Reflection and Action** – in these pieces of work trainees are required to reflect in broad terms on their strengths and weaknesses as teachers (based on observation feedback and their own reflections), and to plan development activity for themselves that will help to remedy some of their weaknesses. At CELTA (preservice) level this assignment is generally done once, towards the end of the course, and is relatively brief. At Delta level the assignment spans the length of the course and is made up of three to four separate entries.

3. **Delta Experimental Practice** – this is an assignment which involves each trainee investigating a new area of practice through reading, practical experimentation in the classroom and reflection on the success of the experiment(s).

In each of these tasks, trainees' written reflections are assessed against the criteria. An honest appraisal of strengths and areas for development will be expected, and this can be challenging for some trainees who are not accustomed to describing what they have *not* done well (although other trainees find it equally difficult to evaluate themselves positively). There may also be a linguistic hurdle to overcome for trainees who must write their reflections in a second language, and this may need to be taken into consideration as part of assessment. Increasingly, there is a view that trainees should be allowed to submit written reflection tasks in their first language in order to enable the most accurate assessment of their skills in this area (Beaumont, 2019). At the same time, trainers need to be clear that the ability to talk or write about teaching is not the same as the ability to teach (Delaney, 2019). This is sometimes strikingly evident on in-service courses that involve several hours of training sessions before trainees are observed – just because trainees can 'talk the talk' does not mean they can 'walk the walk'!

Managing assessment challenges

If assessing teachers seems difficult, that's because it is! And that is particularly true when you are still new to a particular course or qualification, because part of the challenge is to become familiar with the standard of teaching represented by the assessment criteria, which can cover many different areas. Assessment also tends to be time-consuming, especially when it involves observation, which is a lengthy process, or when it involves marking individual assignments which have to be understood in their own terms (rather than, say, test answers which can be marked much faster). Inevitably, there is usually a lot of paperwork to deal with too, which adds to the burden on time. But at the heart of the issue is the fact that teaching is a complex, context-dependent activity that doesn't lend itself to simple description. If assessment of teaching is easy, the results probably aren't very meaningful.

Understanding how the complexity of the classroom relates to the expectations represented by assessment criteria is challenging, but it comes with time and increasing familiarity with applying criteria (and through standardisation; see below). It is useful to remember that in many assessment situations you will be able to run your thoughts past a co-trainer, who can also help to indicate how grade boundaries translate to classroom action. But technology – specifically video recording – can also be a help, particularly when it comes to dealing with the issue of filtering out classroom 'noise' that we highlighted in Chapter 6. The demands on a trainer's attention during an assessed observation are very high, and so it is only natural that having the chance to review and recap certain parts of the lesson on video makes life easier, and thereby increases the reliability of the assessment (by making more evidence available).

Overcoming inherent limitations of assessment criteria

Inevitably, written criteria are limited in their ability to capture and describe 'good teaching' across the many contexts in which they will be used. This leads to two problems. First of all, there is a need to make sure that trainers interpret and apply criteria in the same way, particularly where a course is delivered by more than one trainer (which is usually the case). This is because trainees are entitled to know that they will be assessed in the same way regardless of which trainer is assessing. Secondly, it is difficult as a trainer working with a set of criteria for the first time to know precisely what is expected from each trainee in order to consider that each criterion has been met. A criterion such as 'monitoring learners appropriately in relation to the task or activity' (from CELTA) can be met to varying degrees and in different ways in different contexts. Therefore, standardisation is needed so that trainers themselves know what is considered satisfactory and what is not.

The exact procedures for standardisation can vary, but an approach used by many institutions is to ask new trainers to mark a lesson plan or a recording of a lesson that has been kept for the purposes of standardisation. The marks are then compared with the 'correct' marks that have been agreed by existing trainers, and any discrepancies can be discussed and explained. The new trainer would then shadow mark real assessments (whether Practical, Professional or Personal) and compare their marks to the marks given by the main trainer to ensure the interpretations of different trainers are as consistent as possible.

Offering guidance for trainees on assessment

We have often observed that trainees don't seem to have a clear understanding of the criteria they are being assessed on. This is a pity because it suggests that they might be able to perform better if they knew what was expected of them, and because when trainees understand how they're being assessed they are better able to evaluate their own practice once they leave the course. Some trainees also react negatively to assessment, and demystifying it can help them to feel more positive about observations, exams or assignments.

One of the simplest measures that trainers can take is to set aside time to share and discuss assessment criteria with trainees at various points in the course. That is not to say that you should take them through each criterion one by one, but rather that you should explain the expectations of each assessed part of the course (e.g., assignments, teaching practice, lesson plans) in terms that the trainees will understand. The criteria themselves may not always be particularly transparent, especially to preservice teachers, so it's important to convey expectations in ways that are more meaningful, such as during input sessions or in feedback conversations. The kinds of practices you may have used with your students to develop learner autonomy are also relevant here: making learning objectives explicit, encouraging trainees to self-assess using selected criteria, and referring to criteria explicitly when giving feedback.

Managing tension between assessment and support roles

We've discussed the supportive role that trainers need to play in Chapter 5 on mentoring practices, but the role of assessor is quite different, and yet trainers are generally expected to carry out tasks that encompass both. In practice, this means giving encouragement, help and advice at some times, and grades and feedback at other times. This may, unfortunately, create rather than resolve tension between assessment and teacher development, and foster feelings of negativity in trainees, particularly about observation.

We feel that it is important to acknowledge both roles and to perform both, rather than (as often happens) downplaying the role of assessor in order to engender trust and encourage contributions from participants. Trainees should know that the tutor's interpretations of the assessment criteria are what will underpin assessment decisions, and so those interpretations should be made explicit, whether that's during group feedback or at other points in a course, such as input sessions.

The same tension can arise when trainees are asked to evaluate or comment on their peers. For many trainees it feels uncomfortable to do this, because there is an understandable desire to avoid delivering negative feedback, but also because many trainees believe that the tutor, as the expert in the room, should be the only one to pass judgement. The result is that peer feedback is often quite bland (what one of us calls 'the trainee appreciation society'), and the sessions themselves can feel awkward, as trainees guess what the trainer wants to hear.

There are several steps that can be taken to improve this situation, starting, as mentioned above, with ensuring that trainees have a clear understanding of the relevant assessment criteria and how they are being applied. We feel that carefully structured group feedback discussions are essential, and that the trainer's questions need careful thought in order to encourage a focus on evidence from the classroom and observations of what was effective or not. We discuss this further in Chapter 8. A useful way of circumventing the guessing game nature of some group feedback is suggested by Delaney (2019): have trainees discuss their feedback without the trainer present and come to some (anonymous) conclusions, before the trainer returns to discuss them.

Summary

Assessment processes can seem very familiar, which raises the danger that we don't give them the attention they deserve. We've all taken dozens of tests as students, and most of us will have been observed many times in our teaching careers, so it's easy to accept these practices and get on with administering them without thinking very carefully about what they are meant to achieve. But as with all other areas of teaching, trainers should understand the principles behind the practices they model, and assessment is no exception. A rigorous approach is essential to ensure that trainees and other stakeholders have faith in assessment processes.

Assessing students goes beyond isolated practices or instances of assessment; the way that assessment is practised and discussed has a profound impact on the culture of teaching and learning in an institution. Ideally, it should be seen not as a judgement that is set in stone for all time, but as a valuable signpost on the road to further learning. In addition, the process of assessment should help to set teachers up to self-assess as part of their own development, so that they can continue to improve their teaching once they leave training: 'encouraging teachers to regularly assess their own teaching competences and reflect on these self-assessments should be an integral part of teacher development' (Rossner, 2013, p. 121).

TRAINER VOICES

Scan the QR Code and watch the videos 'Assessment challenges' and 'Standardising assessment' to hear how trainers ensure that assessment is carried out effectively in their contexts.

TO FIND OUT MORE

Delaney, J.-A. (2019). Assessment and feedback. In S. Walsh, & S. Mann, *The Routledge Handbook of English Language Teacher Education* (pp. 385–401). Abingdon: Routledge. (This chapter provides a useful summary of the main issues in assessing language teacher skills and knowledge.)

Wilson, R., & Poulter, M. (2015). *Studies in language testing 42: Assessing language teachers' professional skills and knowledge.* Cambridge: Cambridge University Press. (This collection of papers deals with language teacher assessment in detail.)

8 Giving feedback on teaching

It's really important that you allow the teacher time to think and allow the teacher time to talk.

Peter, teacher trainer, Cyprus

Teacher educator John Fanselow wrote that 'to teach is to give feedback' (Fanselow, 1987, p. 267) and there's an argument that his maxim is just as applicable to training: feedback is absolutely essential to teacher learning at the levels of *Knowing how* and *Knowing to*, where it leads to sustained changes in classroom practice.

It can be helpful to think of teachers' professional learning in terms of adding effective practices to their teaching, while subtracting habits that are ineffective or even counterproductive. Teachers can do a great deal to add effective practices on their own, and you can probably think of techniques or activities that you were able to include in your own lessons after hearing about them from a colleague, or in a training session, or reading about them in a book. But ineffective practices, or ideas bluntly applied, can be harder for teachers to notice on their own, and feedback from you, the trainer, then becomes an important factor in improving teaching. Feedback is a critical part of helping teachers attain adaptive expertise, developing their professional knowledge from the level of *Knowing about* to the levels of *Knowing how* and *Knowing to*. Trainers are not the only potential source of feedback – colleagues and even students may also be in a position to offer useful insights – but it is an indispensable part of the trainer's role and it therefore needs to be carried out effectively.

But of all the skills involved in training teachers, we would argue that delivering feedback is the most challenging. There's often a lot at stake, particularly for practising teachers, and it takes careful preparation and sensitivity to manage feedback in a way that leads to professional learning and increased confidence. It's also an area, unlike delivering sessions or observing lessons, that benefits less from overlap or analogy with teaching (although there is still *some* benefit), and so it requires specialist preparation – you need to know what you're doing when you deliver feedback. Our experiences of receiving feedback as teachers mean that we all have ideas about what it usually involves. However, many of those experiences are not positive, and even for those that are, attempting to replicate the way that someone else has delivered feedback without an understanding of how it relates to roles and context may have minimal impact, or even negative results: 'to borrow only certain outward features of the approach without understanding what its real power is would be like using an airplane only as a car or a sophisticated computer only as a typewriter' (Blair 1982, p. 103, cited in Gebhard, 1990, p. 161).

So it's essential to understand the rationale behind each of your options for delivering feedback, and to choose the most appropriate options depending on the individual characteristics of each situation. Many of these characteristics relate to the training habitat (see Chapter 2), and in this chapter we'll revisit this idea to examine what elements of the training habitat are relevant to delivering feedback, and how you can weigh them up to make the best decisions for your situation.

Defining feedback

We define feedback as the things that we say or write to teachers to help them develop their knowledge, skills, beliefs and attitudes. It can be positive, reinforcing existing knowledge and skills, or it can focus on areas for improvement, and in most cases it should balance both of these. Sometimes feedback will be quite direct ('try not to talk to students while you're writing on the board with your back to them') and at other times it involves helping teachers to reach deeper understandings on their own, through questioning and elicitation. Sometimes it is given immediately, for example during a training session, and at other times it is delayed, as is usually the case when it relates to the observation of real classes.

Feedback on lesson planning and teaching is our focus here, so although trainers can and do give feedback to trainees on other areas, such as assignments, or in tutorials, these tend to mirror much more closely the kinds of feedback that you give to students as a teacher. Feedback on teaching is rather different because it tends to happen quite infrequently and therefore takes on considerable significance when it does happen. Any of the following can involve feedback on teaching:

- meeting before and after a CELTA or Delta-style assessed lesson

- when a manager or director of studies gives feedback after observing a teacher as part of appraisal

- when teachers observing each other informally meet to discuss a lesson one of them taught and the other observed

- a school-based mentor giving feedback to a teacher after being invited to observe a lesson, either for troubleshooting or for more general developmental purposes

Aims of feedback

The ultimate goal of feedback, like all teacher training activity, is improved classroom practice and, as a result, better learning outcomes for students. Feedback on teaching, given after an observed lesson, will aim to develop what the teacher is doing in the classroom, at the levels of *Knowing how* and *Knowing to*.

In many cases feedback aims to improve not just teaching skills, but also reflection skills (see Chapter 7). That's because feedback conversations are an important opportunity to invite teachers to reflect in the presence of a trainer so that they can be supported in reflecting effectively. Most teaching takes place without an observer in the room, so it is important that teachers are able to evaluate their own effectiveness, and feedback conversations are one of the best ways we can model that evaluation process. Following evaluation, we want teachers to be able to take responsibility for decision making upon themselves, whether those decisions relate to their students' learning, or to their own. The ideal endpoint is for teachers to reach a stage where they don't need an observer in the room, because they can already perceive what students are doing and identify the most effective ways to respond:

> Teachers should be more than programmed automata delivering pre-selected material; they should be actively engaged in critically examining what they do in classrooms. Thus, the ultimate aim of providing advice is to produce a teacher or trainee capable of such independence of thought and action. (Randall & Thornton, 2001, p. 2)

Feedback conversations are therefore critical stepping stones towards developing adaptive expertise in trainees, and making them evaluative practitioners.

You may be starting to see the three Ps (see Chapter 2) re-emerge here. The observed lesson itself, and subsequent discussions of how effective particular practices were, or which ones might be more effective, are in the domain of the Practical. The aspects of the feedback conversation that are designed to support trainees' noticing and reflection skills cover the Personal. And although it may not immediately appear relevant, the Professional also has a role in feedback on teaching. It is through feedback conversations that teachers learn how we label and talk about classroom events, and this provides them with the ability to notice and describe what goes on in the classroom in terms that will enable them to explore external resources and seek help or inspiration. Dan Lortie explains why this is so important:

> [When a beginner teacher] identifies a difficulty, he may request help. But there is a secondhand quality to such assistance: if the advisor is not someone who regularly visits the classroom, the teacher must describe the situation. . . . The beginner's perceptions and interpersonal skills mediate between external advice and classroom events; his learning is limited by his personal resources – the acuity of his observation and his capacity to take effective action. (Lortie, 1975, p. 73)

Feedback conversations, then, are a way of connecting the Professional elements – the concepts and terms – that teachers have gathered from elsewhere (training sessions, reading, discussion) to their physical manifestations in the classroom. And they are a way of adding to those concepts and terms where necessary, so that teachers are able to better perceive what's happening in their classrooms in the future, and do further research or ask the right questions when a problem arises.

When and how to give feedback

Two very simple options for when and how feedback might be given are 'hot' or 'cold' (Scrivener, 2011) and either written or spoken. Hot feedback is given immediately or very soon after teaching (e.g., after a 15-minute break), when the memory of the class is still very fresh. That means that details of what happened in the lesson, or of what the teacher was thinking or feeling, will probably be recalled more accurately, which can be helpful. The downside is that it can be hard for teachers to step back and reflect on the lesson with a sense of perspective so soon, and perceived triumphs or failures can seem much more significant than they really were. Cold feedback takes place later, perhaps the day after the lesson, when trainees can look back on it a little more objectively, but when it is still possible to remember what went on. Jim Scrivener (2011) suggests that it can be useful for teachers to note down their thoughts both hot and cold, and then compare them side-by-side to see which perspective seems more realistic, or a better guide to development. Whether the feedback discussion is hot or cold, it is good practice to have the teacher reflect 'hot' in writing beforehand and then pass those reflections to the observer ahead of the meeting. This allows the teacher to get their thoughts on the lesson somewhat clear and gives the observer an early indication of how much their views align.

A feedback meeting between teacher and observer might be hot or cold, but it is unlikely that there would be both. In contrast, we believe that when it comes to *how* feedback is delivered, teachers should always receive both written and spoken feedback after an observation. The written feedback is an important record and future reference point for the teacher, and we will discuss this further later in the chapter. We suggest that spoken feedback, on the other hand, should be treated as the principal form of feedback, and delivered before written feedback in most cases (the exception being when feedback is almost entirely positive). This is because:

- It is easier to ensure that feedback has been understood in a face-to-face conversation.

- A conversation provides the opportunity for questions and elicitation, meaning that teachers can be guided towards uncovering insights for themselves, rather than simply being told in writing.

- Having reached those conclusions themselves, teachers are more likely to remember them.

- Teachers are arguably more likely to take steps to improve their practice if they identify for themselves the necessary action.

- A conversation allows the teacher to explain their thought process during the lesson, which means that you can target recommendations in written feedback on the right area(s).

- There is some evidence that trainees consider spoken feedback to have a bigger impact on their teaching (Delaney, 2019).

Despite all these advantages, there is 'the central conundrum of all teacher observation and feedback' (Randall & Thornton, 2001, p. 20) to contend with as part of spoken feedback: the possibility of upsetting or prompting defensiveness in a teacher with criticisms of their teaching. This possibility is often associated with assessment, even relatively informal kinds of assessment, because it is more likely than not that shortcomings in teaching will be identified. Nevertheless, this is an unavoidable reality of providing feedback on teaching: in order to be useful, feedback must deal with elements of the lesson that were not successful as well as with those that were, and broaching these is difficult.

> Any observation of a lesson is going to involve, by its very nature, judgments about what has been seen. . . . Unless the feedback is to become so bland as to be of no use in moving a teacher on, the observer will need to make judgments about what went on in the lesson. These need to be expressed to the one being observed, and any criticism will at least have the capacity, if not the actuality, of causing pain. (Randall & Thornton, 2001, p. 20)

Of course, criticism, properly expressed, will also have the capacity of enabling improvement in teaching, which is our primary goal. The best approach observers can take is to be honest with teachers about the judgements they are likely to be making during an observation: what standards or criteria will they use to evaluate what they see, and for whose benefit will those judgements be made?

Obviously, there is a lot happening in these conversations, and in order to strike the right tone and get the outcomes we want, some understanding of the social context of each feedback conversation is very important. To a large extent this is a question of putting ourselves in the shoes of the teacher and understanding what feelings and preconceptions they are bringing to the feedback conversation, so that we can approach it in the most effective way. We can think about the social context for feedback conversations in terms of three interrelated factors – Interpersonal, Institutional, and Intentional, as detailed in Table 8.1.

Table 8.1: The social context of feedback conversations (based on Randall & Thornton, 2001)

Interpersonal factors	Concerning the level of formality in the relationship between the teacher and observer, the degree of trust between them, and their perceived status	◦ Age gap ◦ Level of experience (of teacher and of observer) ◦ How well teacher and observer know each other, both personally and professionally
Institutional factors	To do with the professional setting of the feedback conversation, institutionally, or in terms of the wider educational system	◦ Observer's role title and connotations it carries ◦ Whether the observation is part of preservice or in-service training activity ◦ Administrative requirements set by the institution, the training/awarding body, or the education system ◦ Cultural expectations of the education system and the specific sector (e.g., primary/secondary/tertiary; state/private)
Intentional factors	Determining if the intention of the observation and feedback is balanced towards support and development of teaching, or towards assessing the teacher's competence	◦ Whether 'good teaching' is specified by clearly-defined criteria ◦ Whether a grade must be given ◦ Whether the observed lesson is assessed as part of a wider programme of study, or is an unassessed component of it ◦ Whether the observer will report details of the observed lesson to others

There are no hard-and-fast rules we can draw from these contextual factors. Instead, it is the observer's responsibility to be aware of them and to weigh up how they might affect the dynamic of the feedback conversation by promoting a sense of equality between the teacher and observer, or a sense of hierarchy. With experience this becomes second nature, but it is worth doing more deliberately when you start observing.

To give an example, a colleague of ours in the Middle East found herself in a fairly unusual social context for an observation as a school inspector observing a lesson given by the same teacher who had taught her as a child some 20 years earlier! In terms of Interpersonal factors there was a pre-existing relationship (albeit one from many years ago), there was a considerable age gap, and also a gap in experience, although the inspector had gained more varied experience in her teaching career than the teacher she was observing. These factors alone would have tilted the balance of seniority towards the teacher, but the Institutional and Intentional factors acted to shift seniority towards the inspector: her title and role for the Ministry of Education carried significant weight, and was supported with extensive inspection criteria and associated administrative requirements. The result was that our colleague, the inspector, was in a position to make the atmosphere in the feedback meeting one of mutual respect and of openness, despite circumstances that might otherwise have led either side to feel quite apprehensive.

TASK 8.1

...To trainer

For each of the training contexts in the list below, consider what Interpersonal, Institutional and Intentional factors the observer ought to take into account ahead of the feedback conversation. You could review the case studies from Chapter 6 (Marie, Moses and Carmen) to help with this.

- Intensive preservice training course (e.g., CELTA)
- Peer observation between two colleagues
- Routine observation of a teacher by their academic manager

For notes see page 231

Setting up and preparing feedback

After the observation, you will need to review your notes from the lesson and decide what to address in feedback. This is almost always a process of deciding what *not* to talk about, because the data from the lesson will be too rich to cover in full. Trying to talk about everything that you saw would be overwhelming for the teacher, and would take a very long time! We suggest reviewing your notes and preparing your feedback soon after the lesson – certainly the same day – so that you are not hampered in remembering what took place.

Every lesson is different, and sometimes it will be quite easy to prepare feedback, while at other times it can be difficult to know what to highlight. In general, we find that feedback on preservice courses is more straightforward, because the areas for improvement tend to be more predictable in trainees who are just starting out. Shaping your notes into feedback to experienced teachers, particularly when they are experimenting with new techniques in the observed lesson, can be more challenging. Our case studies illustrate how observers take different approaches depending on what works in their contexts:

CASE STUDY 8.1: MARIE, THE CELTA TRAINER

On most of the courses I work on at the moment we conduct group feedback after teaching practice, so there's a 15-minute break after the lesson ends and we stay in the classroom for our feedback discussion, moving the chairs into a circle. I type my notes and shape them into written feedback while I'm observing, so the 15 minutes is just enough time to get myself ready for the discussion. I make sure that I read the teachers' reflection sheets – I used to forget to do this – so that I can refer to them when we talk, and I print out the written feedback ready to give to the teachers once our discussion has ended. I've worked on courses where we do feedback the next morning, which is less of a rush for me, but I find the trainees are better able to recall details of the lesson when the feedback discussion happens straight away.

What I often do is have the trainees write positives and negatives from all the lessons we've observed that day on the board in the classroom in the 15-minute break, and we take those as the starting point for our discussion. I try to mix things up so that we're not doing the same thing every single time, but I do come back to this technique a lot because I find it so effective.

CASE STUDY 8.2: MOSES, THE TEACHER

My colleagues and I have busy teaching schedules, so it is usually not possible to talk about feedback immediately after the lesson. We normally have our feedback meeting in an empty classroom at lunchtime, because that's the only place and time that's available. I confess I don't do a lot of preparation for these meetings; I just bring my notes from the lesson and tell my colleagues what I noticed.

CASE STUDY 8.3: CARMEN, THE MANAGER

I only give feedback after the formal observations, not after my learning walks – they're too short and they're for my benefit, not the teacher's.

For my formal observations we usually have to arrange the feedback meeting for a day after the lesson because the teachers and I have busy schedules. I try to make it as soon as possible afterward, but sometimes it's a week later. I don't like waiting so long, but sometimes there's no other choice. It's often at the end of the day so that there's not the pressure to finish by a particular time. When we fix the date and time I make sure the teacher has a reflection sheet to complete and I ask them to send it to me the day before the meeting.

For the place where we meet I try not to do it in my office because it feels kind of like 'my territory' and I don't want it to feel like it's *my* meeting. So oftentimes we have the meeting in a classroom and sit side-by-side to avoid any sense of confrontation. But again, sometimes there's no choice. The priority is somewhere quiet and private. Before the meeting I get all

> my paperwork ready – lesson plan, materials, the teachers' reflection, and my written feedback. Sometimes I'll ask for examples of student work from the lesson too. One thing I've started doing is using these documents as a focal point during the meeting, and this seems to help create a sense of collaboration and shared problem-solving, as opposed to confrontation. I think that's really positive.

What we see in these three descriptions of how Marie, Moses and Carmen prepare for their feedback meetings is how the atmosphere in the feedback meeting can be changed with some subtle alterations to the way it is set up. Carmen, for example, chooses the location for the meeting carefully so that it takes place in the classroom (the teacher's 'domain') and plans to sit alongside the teacher so as to minimise any sense of conflict, assessment or judgement. She even uses the idea of a 'third point' (Grinder, 2006) to ensure that the focus of the discussion is on teaching practices, not on the teacher as an individual – by having a document on the table as the focus of discussion, she is able to direct her comments towards this third point rather than directly at the teacher. This avoids a sense of confrontation and allows the teacher to save face (a technique that can also be performed rhetorically, by focusing the conversation on the behaviour and responses of learners, rather than on the teacher's actions). This is arguably very important in Carmen's context, because her role as manager means there is a strong sense of hierarchy in her meetings with teachers, and she needs to work hard to mitigate the perception that the teachers need to perform well or risk losing their jobs!

Marie also tries to use seating and a third point to make the dynamic of her feedback meetings more favourable. Sitting in a circle creates a sense of equality, and because she can use the trainees' comments on the board in the classroom as the focal point for discussions, she also exploits the idea of three-point communication. In addition, by working from the points that the trainees have highlighted, she skilfully combines the development of their reflective skills with a technique that gives them a say in how the discussion unfolds. All of this combines to foster trust between Marie and her trainees, and between Carmen and the teachers she observes, and this is essential to productive feedback conversations: 'the atmosphere created in the feedback session must be one in which the teacher feels free to talk and explore the situation with the [observer]' (Randall & Thornton, 2001, p. 95).

TASK 8.2

...To trainer

After reading the Case studies 8.1, 8.2 and 8.3, can you list the tasks that should always be completed in preparation for a feedback conversation?

For notes see page 233

Spoken feedback one-to-one

On preservice courses it's quite common for feedback to take place in groups, and so we'll cover those situations separately (although many of the principles of feedback conversations with individuals will still apply). In other situations, most observation feedback takes place one-to-one, and we deal with how to manage those conversations first.

It can be useful to have a handful of remarks and questions ready to open the conversation. Often the teacher will be feeling nervous and you will want to set a relaxed tone for the meeting and put them at ease. Here are a few examples:

What a lovely group of students!	Sets a positive tone, takes the spotlight off the teacher for a moment, and acts as a conversational 'third point'.
So was that a fairly typical lesson with that group?	Again, takes the focus off the teacher and onto the students, and opens the door for the teacher to highlight anything that wasn't representative of their usual teaching.
How do you feel the lesson went?	A very common question, but one that we tend to avoid because it is vague and immediately puts the burden of evaluation onto the teacher. It can be useful, however, if you sense that the teacher is unhappy with the lesson – they may well raise some of the weaker aspects of the lesson and you can steer the conversation towards the positives once they have let off steam.

A five-stage model for feedback discussions

Once the discussion is underway, we use a five-stage model to structure our feedback conversations, as shown in Table 8.2.

Table 8.2: Five-stage model for feedback discussions

Stage 1	What happened in the lesson	It's important to begin the discussion by establishing a common understanding of events in the lesson.
Stage 2	Whether aims were achieved	The question here is 'How successful was the lesson in terms of the objectives set by the teacher?' The teacher should be able to answer this.
Stage 3	What the teacher might do differently	This is a hypothetical discussion, but an opportunity for the teacher to demonstrate that they are aware of the areas they can improve.
Stage 4	How the teacher will follow up on this lesson	This part of the conversation is grounded in reality – however successful the lesson was, the teacher needs to consolidate the learning that took place and remedy any gaps.
Stage 5	What the teacher has learned	Here we see how well the teacher is able to reflect and use reflection to guide future professional learning.

Since one of the aims of feedback is to develop the teacher's ability to self-evaluate, for each of these stages the teacher should be the one doing most of the talking, guided by you as the observer. Very inexperienced teachers will need more input from you as part of their feedback discussions, but teachers who have more experience and knowledge should be guided as much as possible towards their own conclusions by questions and elicitation. Unfortunately, the word *feedback* suggests a different kind of conversation in which the observer does the talking and delivers a verdict on the lesson they saw, and so many teachers come to the feedback discussion with expectations of listening rather than talking.

For this reason, there's a need to be very explicit about what you're doing at each stage and why. For example, when beginning the discussion explain that you want to start by establishing a common understanding of what took place in the lesson before evaluating the effectiveness of specific teaching moments or analysing perceived problems. Stating aims like this is especially important in cross-cultural interactions – when trainers and teachers from different cultural backgrounds meet there may be 'crossed wires' if roles, topics and goals are not clearly laid out (Randall & Thornton, 2001, p. 139) – but also because teachers frequently seem to misunderstand the trainer's goals in feedback, even when they share the same cultural background. Our experience is that many teachers expect the observer to deliver a grade or judgement, and completely miss the observer's aim: to use the observed lesson as a vehicle for improving reflective practice in general terms, and for helping the teacher identify and plan to implement specific teaching practices that might improve learning outcomes.

Stage 1: What happened in the lesson

In most cases, the feedback discussion relies on the teacher and observer accurately remembering events from the lesson (the exception being if there is a video recording, but even then, it won't show everything). So it is a good idea to begin by talking through what happened to make sure that there's basic agreement about what took place. It's best if the teacher does most of the talking because you can learn a lot about how they perceive the classroom from their descriptions – expert teachers tend to focus more on student behaviours, while less experienced teachers generally focus more on their own actions. There are a few different ways that you can invite the teacher to recount what happened:

- **Chronologically** – running from the beginning of the lesson until the end. This is logical, thorough and easy on the teacher, but it can also result in quite a lengthy, unfocused feedback conversation.

- **Flashpoints** – ask the teacher to describe the moments in the lesson that they remember most vividly, or that seem most significant to them. This can be challenging for inexperienced teachers, who may focus on moments that they felt were 'failures' (but which may have had little impact on the lesson).

- **Highs and lows** – ask the teacher to pick out moments or things that they feel went well, and those which they are not so happy with. This can be useful for teachers who struggle to take a balanced view of their lessons.

- **Your selections** – you give the teacher a range of moments or themes (e.g., 'giving instructions') and they recall what happened in relation to each one. This gives the observer the most control over the conversation and can help keep the discussion on track, but it takes the onus off the teacher to notice classroom events, and might increase the sense that there are 'right and wrong' answers that the observer expects to hear.

- **Pre-selected areas of focus** – if the teacher identified specific areas for which they wanted feedback as part of the pre-observation meeting, they should of course be included within this part of the discussion.

It often makes sense to combine this first stage in the discussion with stage 3 – thinking about what could have been done differently. The alternative to doing that at times when the teacher alights on a part of the lesson which was not so successful is to talk about what happened in the lesson in full, and then return to those moments afterwards to think about how they could be improved. That approach may be more appropriate if there is a common underlying cause to the problems at each stage (which may be the case with issues such as poor timing, for example).

TASK 8.3

...To trainer

You might find that, in their description of the lesson, the teacher doesn't mention some of the moments or issues that you felt were most salient. In that case you will need to raise those points yourself. How many ways can you think of to do that? Make a list of useful phrases.

For notes see page 233

Stage 2: Whether aims were achieved

After reviewing what happened during the lesson, the next stage is to evaluate how effective it was. Doing this by referring to the lesson aims creates a link to the pre-observation meeting and encourages the teacher to reflect not just on what happened during the lesson itself but also on the decisions made during planning. In this way the feedback meeting is an opportunity for the teacher to improve their planning skills as much as it is an opportunity to develop their classroom practice.

In addition to discussing aims, however, it is important to prompt the teacher to reflect on any incidental learning that may have taken place. If students have benefitted from elements of the lesson that were not pre-planned, there is value for the teacher in reflecting on why and considering how those same elements could be deliberately incorporated in future. This part of the discussion may be especially necessary if the teacher's aims were not well formulated – it is very common for novice teachers to phrase their aims in terms of what they will do in the lesson, rather than in terms of what students will learn (e.g., 'By the end of the lesson we will have practised reading'), and that makes the aims pretty useless as a benchmark for evaluating the lesson.

Probably the most important skill for the observer in this part of the discussion is leading the teacher to think about what evidence there is for student learning. It's quite common for teachers to point out at this stage that students were engaged and enjoyed the lesson, which is undoubtedly positive, but it is not the same as evidence of learning. So a crucial part of this stage of the discussion will be eliciting from the teacher the student talk, or written work, or behaviours that point towards successful achievement of their aims, or towards increases in learners' capabilities and understanding. It may be that they didn't notice these or that they can't remember them, and your role will then be to share what you observed in the lesson and invite the teacher to judge what learning took place on the basis of that evidence.

Stage 3: What the teacher might do differently

No lesson is perfect, and so there is always something to talk about at this stage, but the degree of change required can vary greatly. It may be a question of improving on a lesson that was already quite effective, or a case of addressing some serious shortcomings in teaching or planning. Either way, the first step is for the teacher to recognise that there was indeed room for improvement, and hopefully the previous two stages have pointed in that direction and brought some of the weaker areas of the lesson into the discussion. If the teacher has completed a written reflection then you will also get a sense from that of how many of the weaker aspects of the lesson they've identified themselves.

We suggest using the following four steps to guide the conversation. If the teacher hasn't identified the issue(s) you want to deal with, you will need to begin by raising them yourself, but the steps remain the same for each issue:

1. **Begin by describing what you observed**

   Often, the teacher will already have described what you want to discuss and you may simply need to elicit further detail. The aim is to agree on what happened: what the teacher's words and actions were, and how the students responded (or vice versa).

2. **Clarify the consequences/implications of the teacher's decisions**

   When giving negative feedback it is vital that the teacher understands why different choices may have been more appropriate. In this step, the focus is on the students and their learning, and (evidence of) how it was negatively impacted.

3. **Understand the reasons for the teacher's decisions**

   In order to help the teacher understand what to do differently you need to know the reason behind their choices in the observed lesson. Was it:

   - a gap in their teaching knowledge (which could be a complete gap, with no relevant *Knowing about, or* a gap between *Knowing about* and *Knowing how* and *Knowing to*)

   - a belief about teaching and learning which meant the teacher did not apply knowledge that they already possess

   - a psychological barrier (e.g. nervousness) which meant the teacher did not apply knowledge that they already possess

   The teacher may indicate this without being prompted, but if not, invite them to reflect and consider what their thought process was at the time.

4. **Advise/explore/support**

   Depending on the reason(s) identified in the previous step, you will need to advise, to help the teacher develop their knowledge; to explore and challenge beliefs by inviting the teacher to unpick what they believe and why; or to support the teacher in overcoming a psychological block by offering encouragement.

When the observed lesson includes many potential areas of improvement one of your main tasks will be prioritising. A long list of things to do differently is demoralising for teachers and may leave them wondering where to begin. A useful question to ask yourself is 'What is the one thing that will help this teacher improve?' If it is a significant gap in their practice, it may be more effective to devote a good chunk of time in the feedback meeting to working on improving it, rather than trying to tackle several problems at once.

Stage 4: Following up on the lesson

In this stage the focus shifts from the hypothetical world of discussing what could or should have been done differently into the real world, and the question of what the teacher will do in the next lesson. They will either want to consolidate and build on the learning that took place in the observed lesson if it was successful, or want to remedy any gaps in understanding that resulted from the lesson.

Your aim as the observer in this stage is to evaluate how well the teacher is able to view the course as a cohesive whole, rather than a series of isolated lessons, and how well the teacher is able to use each lesson to evaluate the learning that took place and what was revealed about the students' ongoing needs. Non-expert teachers tend to find it more difficult to make these connections between lessons, and may need some help to see how the observed lesson can inform the planning of the next one, for example by highlighting earlier parts of the discussion and using them to elicit appropriate next steps. This is another instance, therefore, of how the feedback discussion can support lesson planning and not just classroom practice. Expert teachers, on the other hand, should be able to describe the links between the observed lesson and their plans for the next one much more readily.

Stage 5: What the teacher learned

Ted Wragg argues that 'in order to make an impact, any formal appraisal of teaching competence must be both retrospective and prospective, looking back at what has been achieved and forward to what might be done in the future' (Wragg, 1999, p. 101). So the final part of the feedback discussion should review what the teacher has learned from the whole observation cycle (the pre-observation meeting, the observed lesson and the feedback discussion) and look ahead to the actions they can now take to improve their teaching practice further. At this stage the teacher may need to be directed towards certain resources, or to be told about specific approaches, methods or techniques that may be useful and which they are not currently aware of. Some of this information can be provided afterwards, perhaps by email, which helps to keep the meeting focused and allows the teacher to digest it in their own time and refer back to it later as they try to adapt their teaching.

It is a good idea at the end of the feedback discussion to ask the teacher to summarise the meeting and reiterate any action points – this acts as a check that your feedback has been received as you intended, and can help to highlight anything that might have been forgotten or misunderstood in time for you to clarify it.

TASK 8.4

...To trainer

Watch the feedback meeting between Peter, the trainer, and Theresa, the teacher. What do you like about Peter's approach? What would you do differently, and why?

Spoken feedback with groups

Group feedback is more likely to take place on preservice courses, because trainees starting from scratch will tend to share similar learning needs – for that reason we focus in this section on preservice trainees. Once teachers begin to start gaining experience their needs diverge quite significantly and individual feedback becomes essential. The group setting means that less time is spent discussing each lesson than in most individual feedback meetings, but beginning teachers will probably benefit from more succinct, focused feedback about how to improve. It's also the case that on a preservice course they will have an opportunity to teach again and implement that feedback very soon, so it makes sense for group feedback meetings to offer trainees advice on just one or two areas for improvement.

While there are many similarities in feedback techniques between individual and group scenarios, the preservice course context in which group feedback is most likely to take place introduces a number of distinctive elements:

- Other trainees are observing too, so you need to address what they've seen and bring them into the discussion.

- Running feedback with a group of trainees introduces more possibilities for demonstrating teaching techniques in the feedback discussion.

- The group situation means that there is the potential for trainees to lose face in front of their peers.

- The course context means that observed lessons must be graded, with the grade given as part of the feedback.

- Two or three teachers will be receiving feedback, so the time available will need to be split fairly evenly between discussion of each lesson.

As with individual feedback, you'll want to start by setting a positive tone. You may be discussing several lessons in one sitting, so it is a good idea to begin feedback on each lesson by asking the teacher to remind the group what their aims were and what the lesson was about. This is a good way to align everyone's thinking, ready to contribute to the discussion, and it's an easy way for the teacher to start talking.

Once you've established aims in this way, the structure in Table 8.2 (see page 160) is a useful template for managing the discussion of each trainee's teaching, and our experience has been that it is generally preferable to focus on each trainee's lesson, or part of a lesson, in turn. There are various ways of approaching these discussions: the group might start with comments from the trainees who completed peer observation tasks, you could use the trainees' written reflections as an initial conversation starter, or you could use the technique that Marie describes in Case study

8.1, using a list of talking points drawn up by the trainees as a point of departure. With each of these, let trainees do the talking – eliciting what they saw, evaluating the positive and negative aspects and suggesting improvements with the aim of improved student learning in mind.

It is often necessary in these discussions to steer the focus onto the students and onto what they learned from the lesson. That's because trainees will naturally focus more on their own actions, and we want to encourage them to evaluate lessons in terms of student learning. But it can also make it easier for you to deliver negative feedback if that's what's required, by pointing towards the consequences of any weaknesses in teaching. Trainees tend to be reluctant to deliver negative feedback, partly because they feel that as novices it's not their place to do so, and partly because they are more concerned with maintaining positive relations with their peers (Delaney, 2019). So be prepared to interject to keep the discussion on track, and to summarise the key feedback for each teacher before moving on to discussion of the next lesson.

When a lesson is graded 'not to standard' the teacher will inevitably be disappointed. It is important that the reason for the grade is clear to the teacher, and that means that if they or their peers seem unaware of the problems with the lesson you will have to communicate them yourself. The overall message should focus on the bigger picture: the necessary next steps and the teacher's path to improvement. If the lesson is not the first below standard grade that the teacher has received and they are in danger of failing the course, then it may be appropriate to conduct a short initial group feedback discussion (perhaps just dealing with aims and peer observation tasks) before conducting the remaining feedback with each teacher individually. This means that the teacher who is struggling is able to get the support and advice they need in a private setting – essentially a mini tutorial.

Written feedback on teaching

In general, observations should always be followed up with written feedback (the informal nature of much peer observation makes it the exception). It provides a record of the observation and of the feedback meeting, and it acts as a reference for the teacher. That's important in the days after the feedback meeting, when the teacher will (ideally) review the feedback and begin to start thinking about how to act on the suggestions for improvement that were given. Without written feedback, it's difficult to remember those suggestions or the rationale for them, and it's also more difficult to ask others, such as colleagues, for help unless you have a clear idea of what you're trying to work on.

CASE STUDY 8.4: MARIE, THE CELTA TRAINER

I write my feedback to the trainees during their lessons, so I am shaping my notes into feedback almost as soon as I have written them – I type everything, and I don't think I could do this if I was handwriting. The downside of writing the feedback so soon is that I'm not able to include any comments acknowledging the trainee's spoken reflections in feedback, but I do make sure I look at their written reflection sheets.

We have a one-page template for TP feedback, which makes the job easier because it forces me to be succinct (I tend to write in bullet points rather than continuous prose) and because I've used it countless times now. It has a box for strengths, then two for areas to develop: those which were identified in previous lessons and a blank box for those identified in the current lesson. The final space is for overall comments. So there's always a balance of positive and negative. My priorities are to give clear action points to the trainees and to motivate them to act on them in the next TP, and if the grade for the lesson is above or below standard, to make it clear why. I always ask the trainees for feedback on my feedback(!) at the end of each course and it has been a useful way of understanding how to make my messages clearer.

CASE STUDY 8.5: MOSES, THE TEACHER

I don't give written feedback to the colleagues I observe, but sometimes they ask to see my notes and we see each other every day anyway, so we are always talking about what we are trying to improve on. But I can tell you what I prefer when I receive written feedback after an observation! I want the feedback to match what I have heard in the feedback discussion, I want the observer to be clear and tell me how I can improve (not only to point out weaknesses), and for the same reason I do not like it when supervisors ask many questions in the written feedback. I will not see them to check my answer, so I do not believe it is a useful technique.

CASE STUDY 8.6: CARMEN, THE MANAGER

Well, for me, writing the feedback takes a long time because I think about it very carefully. I try to give a lot of details to the teachers and include examples from what I saw in the lesson because they don't have observations frequently, and I want them to feel that the process was worthwhile. I make time in my schedule to write the feedback because it should be given promptly after the feedback meeting.

For the action points, I give only a few so that the teachers are not overwhelmed. The exact number depends on what they are, because some areas need a lot of work but other weaknesses can be fixed easily. But three is a good number, I would say.

Together, the approaches to written feedback described by Marie, Moses and Carmen offer some useful guidelines for how to approach the task of putting feedback down on paper. These are shown in Table 8.3 below, grouped according to whether they relate to the process of writing feedback, the content of written feedback, or the style in which it is written. Some of these guidelines may be limited by the training context, particularly when the observation is assessed. For example, in Marie's context there is very limited time to write feedback, so the question of when to write it is largely preordained. In other assessed contexts the observer may be instructed to write feedback in the third person rather than address it to the teacher. But we feel these guidelines are applicable to most observation situations.

Table 8.3 Guidelines for preparing written feedback

Process	○ Plan when you will write feedback.
	○ Deliver written feedback promptly.
	○ Consult trainee's written reflections (and spoken reflections if possible) before writing.
Content	○ Balance positive and negative comments.
	○ Ensure that written feedback aligns with spoken feedback.
	○ Refer to feedback / action points from previous observations in order to comment on progress and development.
	○ Include specific examples from the lesson to support your comments.
	○ Make action points as clear as possible, don't offer vague advice.
	○ Give practical advice on exactly how to address teaching shortcomings and/or links to resources that give such advice.
Style	○ Address comments to the teacher, using their name.
	○ Aim to motivate the teacher to act on your feedback.
	○ Use bullet points if you wish.
	○ Don't overuse rhetorical questions.
	○ Limit action points to a manageable number.

Besides the training context, the other factor that will influence written feedback is the template that observers are required to use when writing it. For assessed contexts like Marie's, or in managerial contexts like Carmen's, a template will be provided by the institution, and will shape what and how much you are able to write (although templates will vary in how rigidly they must be adhered to).

TASK 8.5

...To trainer

Below are examples of written feedback templates from a CELTA course and an observation by an academic manager.

What similarities and differences do you notice between the format and layout used for each of these?

TP:	Trainee Name:	Date:
	Tutor Name:	
Area:	**Tutor's overall comments**	**Action points**
Your TP preparation and planning		
Your teaching practice		

Overall Comments

Lesson **for this stage of the course** was:

BELOW STANDARD	AT STANDARD	ABOVE STANDARD

Signature of TP Tutor: _________________   Signature of Trainee: _________________

Date: _________________   Date: _________________

Figure 8.1: CELTA observation feedback template

Teacher		Observer	
Lesson date/time		Class name	
Classroom		No. of students	

Course and lesson planning

Classroom management

Use of resources and materials

Subject knowledge

Understanding of learners

Overall

Action points

Figure 8.2: Academic manager observation feedback template

The two templates above share many similarities: nearly all written feedback begins with the details of the observed lesson (e.g., date, time, number of students), and it is common for written feedback to end with an overall comment and action points. The differences between the templates reflect differences in context. For assessed observations a grade and the observer's signature are commonplace, and if the observation is part of a course then there may be other details given relating to the course and the stage at which the observation is taking place. For performance appraisals the feedback template will be used with teachers across the institution, and it will therefore reflect the priorities of the institution (e.g., the themes used in Figure 8.2 are set by the institution because they have been deemed important by management) rather than the developmental needs of teachers.

Summary

Feedback is an essential part of the observation cycle, and can have a significantly positive impact on teaching outcomes when it goes well. But it is a challenging and complex part of a trainer's role, and although that makes it rewarding it also means that it may take longer to get to grips with than other aspects of training.

Developing skills as an observer

Now that we've looked at the observation cycle from beginning to end, it is worth considering what you can do to develop this area of your training. Getting as much practice as you can observing other teachers is probably the most useful thing you can do, but it also helps to be observed yourself and see how other observers approach the role. When it comes to feedback, it is enormously helpful to be able to observe a feedback meeting, but very difficult to arrange in reality. Instead, we recommend asking trainees for feedback on your feedback, as Marie suggests in Case study 8.4. The best time to do this is when they have had an opportunity to act on the feedback by experimenting with changes in their teaching practice. If those experiments weren't successful, or didn't happen at all, try and find out why, and whether there is something that you can add to your feedback technique to make it more successful in future.

TASK 8.6

...To trainer

Scan the QR Code and watch Theresa's lesson again. Then, use the academic manager observation feedback template (Figure 8.2) to write feedback for the lesson. Compare your feedback with Peter's example and commentary in the notes. What similarities and differences do you notice between the example and your own feedback?

For notes see page 234

TRAINER VOICES

Scan the QR Code and watch the videos 'Opening the conversation' and 'Trainees who don't take on feedback' to hear how trainers manage their real-life feedback conversations. Which techniques would work best with the trainees you observe?

TO FIND OUT MORE

Randall, M., & Thornton, B. (2001). *Advising and supporting teachers.* Cambridge: Cambridge University Press. (Gives thorough and detailed coverage of the issues involved in giving feedback to teachers, and includes tasks to help develop feedback skills.)

9 Training courses and programmes

Here we consider:

- The difference between a course and a programme
- The benefits of courses and programmes
- What is involved in working on a course: before, during and after
- What is involved in working on a programme: before, during and after

In my experience, you can't ask too many questions to try and find out who you're giving the training to, what kind of limitations there might be, what opportunities there might be.

Olha, teacher trainer, UK

So far we have considered training activities – sessions, mentoring practices, observation, and assessment – in isolation. In this chapter we examine what is involved in planning and delivering sustained training, and how training activities are combined to form successful courses and programmes of teacher learning.

Why courses and programmes matter

Training courses and programmes combine different elements of the trainer's toolkit to promote teacher learning that has greater impact than the sum of its parts. One-off professional learning opportunities, such as a single training session or observation, can have a limited effect, but lasting and meaningful change to a teacher's practice needs sustained effort and a range of activities that guide teachers from input, to implementation, to reflection on the impact of their learning (Richardson & Díaz Maggioli, 2018; Weston & Clay, 2018). In this way, improving teaching is a bit like getting fit: going for a jog is likely to do you some good if you aren't generally very active, but the impact on your health pales in comparison to a sustained, well-planned and consistent pattern of regular exercise.

If we enrol on a course or programme, we expect it to have more far-reaching effects than a single training session or observation, and so we usually expect those outcomes to be certified, while also accepting that there is probably a cost involved. There is a distinction to be made here between courses and programmes based on the nature of the work involved for trainers. Courses are schedules of teacher learning that are fairly fixed, which are repeated for different cohorts, and which participants choose to join, usually in the expectation of receiving a qualification if they perform well enough (examples would be CELTA, CertTESOL or an MA course). Programmes, on the other hand, are planned at the request of decision makers in the educational context (so they are always in-service), with reference to a specific group of participants in order to address their specific needs in that context. A programme may include discrete courses as part of the activities that participants do, and many programmes are open-ended, continuing year after year. Examples would be an ongoing programme of training for teachers in a particular institution, planned by the professional development unit there, or a programme for a national ministry of education that aims to improve teaching outcomes in primary schools across a whole region.

TASK 9.1

From teacher ...

When you think about the training that you have been involved in as a teacher (rather than as a trainer), what is the balance of courses, programmes, and standalone training events (e.g., a single training session, or observation)?

For notes see page 236

Courses and programmes offer several things that isolated training events can't. For a start, they offer trainees more variety because they can include group and individual work, and training activities that take place both in and out of the classroom. That means that trainees can develop knowledge at different levels, for example *Knowing about* in training sessions, and *Knowing how* in teaching practice. Besides tackling trainee knowledge in a multifaceted way, the variety that courses and programmes offer creates opportunities for collaborative, teacher-led professional learning. In other words, trainers don't need to be at the forefront of all the activities that make up a course or programme, and in fact if trainees are able to work together at times without the trainer being present, they may develop valuable classroom problem-solving skills. Examples of this kind of collaborative teacher development are given in Table 9.1 below.

Table 9.1: Collaborative teacher development activities

Collaborative action research	Teachers work together to systematically research a particular aspect of their teaching context, with the aim of improving their practice (see Burns, 1999).
Video discussion groups / video clubs	Teachers record themselves teaching and then meet to watch short clips and discuss successes and potential solutions to classroom problems (see Mann et al., 2019).
Reading group	Teachers select an article or book chapter to read ahead of meeting to discuss it with a view to improving their teaching (see Richards, 2017).
Team teaching	Teachers work in pairs to plan, deliver and reflect on lessons together (see Richards, 2017).

Another significant benefit of courses and programmes is that they offer sustained professional learning. While one-off training sessions can be helpful, particularly if they deal with very specific areas, professional learning should last at least six months if it is to have lasting impact on trainees' teaching practice (Cordingley et al., 2015). That doesn't mean that teachers need to attend daily training sessions for months on end. What it does mean is that incorporating change into day-to-day teaching needs time, and that time must be used effectively: teachers need to focus their attention on a particular area of their teaching many times and in many ways in order to really improve what they do at the level of *Knowing to*, and courses and programmes help them to do that in structured ways.

Working on a course

Although courses can be demanding, they are also extremely rewarding. It is enormously satisfying to see trainees make clear progress in their teaching practice and in their professional understanding, and to support their development both in and out of the classroom. When the course leads to a recognised qualification, it can make an enormous difference to your trainees' career prospects. You may even bump into some of your trainees further down the line and work alongside them as teaching colleagues, or even co-trainers, which is a great endorsement of the quality of your training!

Obviously, designing and delivering a course or programme is a major undertaking, but at this point in the book we've already covered many of the components that go into them. Let's begin exploring course delivery with a case study.

CASE STUDY 9.1: YI ZHANG, CELT–S TRAINER

I work for a chain of private language schools in China. It is very large, we have approximately 6,000 teachers working for us. My job is teacher trainer and I travel to our schools to train teachers on the Cambridge CELT-S course, which is for teachers of teenagers. It is a blended course, so teachers learn online for six months before I arrive and then they attend my workshops. Usually there are 12–16 teachers in the group, but sometimes I work with another trainer and we make two groups if there are many teachers. The course that I deliver is one week long but the teachers have already seen the concepts online and completed some tasks about them, which I grade. For the workshops I use the course materials that are provided by Cambridge Assessment. The trainees are observed twice. The first time I give written feedback but they do not receive a grade, and the second time is a summative assessment – they receive a grade for their lesson.

	Mon	Tue	Wed	Thu	Fri	Sat
09:00–09:30	Orientation	Module 3: Skills teaching in the secondary classroom	Observation	Module 5: Developing language use in the secondary classroom	Module 7: Resources for learning in the secondary classroom	Observation
09:30–12:30	Module 1: Managing the secondary classroom					
12:30–13:30	Lunch					
13:30–16:30	Module 2: Language learning and the teenage learner	Module 4: Language awareness for teaching	Observation	Module 6: Planning language learning in the secondary context	Module 8: Assessing language learning in the secondary context	Observation
16:30–17:30						Closing

Figure 9.1: Yi Zhang's CELT-S course schedule

Before the course

As a new trainer, you should be working alongside an experienced training colleague when you deliver your first few courses, and the design and shape of the course will be largely set in stone when you come to work on it. So the task of preparing is more a case of familiarising yourself with the existing course timetable, documentation and session materials, rather than a question of designing and planning things from scratch. The main course trainer should be able to offer plenty of guidance as to what you will need to get ready yourself, and where to find resources that have already been prepared.

Your main goal should be to thoroughly familiarise yourself with:

- the course aims and objectives

- the course timetable

- the assessment requirements and how assessment will take place

- how the different parts of the course will be divided between you and any other trainers

- the names of trainees and why they've chosen to enrol on the course (if they've given this information during the enrolment process, e.g., at interview)

There's no question that the work of the trainer on a course begins well before the first meeting with trainees. Besides the work of getting acquainted with the course material there may be preliminary tasks to complete such as:

- interviewing and selecting trainees

- sending pre-course tasks to successful applicants

- conveying course information / clarifying expectations of trainees

- arranging students for teaching practice sessions

The lead trainer on the course will probably have responsibility for these tasks, but you should expect to have to help and learn what to do in preparation for future iterations of the course, when you might take on those duties.

During the course

Describing a day in the life of a CELTA tutor, Chia Suan Chong explains that her day begins at 8:30 am with preparation for her first training session. At 6:30 pm, ten hours later, she goes home. Even then, she says, 'the day often does not end here. I tend to prefer to mark assignments in the comfort of my own home' (Chong, 2012, p. 54). This is a long day, but it is not unusual for a teacher trainer working on a full-time course. The schedule for Yi Zhang's CELT-S is similarly demanding (bear in mind that it details only the activities that trainees will be involved in, not Yi's preparation and follow-up tasks outside these hours), and it is certainly not unheard of for trainers to work longer hours than these.

Given this kind of time pressure, being organised when you deliver a course is absolutely essential. Before the course starts, you will want to:

- Have a clear schedule for each day of the course, so that you know what should happen when. Don't forget to schedule in breaks for yourself and time when you are *not* available to trainees or colleagues; this is important.

- Have your sessions planned (and materials prepared, ideally).

- Know what paperwork is required of you (e.g., observation feedback, portfolio entries, marking of assignments) and when you will be completing it.

- Know what paperwork is required from participants at each stage, so that you can help them stay on top of it and do well.

- Be in a position to answer questions from trainees about assignments, deadlines, procedures, the timetable, etc.

The good news is that courses such as CELTA and CELT-S tend to follow a repeated format and schedule, and the content of input sessions doesn't change drastically. So if you find yourself delivering the same course several times, all these tasks get much easier because you are much more familiar with what is happening at each stage.

Not all courses are run on a full-time basis like Yi's. Part-time delivery is also quite common, with trainees often attending at evenings or weekends in order to meet other commitments. If you're working on a part-time course then all our suggestions above still apply, but you will of course have more time between sessions with the trainees to prepare yourself, which can be an enormous help to a new trainer. Trainees can also benefit from having time to review and reflect on the content of training sessions and teaching practice feedback. The extra time has its disadvantages too, though: it can be more of a challenge to maintain focus and motivation among the trainees over an extended period in which other commitments are competing for their attention, and the long gaps between trainees' teaching practice lessons can make it harder for some to make progress.

CASE STUDY 9.2: BAHAR, CELTA TUTOR

I work at a university in İzmir, Turkey. I work in the School of Foreign Languages and I am in charge of teacher education and teacher training programmes within the school. Our school has been a CELTA centre for 17 years; besides full-time CELTA courses, we also offer part-time courses depending on the demand.

We spread our part-time courses over three months. Two evenings a week (around three hours) are allotted for the teaching practice lessons (TPs) followed by feedback sessions; and the input sessions are presented at the weekend, usually on Saturdays. Input sessions are followed by lesson planning sessions in preparation for the weekly TPs. The CELTA candidates prefer part-time courses because it is convenient for those who teach during the day, which is almost all of them (this is common for CELTA courses in Turkey). Although the course length might be too long for some teachers, they say they like the part-time programme as it is less intense and less stressful. Unlike the month-long full-time CELTA courses, which many candidates may find challenging and highly stressful, part-time courses give the candidate teachers more time and flexibility for planning and preparing their lessons and working on their written assignments.

As a CELTA tutor, I love both part-time and full-time courses with the pros and cons of each type.

Working with other trainers

In many courses, you will work with a co-trainer, perhaps even two or more. This is especially likely in your early days as a trainer, when you may have a main course tutor to help support you while you get to grips with the course. Being able to work closely with your co-trainer is very important – many hands make light work, and having two trainers on a course can help to ease the workload, but only if you communicate with one another. Chong (2012), for instance, explains that the two daily input sessions on her CELTA course are split between her and the co-trainer; they take one each. But for this to work she starts the day by checking with the other trainer what they will be covering in their session, and her 'break', scheduled for the time that the other trainer is with the group, is spent planning the following day's session. Even lunch is spent working: 'the lunch hour is often used to exchange notes with fellow TP tutors regarding the progress of the trainees and the best ways to go about developing them' (Chong, 2012, p. 54). For courses that involve assessment of trainees this kind of discussion is very important, as you will need to work with your co-trainer to build a picture of each trainee's performance and agree upon each assessment, ensuring that all trainees are treated equally – CELTA courses, for instance, require tutors to double-mark a proportion of candidates' assignments, meaning that one tutor will check the grades and comments given by the other tutor. Blind double-marking, in which both tutors mark some assignments independently, and compare their grades, is encouraged as a way of agreeing and verifying standards.

As well as being close colleagues on the course, co-trainers are also a source of support and development. Working on an intensive course can be draining, and having an encouraging, positive co-trainer can make all the difference. More experienced co-trainers are also an excellent sounding board for your reflections or questions, and most will be happy to fulfil this role and support your professional development. Nevertheless, if you think you will need a lot of help, or if the co-trainer is acting in a formal capacity as your training supervisor, it is preferable to agree a schedule for these conversations (which are a form of mentoring, see Chapter 5) before the course starts – as the main course tutor your co-trainer is likely to have even more on their plate than you, so it is only fair to ensure that they can plan their time effectively.

After the course

From the trainees' point of view, the end of the course should mean that certificates are given, perhaps alongside more detailed feedback. For most accredited courses the certificate itself doesn't include qualitative information about the trainee's performance, and it is therefore not unusual for the training centre to provide its own report which does bear comments of that nature from the trainers, and you may have to write those. On some courses, particularly preservice ones that form the launchpad for a teaching career, trainees may ask for references. Your training centre is likely to have a policy in place and may prefer to deal with references in a centralised way, rather than having individual trainers deal with them, but make sure you know what the policy is and communicate it to trainees so that they know what they can expect.

From the training centre's point of view, the course should be evaluated, and there may be administrative tasks associated with evaluation on the final day of the course, such as having trainees fill in feedback questionnaires. These should be as anonymous as possible to encourage frank responses – leave the room and ask one of the trainees to collect completed forms in an envelope, or provide an online form so that trainees can't be identified by their handwriting. Although it is tempting to send digital questionnaires once the course has ended, we find that invariably the only way to get all trainees to complete them is to set aside time during the course itself, before they all go home.

From your own point of view, it will be important to reflect on what the course meant for you as a trainer. You might want to consider:

- Course outcomes – did the trainees learn what they (and you) had hoped they would learn?

- What did you do particularly well in helping them achieve those outcomes?

- What could you have done better?

- What would you like to improve on from your own perspective? Are there ways that you can make the course less stressful or more rewarding for yourself?

- What developmental goals for your work as a trainer will you take on to the next course?

You can do this on your own, of course, but we have found it helpful to go through this process with one another when we work together, or with the co-trainer on the course. It's helpful to have a different perspective on the same course, these conversations are one of the most valuable resources for trainer learning, and if you work together again in the future you can be accountable to each other for implementing the improvements that you discuss. You'll probably have these reflective conversations to varying degrees throughout the course, but you might want to document them at some point, and the end of the course is usually the best time to do that.

Finally, don't forget to celebrate the completion of the course – for the trainees and for you. Hopefully it will have been a meaningful learning experience for everyone, but it is also sure to have been a lot of hard work, and there's nothing worse than having the course go out with a whimper. At the very least it is usually worth marking the occasion with a photo, and if you've built up a good relationship with your students it might be nice to arrange a social gathering, but you'll have to discuss plans with the group before the final day.

Working on a programme

Programmes are unlike courses in that they are prepared for a specific group of trainees, and may be open-ended. So although they still need to be well-organised, potentially working alongside other trainers, and integrating training skills, they also require thorough design, planning and preparation, and you may be accountable throughout the life of the programme to the programme sponsor (the person or institution that is paying for it). Examples of programmes might include:

- A short series of workshops designed and run by an academic manager at a small private language school who wants to improve teachers' ability to teach with technology.

- A selection of optional weekly workshops run by a chain of schools for teachers at every branch in the chain. The programme is ongoing, running throughout the academic year, and some of the workshops form courses which are certificated in their own right. All the workshops take place at the largest school in the chain, so they're also an opportunity for teachers from different branches to get together.

- A country-wide training initiative for a ministry of education that wants to encourage all secondary teachers across the country to adopt a more communicative methodology.

A programme might, therefore, be as short as an afternoon, or it could span many years. If you are working on a programme as one of a team of trainers, the relevant considerations will be more or less the same as they are for courses. So we will focus here on programmes from the point of view of the programme designer and lead trainer, and on relatively small-scale programmes that illustrate the main concerns.

CASE STUDY 9.3: KAREN, PROGRAMME DESIGNER

I work on designing programmes for all sorts of contexts, but what they have in common is that they are tailored to the needs of a particular institution or group of teachers. That means that there are certain parameters to work within: a fixed budget, a timescale for the whole programme, a certain number of study hours for participants, and so on. It's almost always a process of compromise and of trying to maximise the impact of the time and money available. But it also tends to be a process of working out what the sponsor (the institution or ministry) wants, what the teachers want, and what might have the most impact on student outcomes, because those things don't necessarily align.

Before the programme

A programme, once designed and prepared, can potentially be delivered multiple times if it is not open-ended, particularly if the target audience is a large group (as in the case of a national ministry of education). If that happens, those subsequent iterations of the programme look similar to courses in terms of planning: the main task for trainers is to familiarise themselves with the programme documentation so that they can deliver it confidently. But the very first iteration of any programme is quite different to preparing for a course, because everything needs to be created from scratch. It is that process that we will consider now.

Since programmes are 'made to order', there is a wide spectrum of possibilities for how any given programme could look, from something relatively simple at the level of a single department in an institution, to a complex, large-scale programme at the level of a whole national education system. The way the programme eventually looks is determined by the programme designer's decisions in balancing perceived needs (usually those identified by the sponsor), the elements of the training habitat (see Chapter 2), which usually point towards more 'bottom-up' choices that reflect the views of teachers, and the time and resources made available for the programme.

This balancing act nearly always tends to tilt towards the sponsor's requirements and the available resources, and away from teacher needs – it is very common for the voices of trainees to be unheard, ignored, or deprioritised in programme planning. In our experience that's usually not a conscious decision, but a consequence of organising things at short notice and for participants whose needs and wants may be difficult to canvass. In some situations, a needs analysis is avoided because it might spotlight problems that can't be solved with a training programme, or that might reflect poorly on the managers sponsoring the programme.

The exceptions to this problem around teacher needs are open-ended programmes which are run 'in house' by institutions for their own teachers. In these cases, those designing and delivering the programme content are colleagues of the teachers who are participating, so there are ample opportunities for needs analysis and the trainers involved in the programme can easily evaluate as they go, with input from the teachers participating, and make changes to improve the impact the programme is having.

CASE STUDY 9.4: DIEGO, TRAINING MANAGER

In Chapters 2–4 of this book we presented the process of producing a training session in three main steps: designing an outline, selecting appropriate activities and materials, and delivering the session, with evaluation running through all these. The process of creating and delivering a programme is not dissimilar. There's an initial stage at which needs and aims (of sponsor and participants) are established, the programme is planned out, and then of course it must be delivered. Evaluation of the programme might be considered the final stage, but as discussed in Chapter 4 it permeates all design and planning activities, and in programme design evaluation is really a cyclical process – in its initial stages a programme is informed by the cumulative learning of previous evaluations, evaluation data can be gathered throughout, and when the programme is over, the lessons learned during its delivery will be applied to future programmes.

Where programme design does differ from the process for training sessions is in the level of complexity involved. There are many more decisions, course components and variables to be accounted for in programme design, and that means that there is a logistical side to programme design in addition to considerations of needs, aims, training activities and delivery.

Martin Parrott includes some of these logistical elements in his list of 'design variables' (Parrott, 1991, pp. 43–45), the headings of which form a useful checklist:

1. **Aims** – what are the aims for the sponsor? What are the aims for participants?

2. **Selection** – who selects the trainees and on what basis? What's the nature and what are the needs of the resulting cohort?

3. **Location** – will the course be delivered locally or will teachers travel? What proportion and which elements, if any, will be delivered online? Will face-to-face training take place in a school setting, or in a conference centre?

4. **Format** – is the course part time or intensive, and will it take place in addition to teachers' regular timetables or will they be given time to attend/study?

5. **Length** – what is the planned study time for each participant, and over what time period?

6. **Staffing** – what expertise is needed from the trainers, and is it available at the time and place currently planned?

7. **Content** – is there a balance of workshops providing *Knowing about*, and more tailored in-class support (e.g., observations, collaborative activity or mentoring) for *Knowing how* and *Knowing to*?

8. **Training methodology** – what is the balance of the different elements (workshops, observations, webinars, etc.)? What is most practical in the circumstances?

9. **Assessment** – is there an assessed component? Is it formal or informal?

The logistical elements in Parrott's list are not really separable from those related to teacher learning – there is no perfect world in which you have unlimited time and resources to work with. So it makes sense to establish what time and what resources are available, and then think about the most appropriate ways to meet the needs of the participants. There is rarely one best solution. Instead, you will probably have several possible programmes, each with their advantages and disadvantages. It's helpful when deciding between them to remember that the goal is impact – improved student learning – and to try and select the option that maximises impact in relation to the resources it requires.

There are certain research-based principles of programme design that can help to maximise the impact of a programme on teaching and learning. One way of thinking about these principles is through the acronym INSPIRE (Richardson & Díaz Maggioli, 2018):

Table 9.2: Richardson and Díaz Maggioli's principles of programme design: INSPIRE

Impactful	Programmes should have a positive impact on student learning, and should be designed around the aim of achieving impact on learning.
Needs-based	Programmes should address the needs of teachers and learners in context.
Sustained	Programmes should span at least six months, with a regular 'rhythm' (Cordingley et al., 2015) of professional learning activities.
Peer-collaborative	Programmes should incorporate opportunities for teachers to learn alongside, and from, colleagues.
In-practice	Programmes should encourage teachers to experiment with new teaching practices in their classrooms.
Reflective	Programmes should encourage teachers to reflect on the impact of new practices and on how they might need to adapt them to their classrooms.
Evaluated	Programmes should encourage teachers to become evaluative practitioners in their classrooms, and the programme as a whole should be evaluated by trainers and the institution.

In addition to these principles, Cordingley et al. (2015) stress the value of creating a sense of shared purpose amongst trainees, who should be clear about what the programme is aiming to achieve and their role in its success. They also emphasise the need for the various teacher learning activities on the programme to align, and to be congruent with the principles of teaching that the programme aims to convey.

Since all programmes are different there's really no magic formula for putting one together. But our model of the three Ps (see Chapter 2) is as relevant as it has been for other activities: your programme should include Practical components, Professional components, and Personal ones too.

CASE STUDY 9.5: DIEGO, TRAINING MANAGER

The professional development team that I'm a part of runs a huge programme for our teachers, and coordinating it all is a pretty big task. The activities we're running include:

- the four training days annually
- teachers' collaborative project groups
- regular developmental observations
- a mentoring programme
- weekly one-to-one lesson planning with less experienced teachers
- group planning sessions for teachers using the same coursebooks
- a structured peer observation programme
- self-contained online courses on our VLE [virtual learning environment], e.g., language awareness

> Some of these things are compulsory for the teachers and others are
> optional (such as the online courses) so teachers can have some
> control over their development activity. The principle that we use is that
> we try to make it as easy as possible for teachers to access training and
> development, so each teacher can build a programme that works for them.
> To make that work we try to stick to a predictable routine for the teachers,
> so they always know when meetings will be held, where to go for support,
> and so on.

During the programme

As with a course, the pace and intensity of the work on the programme
is likely to be significant, and it is important to be well-organised. One
additional task for programmes, which tends not to be an issue on courses,
is reporting on progress to the programme sponsor. As a trainer this can
seem like an irritating distraction from the more important time spent
on teacher learning, but it is understandable that sponsors want to know
that teachers are engaging with the programme and that it is having a
positive effect.

Managing expectations is the key to success when it comes to reporting –
particularly in terms of when reports will be submitted, and what data
they will include. Generally, it is sufficient to include a record of each
trainee's attendance on the programme, and what assignments they have
completed. What you should aim to avoid is a situation where the sponsor
is demanding detailed feedback on individuals at a point in the programme
when you are busy focusing on other things, so being clear at the early
stages is key.

After the programme

As with courses, participants may expect a certificate, or some form of
formal record, that provides recognition of the time they've invested in
the programme and their achievements on it. This is especially important
for programmes that include optional components, such as the one Diego
describes in Case study 9.5 – when teachers have gone the extra mile to
improve their practice, it's only natural that they expect to be able to show
proof of their efforts. As with courses, evaluation will be necessary, but
even more so for a programme because significant amounts of time, effort
and money may have been spent on it.

The methods of evaluation that we discussed in Chapter 4 are just as
relevant here in thinking about how to evaluate programmes. In fact, there
is a much clearer impetus for evaluation of programmes than there is for
individual training sessions. For programmes, evaluation is an essential
means of demonstrating to the sponsor that the programme has been
successful (or of explaining why it hasn't). However, the degree of planning
involved is greater because there may be more data to gather, and more
people to gather it from. Analysing that data can take considerable time,

and it can't be rushed. So make a realistic schedule for your evaluation activities at the planning stage, even if the bulk of that work is done when the trainees have left the programme and gone back to their classrooms. If you're working on an open-ended programme, consider how you can build evaluation into the regular cycle of the programme so that it becomes as routine as everything else, and so that it can inform your reports to the sponsor.

Summary

From the case studies in this chapter, you should be able to see that the essential training skills – planning and delivering training sessions, observing lessons, supporting and assessing teachers – are all skills that we have covered in this book so far. That means that you can make all of them part of your trainer toolkit, and delivering a course or programme is often simply a matter of putting them all together. That's not to say that courses or programmes are easy, but by the time your first course has finished you will feel far more confident as a trainer. Working in the training room day after day has a far greater effect on your professional development than conducting the odd training session or observation here and there. We discuss how you can find your way onto a course or programme as a trainer in Chapter 10.

 **TRAINER VOICES**

 Scan the QR Code and watch the video 'Course planning' to hear how courses are designed in the trainers' different contexts.

 **TO FIND OUT MORE**

Malderez, A., & Wedell, M. (2007). *Teaching teachers: Processes and practices.* London: Continuum. (Addresses course and programme design in detail, with a good balance of theoretical and practical advice.)

Parrott, M. (1991). Teacher education: Factors relating to programme design. In R. Bowers, & C. Brumfit, *Applied linguistics and English language teaching* (pp. 36–46). London: Macmillan. (This is an accessible and helpful summary of the main issues in programme design, presented through some well-chosen case studies.)

10 Trainer development

Here we consider:

- Why trainer development is important
- What the role of trainer entails
- What skills are needed to be an effective trainer
- How those skills can be developed
- Building a career as a trainer

The idea is to keep in constant movement, not to become static, not to feel that there's nothing else to learn. There's always room for improvement.

Ricardo, teacher trainer, Mexico

Anyone who has taken a flight will have heard the words 'make sure your own mask is fitted before helping others' in the pre-flight safety presentation. We should adopt the same principle when it comes to professional development: make sure you are in control of your own development as an educator before trying to guide the development of your trainees. That's where the analogy ends – development should be far more enjoyable than an in-flight emergency!

Why trainer development matters

The first substantial training course for teachers of English to speakers of other languages is thought to have taken place in London in 1935 (Howatt & Widdowson, 2004). It was led by a man named Lawrence Faucett, who published the *Oxford English Course*, one of the first ELT coursebook packages, at around the same time. Faucett had spent several years teaching and training teachers in China and then Turkey, and after further travels in Africa he was invited to give a course in 'teaching English to non-Western peoples' at the Institute of Education, part of the University of London (Smith, 2007).

From contemporary accounts Faucett sounds like a good trainer, one focused on learner outcomes and attending to Personal, Practical and Professional needs. A participant at one of his sessions in 1931 wrote that

> what was especially striking, perhaps, about his method was the diversity of practical devices at his command. . . . Here many of us were obliged to sit up and take notice. . . . With

> Dr. Faucett's methods it is impossible to conceive of any
> student, good, bad or indifferent, being neglected. (Thomas,
> 1931, p. 8, as cited in Smith, 2007)

Of course, Faucett hadn't completed a course in order to acquire his training skills, as no such thing existed at that time. He had studied and researched extensively, but developed his training skills 'on the job', upon a foundation of teaching experience acquired in a wide range of contexts. Although there is more support for trainers now than in Faucett's day (in the form, for example, of the Cambridge Train the Trainer course, or this book!), the 'way in' to teacher training really hasn't changed very much. It is still a largely informal process that depends on demonstrating teaching expertise in order to be given opportunities to deliver training on a more formal level. An *EL Gazette* article affirms this, explaining that 'most teachers follow an organic path into training – they may start by doing some training or mentoring at their school, and then gradually begin to do more and more' (Magloff, 2020, p. 34), which is indeed the path that both of us took.

Unsurprisingly, then, a recent survey of teacher educators found that a quarter had had no trainer training at all (Dragas, 2019, p. 231). Undoubtedly many of those respondents deliver effective training nonetheless, rather like Lawrence Faucett, but the lack of support for early-career trainers inevitably means that some of the training that is being provided is not as effective as it could be. No doubt a more rigorous gateway to training would benefit teachers as well as trainers themselves.

There is another side effect caused by the lack of a clear-cut route to becoming a trainer, which is that the bewilderment surrounding entry requirements makes it difficult to know what you should do to get started in your training career, and what you should do to keep progressing once it has got off the ground. In order to develop as a trainer, feel confident in your role and inspire confidence in your trainees, it is clearly important to have some sense of the different skills you should be thinking about developing.

The principal reason *why* you should develop as a trainer is, hopefully, at this point in the book, quite clear: the processes of change and development that we hope to guide teachers through are processes that we should be personally familiar with, as teachers and as teacher trainers. In the same way that we model techniques in the training room, demonstrating the behaviours associated with successful professional development is an important part of good training. As Malderez and Wedell put it, if trainers 'are going to be managing other peoples' professional learning, they need to be capable managers of their own' (Malderez & Wedell, 2007, p. 103). Happily, there are significant parallels between the development practices that teachers and trainers might use, so many of the approaches and activities we suggest here for your development are equally applicable to the teachers whose development you will support.

CASE STUDY 10.1: ALLEN, TEACHER TRAINER

It was never really a plan of mine to become a teacher trainer. I was managing a branch of a private language school, which did not have an in-service programme, so I decided to start offering quarterly sessions for teachers to collaborate and learn with each other. Teachers really appreciated the school taking an interest in their development, and the school noticed improved feedback from the students. This evolved into my designing and delivering sessions for the whole system.

Eventually, I got promoted, and developing a sustained professional development programme was part of my remit. It became so successful that we started offering our training services to other institutions. I just wanted to make sure that our school was providing the best possible education to our students, and my role as teacher trainer grew from there.

The skills effective trainers need

In Chapter 1 we examined the qualities of effective teachers to build a picture of what trainee teachers need to know and what skills they need to learn. Similarly, understanding what trainers do helps to provide a picture of the skills that we need to develop in order to be effective as trainers. It might seem odd to be talking about the skills trainers need at this point in the book, but now that you have a deeper understanding of more specialised areas of training, it's a good time to recap some key principles, and to 'zoom out' and look at the bigger teacher education picture with a better understanding now of what the different parts are and of how they fit together. This is particularly true when it comes to your development as a trainer: your development activity will involve focusing on certain areas in depth, but to decide which of those areas to prioritise you may need to be able to take a bird's-eye view of your skillset and how it relates to the role of trainer.

The trainer's primary responsibility 'is to be a facilitator for teacher learning' (Waters, 2005, p. 212), in other words, to help teachers learn, whether that learning happens in the classroom or outside it, amongst colleagues or alone. All teachers are different, and teacher learning is multifaceted, so in order to fulfil this function, trainers have to wear many different hats. In the pages of this book we've seen how trainers must work as designers of learning experiences, mediators of research, agents of change, mentors, observers, course planners, and other roles besides. The range of knowledge and skills required of trainers to be effective facilitators of teacher learning is therefore quite extensive, and it's worth breaking it all down so that we can think about trainer development more clearly.

Four key areas of trainer expertise

What, then, are the main areas of knowledge and skill that trainers require? Most responses to the task above initially identify the following four main areas:

1. **Knowledge**

   First and foremost, trainers clearly need to know how to teach effectively, which is why a robust foundation of teaching experience is an initial prerequisite for the job. We saw in Chapter 1 that 'knowing' in this case refers to *Knowing about*, *Knowing how*, and *Knowing to*, not just in depth but across a breadth of teaching contexts too. For trainers this encompasses knowledge of both the target language and of how to teach it, but beyond that, trainers also need the ability to develop that teaching knowledge in others. Tony Duff highlights that:

   > To be a teacher, you must know the technique. To be a trainer, you must know the technique, know why it is effective, be able to articulate or convey that understanding to others, and know how it relates to other aspects of language teaching.
   > (Duff, 1988, p. 112)

   Equally important is the ability to select specific ideas and practices, knowing what trainees need and will benefit from in their teaching contexts. Trainers need to have a good sense of what their trainees need to learn to operate more effectively in those contexts, as well as an understanding of what their trainees feel is possible in their own classrooms. So expertise in teaching needs to be complemented by an awareness of the educational backdrop: knowledge of a range of methodological approaches, of how the wider education system works, and so on.

2. **Understanding**

   In addition to a sound knowledge base, trainer expertise needs to encompass the domain of the Personal: managing trainees' beliefs, attitudes, experience and prior knowledge to effect changes in their teaching practice. Again, these skills are integral to all the aspects of training that we have covered in this book, and depend on a deep understanding of the trainees as people. Working effectively with trainee beliefs, assumptions and knowledge requires trainers to have a sense of what teachers feel is relevant to their professional lives, and to be able to present new ideas or practices in a way that encourages them to try them out. Expertise in this area isn't simply a question of techniques, but also encompasses soft skills: active listening, empathy, patience, a sense of humour, and so on.

3. **Training groups**

A third area of expertise relates to planning, running and evaluating group training activity, which can obviously vary in depth, from the level of a single session to the scale of a whole programme. Where the latter is concerned, there are likely to be more general skills involved in addition to subject-specific knowledge, such as working with a team, budgeting, scheduling and communicating with various stakeholders. Training groups, rather than individual teachers, entails considering how and why trainees might interact and collaborate to enhance their learning.

4. **Training individuals**

That leaves mentoring, observation, feedback and assessment practices – skills generally involving a closer training relationship with individual teachers – as the fourth basic area of trainer expertise. Again, soft skills are critical to the success of these training practices, but there is considerable domain-specific expertise involved too, as we discussed in Chapters 5–8.

If your ideas in response to Task 10.1 covered these four areas (or gave examples of each) then you are correct, but there are some additional areas of expertise that you may have identified and which shouldn't be ignored. To help make sure that we're not overlooking other domains of expertise, it is worth reviewing some of the more prominent frameworks for trainer development.

Frameworks of trainer expertise

You should be familiar with frameworks for teacher development – for example, we have already looked at how the Cambridge English Teaching Framework (see Appendix 1) might be used to help plan training. There are similar published frameworks relating to trainer development, too. Some of these are divided into levels and exist to enable trainers to profile their development, and others are presented as a list of standards that describe expectations of effective trainers. Trainer expertise is a very under-researched area (Waters, 2005), and as a result experience plays a more significant role in the creation of these frameworks than empirical evidence

(Cambridge Assessment English, 2016). But frameworks can still provide a valuable 'map of the terrain' for trainers interested in developing their professional practice. That is especially true if they are compared side-by-side.

Table 10.1: Frameworks of trainer expertise

British Council CPD framework for Teacher educators	Cambridge English trainer framework	Association of Teacher Educators standards
Knowledge ○ Knowing the subject ○ Understanding the educational context ○ Understanding teacher learning **Skills** ○ Planning teacher learning ○ Teaching teachers ○ Evaluating teachers ○ Supporting teacher professional development ○ Adopting inclusive practices ○ Supporting teachers remotely **Development** ○ Taking responsibility for own professional development ○ Contributing to the profession	**Understanding of individuals and situations** ○ Analysing teacher needs ○ Dealing with individual differences **Knowledge of teaching, training and teacher development** ○ Knowledge of teaching ○ Knowledge of training ○ Knowledge of teacher development **Planning, conducting and evaluating training activities** ○ Planning training activities ○ Conducting training activities ○ Evaluating training activities **Supporting, observing, feeding back on and assessing teaching** ○ Supporting teachers ○ Observing teaching ○ Feeding back on teaching ○ Assessing teaching **Professional development and values** ○ Professional development ○ Professional values	**Teaching** Model teaching that demonstrates content and professional knowledge, skills, and dispositions reflecting research, proficiency with technology and assessment, and accepted best practices in teacher education. **Cultural Competence** Apply cultural competence and promote social justice in teacher education. **Scholarship** Engage in inquiry and contribute to scholarship that expands the knowledge base related to teacher education. **Professional Development** Inquire systematically into, reflect on, and improve their own practice and demonstrate commitment to continuous professional development. **Program Development** Provide leadership in developing, implementing, and evaluating teacher education programs that are rigorous, relevant, and grounded in theory, research and best practice **Collaboration** Collaborate regularly and in significant ways with relevant stakeholders to improve teaching, research, and student learning.

Public Advocacy
Serve as informed, constructive advocates for high quality education for all students

Teacher Education Profession
Contribute to improving the teacher education profession

Vision
Contribute to creating visions for teaching, learning, and teacher education that take into account such issues as technology, systemic thinking, and world views.

Table 10.1 shows summaries of three frameworks of trainer expertise. You will see that the areas discussed above, of knowledge, understanding, training practices for groups and training practices for individuals are all represented. There are additional points of emphasis included in these frameworks, however, that add significantly to the picture of trainer expertise.

The first of these additional points to emphasise is the explicit mention of **modelling** – demonstrating teacher behaviours to trainees – which is central to the trainer's role. It is considered so important by the Association of Teacher Educators (ATE) that effective modelling is the focus of the very first ATE standard for trainers. Of course, as we have also seen in earlier chapters, the real value in modelling is in the trainer's ability to draw trainees' attention to the practices being demonstrated and to link them to underlying principles. So modelling is an important part of trainer expertise but it's also an area of greater depth than it may first appear to be, and is perhaps best thought of as part of trainer knowledge (and indeed, 'demonstrates . . . effective teaching principles and practices' is listed as part of the Knowledge of Teaching competency in the Cambridge English Trainer Framework).

All three frameworks place importance on the trainer's **professional development** as an essential element of trainer expertise. What is emphasised by all the frameworks as part of this is actively contributing to the teacher education profession through the sharing of expertise, for example, through conference presentations, webinars or journal articles. But professional development standards for trainers also link to knowledge that trainers can draw on to guide the development of teachers. As such, the Cambridge English Trainer Framework states that trainers should understand teachers' development needs and be able to direct individual trainees to resources that will advance their development.

As a critical part of professional development, but also as a recurring theme in other domains, **familiarity with research** is a key pillar of expertise in the three frameworks. This includes up-to-date knowledge of relevant research, but also the ability amongst trainers to inquire into their own practice, experimenting with what works and what doesn't in order to improve outcomes for teachers. Again, there's more depth here than there might first appear: inquiry into one's own practice involves well-developed reflection skills, and the ability to gather evidence from the training room as the basis for reflection. Absorbing insights from published research, on the other hand, involves skills in searching for relevant research studies, critically evaluating them, and applying relevant findings to training in a way that is contextually appropriate.

Finally, the frameworks underline the need for well-developed **people skills**. These are integral to every interaction between trainers and teachers, and therefore to all the other domains of expertise discussed here. In an IATEFL conference workshop aimed at distilling advice to new trainers, participants agreed that 'there are several qualities essential for a teacher trainer with the *first being good people skills*. A trainer needs to be sensitive, approachable, supportive and firm but fair. Trainers have to show empathy with the people they are training' (Davies & Northall, 2019b, p. 219). Such skills are especially important for mentoring practices, and a review of research into mentoring echoes the sentiments from the IATEFL workshop, arguing that mentors 'must be supportive, approachable, non-judgemental and trustworthy, have a positive demeanour, and possess good listening skills and the ability to empathize, as well as the willingness and ability to take an interest in beginning teachers' work and lives' (Hobson, Ashby, Malderez, & Tomlinson, 2009, p. 212). Although these comments referred to teacher mentors, we would argue that they are equally applicable to teacher trainers more generally.

The essential elements from the three frameworks in Table 10.1 can usefully be distilled into six domains (see Figure 10.1 below). We show the domain of Interpersonal skills and professionalism as underlying the other five main domains because such skills are crucial to success in all of them. Figure 10.1 presents what is, of course, a broad view of trainer expertise; we are looking at the wood rather than the trees. There will, therefore, be training skills that might sit comfortably in more than one of these domains, but as we suggested earlier, the value in 'zooming out' like this is in being able to consider where our strengths and weaknesses as trainers lie, and in thinking about what we do to develop our practice.

Figure 10.1: Overarching domains of trainer expertise

Developing yourself as a trainer

It is now possible to start using the domains in Figure 10.1 to consider potential trainer development activities. The advantage of doing this is that we use the same domains to both diagnose and resolve areas of development that need attention. 'Development' in this sense refers to activities led by you, the trainer, for the benefit of your own professional learning. This mirrors the distinction made in the Introduction between teacher training and teacher development: in each case, development is a self-directed process.

How can you lead your own development process as a trainer? One way is to set realistic goals for your development and make a clear plan for achieving them. Professional development is a little like new year's resolutions in this respect – it's easy to name an *aspiration*, but to actually achieve something it's usually necessary to be realistic and specific about what you want to accomplish, and to consider what you will need to do to succeed in the time you have available.

We suggest that you select two of the five main domains in Figure 10.1 to focus on over a specific and reasonable period of time (e.g., six months). If you need more detail to guide your thinking, use Table 10.1 or look at the more detailed frameworks online (they are all freely available). You may find it helpful to compare your thoughts with a colleague; your developmental needs and actions will of course be different but the process of planning for development is the same, and a different perspective may help you to consider areas of expertise or development activities that you hadn't thought of.

Now let's look at some different ways to address trainer development needs. We can use the five main domains of trainer expertise (Figure 10.1) as a way to group the activities. (In reality, of course, many of the activities develop more than one facet of expertise. For example, presenting at a conference can develop knowledge and group training skills as well as your profile as a teacher education professional.)

Developing understanding

The aim of these activities is to develop an understanding of a diverse range of teaching and training contexts, from which to better understand the different needs and perspectives of trainees.

Keep teaching, if possible

There's nothing wrong with a short break from teaching, but it can be detrimental to your training to spend a long time out of the classroom. Teaching contexts evolve, as do students, materials, resources, exams, and so on, and it's important to maintain a connection to the 'chalkface' to be able to remain authentic in the training room. We know some colleagues who take the opportunity to get back in the classroom at summer courses, and others who run free classes as volunteers at local community centres – find a solution that fits into your training, and keep it going.

Explore other contexts: speak to trainers and teachers

It would be impossible to teach or train in every country, but you can develop your knowledge of other contexts vicariously through the experiences of peers. Seek out trainers and teachers who have worked in different contexts to you (for example, through your personal learning network – see below), and ask them to tell you about their experiences.

Look for short-term training opportunities in other countries

If you have completed your training as a CELTA or CertTESOL tutor, you could explore opportunities for working on intensive courses in different countries. These can be an excellent way of learning about a new training context and a new culture over four to five weeks (although don't expect to have much time for sightseeing!) There's no formal site for advertising such opportunities and they usually come through professional contacts, which is why developing as a professional (discussed below) is so important.

Developing knowledge

These reading activities aim to develop your knowledge of teaching, training and teacher learning, in order to improve as a trainer as well as to enable you to guide your trainees towards relevant resources for their own needs. As reading activities, they don't require the cooperation or participation of anyone else, and many are free (provided you have an internet connection!), so they are some of the easiest forms of development activity.

Target your reading

Regular reading is essential for your ongoing development as a trainer, for the sake of your own professional knowledge but also to be in a position to direct your trainees towards the most appropriate resources. Books are not the only option here (see the To find out more sections at the end of each chapter in this book for further reading); periodicals such as *The Teacher Trainer*, *Modern English Teacher* or *Voices* (IATEFL) can all be excellent sources of inspiration and new ideas. So can blogs, such as the Cambridge 'World of Better Learning' blog (www.cambridge.org/elt/blog/).

Explore mainstream education resources

We feel that looking beyond the world of language teaching for professional knowledge is a useful thing to do, and there are some excellent resources aimed at teachers in mainstream education that language teachers and trainers can take advantage of. Organisations like the Teacher Development Trust (tdtrust.org), researchED (researched.org.uk) and the Association for Teacher Education in Europe (atee.education) provide a range of downloadable resources and run regular online and face-to-face events.

You may feel that you want to look even further afield for relevant ideas, and explore fields outside education altogether. Waters (2005), for example, draws on change management theory to shed light on the skills that trainers need.

Make reading research a habit

As we discussed in Chapter 2, one of the trainer's roles is to present trainees with research findings in a form that they can apply to their practice, which means it's essential to be familiar with up-to-date research and know how to interpret it. Research literacy is a vital skill for trainers to develop and includes:

- understanding how reliable data is gathered

- recognising well-formulated research questions

- knowing how data can be analysed to answer research questions

- recognising when results have been well-interpreted

- being able to differentiate sound from unsound research

- communicating findings from research effectively

- using research findings to maximise the impact of teaching

(Brown & Coombe, 2015, p. xv)

The Cambridge Guide to Research in Second Language Teaching and Learning, a collection of short chapters on core topics in research, is a comprehensive resource for developing your research literacy, and the OASIS database (oasis-database.org) is an excellent source of free research summaries. It's a good idea to make reading research a habit; try to set some time aside for reading into a particular topic every two weeks, based on questions that arise from your own practice and in preparing training materials. If you can discuss with colleagues, even better!

Developing group training skills

These activities aim to develop your skills in planning, delivering and evaluating training sessions (or training courses/programmes).

Invite feedback from trainees

Hopefully, you are collecting feedback from trainees as part of evaluating your sessions (see Chapter 4), but you can extend that evaluative approach to other areas of training, such as observation and feedback, and make a habit of building it into your general training practice. For example, Tessa Woodward proposes the idea of 'lecturers' diaries' (1991, p. 215). These are written by the trainer throughout a course or programme, letting trainees evaluate trainers' planning and decision-making processes (including their understanding of trainee needs) in group discussion. Trainees may even give the diary a grade (e.g., 'satisfactory' or 'unsatisfactory') at certain intervals, based on the outcome of their discussions.

Collaborate with other trainers

There are many ways of collaborating with training colleagues to develop both your training skills and theirs. Co-preparing and co-presenting sessions is a particularly helpful way of discovering different ways of doing things. Observing colleagues conducting training sessions, or inviting them to observe you, allows you to pay particular attention to how trainee contributions are responded to. In all cases, make sure you take time to discuss what was noticed and why choices were made, as that's often where the most meaningful insights arise.

Attend training

Similarly, aim to attend as many training sessions as you can as a participant, with the twin goals of improving your teaching as well as your training. Online sessions are especially good for this, because they are easy to find (there is a large back catalogue of webinars on the Cambridge University Press ELT YouTube channel, for example). Pause and re-watch parts to make notes on the content to develop your teaching and notes on the delivery to develop your training.

Is there a balance of the Personal, the Professional and the Practical (see Chapters 2 and 3)? How does the trainer manage resources, tasks, signposting and interaction?

Present at conferences

Conference presentations are not typical training sessions, but they are group teacher learning events, and they can therefore be a good way of forcing you out of your comfort zone and re-evaluating how you do things. In particular, the onus is on you to say something new, and that means knowing your topic inside out, so there is a strong incentive to read and research, as well as to reflect on your own story and how to tell it.

There will be constraints: changing the layout of the room will be difficult or impossible, the size of the group is unpredictable, it's likely to include both novices and experts working in diverse contexts, and you will usually have less time for your session than in your usual training context. Changing attendees' teaching practice is difficult, therefore, but resist reverting to a 'chalk and talk' approach to get your ideas across. Aim to send participants away with new insight into a particular area, some examples of the practical implications, and the tools to look into it in more detail if they wish.

Use video

Video is a hugely under-used resource in both teacher and trainer development, but it has gained more attention in recent years. There are various ways of using recordings as a prompt for reflection, but video clubs – group viewing and discussion of video clips in peer groups that meet regularly – can be an effective approach. If you can get together with training colleagues and take it in turns to share short clips of your practice, there is a good chance that you will learn to reflect in more depth, and focus more on trainee contributions and interaction (Borko, Jacobs, Eiteljorg, & Pittman 2008; Sherin & Van Es, 2009; Van Es & Sherin, 2008).

A period of adjustment may be needed initially, as it can feel uncomfortable seeing yourself on screen, but once that has passed you will find yourself noticing trainee behaviour much more, and you can begin to look for evidence of learning and ways to improve it.

Keep a journal

Reflecting on your training needn't be done in writing – discussions with other trainers or with trainees are also a valid form of reflection. But there are few better ways of *recording* your reflections than keeping a journal. There's no 'correct' way to do this – it's a personal document and you will work out a format that is meaningful to you – but your aim is to record briefly what happened in your sessions, what evidence of learning there was, what you feel wasn't so successful and what you plan to do in future to improve outcomes. It can be a private document, or you might choose to publish it as a blog and seek feedback from the wider ELT community. If writing really isn't your thing, consider audio recording your thoughts and reflections., but try to make time not just to record your ideas, but also to listen to earlier entries from time to time. This is a good way of measuring your progression and of understanding which development activities have proven to be most effective for you.

Developing skills in training individuals

The ability to develop skills in mentoring, observation and assessment of individual trainees can be more challenging, because the activities to do so require time and a personalised response to the trainee in each situation. All the more reason, then, to build in development of these skills early and to seek regular opportunities to put them into practice.

Ask colleagues to observe you

If you are still teaching (and we recommend that trainers do continue teaching to some degree at least), look for opportunities to be observed and get feedback on your classroom practice. It can feel that as a trainer you're not expected to need this kind of intervention, but critical feedback is always a valuable learning opportunity for any teacher or trainer. If you're not still teaching, having a colleague observe and feed back on one of your training sessions can be just as useful, and can also help to remind you of what it's like for trainees when they are 'in the hotseat'!

Shadow mentoring/feedback conversations

Just as observing colleagues delivering training can be very instructive, you can learn a lot from observing feedback or mentoring discussions between colleagues and their trainees. These are obviously difficult to arrange because you are observing a private conversation in which trust is key, so both the trainer and the trainee must agree to your presence. If you can arrange this, however, discussing the conversation afterwards with both mentor and trainee can be very illuminating.

Share mentoring stories

If direct observation of a mentor colleague is not possible, an alternative is to discuss past experiences that a colleague has had mentoring instead – what challenges have they had and how did they deal with them? It is essential that the confidentiality of the mentor-mentee relationship is maintained, but much can be learned from sharing these kinds of narratives.

Developing as a teacher training professional

Activities here are about connecting with the wider second language teacher education profession, meeting and learning from colleagues who may be working in quite different situations, or in similar situations in faraway places!

Create a personal learning network on social media

Social networking sites can be outstanding ways of connecting with other ELT professionals, including teacher trainers. Start by following the pages of reputable ELT organisations such as IATEFL, TESOL, the British Council and ELT publishers such as Cambridge University Press, and search for relevant content using the hashtags #ELT, #ELTchat, #TESOL and #CELTAchat. As your personal learning network (PLN) grows, you're likely to find you have access to a wealth of resources (some more useful than others), and you'll be able to ask questions and canvass opinions on your work, as well as help others who are doing the same thing.

Join a teachers' association

IATEFL and TESOL are both well-known global organisations for teachers of English, and have special interest groups (SIGs) for teacher trainers. Consider joining one of these international teachers' associations as well as a local association, which may provide more opportunities for meeting other trainers in person and for delivering sessions. Don't just sign up to an association, look to actively get involved by joining a SIG committee, contributing to a newsletter or running a webinar – you will get far more from your membership and make new professional connections and friends as a result.

Start a reading group

Reading groups are a fairly well-established development activity, and with videoconferencing tools can be carried out with training colleagues all over the world. We have been a part of several reading groups as both teachers and trainers, and have found that they all have their own character, but tend to work best when they have clear routines, such as a predictable meeting time (e.g., the first Wednesday of every month), an agreed source of texts (perhaps participants take it in turns to provide or suggest a text, or perhaps there is a 'leader' who sources them), and a structure for discussions.

Some groups we have been part of combined the reading group with a blog: participants took turns to summarise discussions and post them to the blog, and others left comments after they had tried out new teaching or training ideas. Ensuring that discussions lead to practical experiments is an important part of a successful group.

Attend conferences

Conferences are an excellent opportunity to expose yourself to new techniques and approaches, make connections and friends within the profession, and see how other professionals present ideas to colleagues in the teaching community. At the annual IATEFL conference there is always a substantial selection of talks on the programme aimed at teacher trainers. There is even an increasing number of conferences aimed specifically at teacher trainers, such as the Cambridge English Teaching Awards Symposium, or the IH London Future of Training conference, both also held annually.

The key to making conferences a productive part of your professional development is to be selective: choose both the conferences and the conference sessions that you attend carefully, and have a clear idea of what you want to gain from them. You might find it helpful to set goals for each conference (and/or each session) you attend, which could relate to teaching (e.g., *I want to come away from the conference with five new ideas to add to my training sessions on pronunciation*) or training (e.g., *I will make a note of the different ways that presenters started their sessions*), and plan which talks you will attend accordingly.

'Go public'

At a certain point you may feel ready to take your ideas to a wider audience, and 'go public', as Tony Wright and Rod Bolitho put it (2007). For example, if you've done plenty of background reading and practical experimentation for a session, it could well be worth writing it up for a periodical such as *English Teaching Professional* or *Modern English Teacher*, or, if it is a more theoretically grounded piece, for the *ELT Journal*. If your submitted article is rejected initially, don't feel downhearted – treat the process as a route to development and learn valuable lessons about how to present ideas in writing through the feedback that you receive.

Another way to get published is to write a book review for one of the publications mentioned. Editors of reviews are often willing to provide guidance and support to new contributors. Book reviewing is also of course a good way to keep your knowledge up-to-date.

You can 'go public' more informally by writing a training blog to tell your 'story' and share challenges and successes with others in the field. Two particularly good examples are Anthony Gaughan's teachertrainingunplugged.com and Matthew Noble's account of his journey towards becoming a CELTA tutor, *Diary of a newbie CELTA trainer*, at celtatrainer.wordpress.com. A more interactive option is to join a live discussion online. Twitter is a particularly good forum for these – look for the hashtags #ELTchat, #CELTAchat and #edchat. You will come across like-minded people, learn about a range of contexts, and build your PLN!

This is by no means an exhaustive list, and perhaps you can think of other activities, but it should at least be a good starting point to help you develop your expertise as a trainer. Find what works for you; it shouldn't be a chore and the key is to enjoy the process of developing as much as the outcome.

TASK 10.3

...To trainer

Many of the trainer development activities we have seen can also be used with trainees. We have used our domains of trainer expertise to group the activities, but how else could you group them in a way that is meaningful to trainees, so that they can use them to develop as teachers?

For notes see page 237

Pursuing a training career

If you're relatively new to training – or a newly qualified trainer – you're probably keen to get your training career off the ground and build up enough experience to feel confident referring to yourself as a teacher trainer as well as a teacher. It's important to look beyond that, though, and consider your long-term career path. Let's take a look at these two stages in your teacher training story.

Getting off the ground

There is no substitute for teaching experience as a basis for a career as a trainer. Hours in the classroom are key (we would suggest 5,000 as a basic minimum, which would equate to around five years for someone teaching 25 hours per week) but the diversity of contexts (ages, study purposes, class sizes, nationalities, etc.) making up those hours is just as important. And as stated in Chapter 1, that experience is a necessary, but certainly not the only, criterion for a successful training career. Nor is there any escaping the fact that trainers need to know their subject well: its terminology, history and development, theories, practices (and how they relate to theories), controversies, relevant texts and resources. Nevertheless, one of the most valuable traits of a trainer is a supportive, collegial attitude towards teachers, and this can be cultivated and demonstrated early in a teacher's career, as they work on acquiring experience and developing their knowledge. As John Hughes (2015) points out, the clues that someone has potential as a trainer can emerge during their teaching experience, demonstrated in a willingness to share teaching ideas or lesson plans with colleagues, to engage keenly in training and development opportunities, or to experiment with new activities and approaches in the classroom.

Assuming you have a suitable basis of experience and knowledge, the survey run by Teti Dragas (2019) identified three main ways into teacher training. A quarter of the teachers moving into training roles had no guidance and had 'just started doing it'. Of the others, 35% were trained 'in-house' and the remaining 40% were trained in preparation for delivering certificate courses such as the Cambridge CELTA or the Trinity CertTESOL (Dragas, 2019, p. 231).

Paradoxically, the most common route to teacher training in Dragas' survey is probably also the most elusive. That's because it is a route that is not openly publicised – those chosen as trainers-in-training (TinTs) on certificate courses are generally teachers working at institutions that run preservice courses alongside English language courses for students. The institutions may have an internal selection process for teachers who are interested in moving into teacher training, but there is no obligation on them to carry this out; the opportunity may be offered directly to a teacher instead.

If you've been selected as a TinT, congratulations! If you haven't and would like to be, you will need to (1) get a teaching job at an institution running preservice certificate courses, and (2) do enough to get yourself noticed as a potential TinT by the training manager there. That is every bit as challenging as it sounds, particularly if you live in Francophone Africa where there are no CELTA centres, or North America, Africa or Australia, where there are no Trinity CertTESOL centres. But if it is your goal, it's important to be seen to be dedicated and able when opportunity knocks.

Being trained in-house is probably easier, but relies on working at an institution with a well-organised professional learning scheme in place that will provide opportunities to deliver training sessions or mentor teachers. We have been fortunate enough to work at schools that ran weekly training sessions, and at others that ran dedicated training days scattered throughout the year – each of these provided ample opportunities for volunteering to deliver training. The number and the nature of opportunities for being involved in teacher learning will depend on the institution. Your training as a trainer in these sorts of scenarios is likely to be fairly informal in the sense that there will probably be no defined TinT pathway, but ideally you will be able to work with a more experienced supervisor who will guide your efforts, provide opportunities for working with teachers, and give you meaningful feedback.

The time frame for these two pathways – preservice certificate TinT and in-house TinT – will vary. TinTs on intensive CELTA courses will typically 'shadow' one or two full courses before being able to act as assistant course tutor, which for many signals 'mission accomplished'. Those who wish to then go on to become main course tutors may be able to do so after three or four further courses. We would argue that that is long enough to provide a healthy footing for a training career in which continuing professional development plays a part. The danger with intensive courses is that they are so intensive that professional development becomes an afterthought, which is why effective development planning is so important, and why a good TinT supervisor can be the difference between success and stress!

If you are like one of the 25% from Dragas' survey who just start doing it, you may find that you need to be more self-reliant and motivated, as you will need to take responsibility for creating your own opportunities to train teachers. If you are successful with these, they can often lead to other opportunities. Allen's story in Case study 10.1 (page 191) is a good example, while one of us started by setting up a teacher reading group and related blog for colleagues. Initiatives like these require energy, determination and enthusiasm, but are ultimately very good preparation for full-time teacher training, which requires all of those qualities in abundance.

CASE STUDY 10.2: WALID, TEACHER TRAINER

After teaching for several years on a pre-degree English language foundation course at a large university in Saudi Arabia, I was selected to join the Cambridge Train the Trainer course. This was a fairly intensive 30-hour course run over five days, but luckily I and my fellow course participants were released from teaching duties for the whole week. The course was highly practical and gave me plenty of opportunities to reflect on my teaching career to date, to learn more about training methods and approaches, and to experiment with new ideas.

Once the course had finished, I was strongly encouraged to seek out opportunities to put into practice what I'd learned, and part of that was to present training to my teaching colleagues. Even though it was not part of the Train the Trainer course, my trainer from the course supported me and my course peers during the whole process of creating our training sessions and observed us when we delivered them. This was enormously helpful as I never once felt that I was alone, nor did I feel unsure about what to do. Subsequently I presented at the university's annual ELT conference, in front of 100s of people, and my trainer also invited me to co-present with him at another conference. Nowadays I take every opportunity to deliver training but also to explore my own PD in as many ways as I can.

Staying off the ground

In most situations, teachers don't need to worry about the logistics of their lessons. It is someone else's responsibility to find students, assign them to a class, create the timetable, and so on. For trainers, the picture tends to be quite different: you can expect to have far more involvement in the processes that surround and support the training itself. For example, on a CELTA course, you may well need to interview prospective trainees, find students for teaching practice sessions, triple-check that trainee names have been spelled correctly so their certificates are right, find an assessor, and more. This means that you will need to be willing to demonstrate initiative and take responsibility for ensuring that things get done outside the training room as well as in it. Unfortunately, this is where some novice trainers can come unstuck – we have trained candidates on Train the Trainer courses who completed the course successfully but haven't had the opportunities to apply what they learned and develop as trainers because they weren't prepared to take the initiative and start creating opportunities themselves.

Full-time trainer jobs are rare. It is much more common for trainers to work on a freelance basis, juggling short-term training contracts with other teaching-related commitments. So again, it is important to be proactive when it comes to looking for work opportunities. Many of the development activities detailed in this chapter can serve two useful purposes beyond simply developing your knowledge and training skills:

- They can provide evidence of your expertise (e.g., conference sessions, blog posts, articles).

- They can put you in touch with people who may be in a position to offer you training work (e.g., online discussions, attending conferences).

These two benefits are the key to finding work as a trainer. You need to be effective when it comes to designing and delivering training, and supporting teachers. But just as importantly, people need to know who you are and that you have those skills. Interacting with other trainers – whether at work or in a developmental capacity – is a useful chance to learn about how they handle this side of the profession. Find out how they promote themselves and how they manage the task of finding work. There are many different ways of doing this, so talking to a range of training colleagues will help you to decide what might be most effective for your own circumstances.

Different destinations

Your journey as a teacher trainer may just be getting started, but where could it take you? There are many possibilities, including:

- Being **employed full-time for a training organisation** such as International House, Bell, Pilgrims, NILE, or the British Council, either delivering training courses to paying trainees or providing in-service training to teachers at the institution.

- Working as a **training consultant**, designing large-scale programmes of training for institutions or even for ministries of education.

- **Managing a team of trainers** on a large-scale training project, with responsibility for their ongoing professional learning as well as for the outcomes of the training they deliver.

- Working as an **assessor** for Cambridge Assessment English, evaluating the quality of training on CELTA courses.

- Working as a **freelance trainer**, combining a range of short-term training posts with teaching and other ELT-related work.

Wherever your teacher training career takes you, we wish you good luck, we hope you enjoy the ride, and we look forward to seeing you at a training event (online or face-to-face) showcasing your new skills!

 **TRAINER VOICES**

 Scan the QR Code and watch the video 'Staying up to date' to hear how trainers attend to their own professional development. Which practices can you adopt for yourself?

 **TO FIND OUT MORE**

Foord, D. (2009). *The developing teacher.* Peaslake: Delta. (Although this collection of developmental activities is aimed at teachers, most can be usefully repurposed for trainer development.)

Wright, T., & Bolitho, R. (2007). *Trainer Development.* Self published. (This is the most substantial text on trainer development in language teaching contexts.)

Notes on tasks

TASK 1.1

Of course, only you can answer questions about your teaching context. But it is important for you to have a clear idea of what the parameters there are, and how they affect your teaching. This is because, as a trainer, you will need to be sensitive to your trainees' contexts in order to effectively support their learning. Understanding how your own teaching is affected by the context you work in is an essential prerequisite for that.

If you have spent most of your teaching career in the same teaching context then we would encourage you to explore other contexts in any way you can. You can do this by:

- exploring coursebooks used in other contexts

- looking at exams used in other contexts

- observing teachers in other contexts (online, if not in person – Sandy Millin has curated a selection of freely available video lessons at https://sandymillin.wordpress.com/2017/11/11/lessons-you-can-watch-online/)

- talking with teachers from other contexts – social media is a good way of doing this, e.g., the #ELTchat group on Twitter

TASK 1.2

	A	B
Opportunities	○ More people for each student to talk to ○ More opinions/experiences for the teacher to work with ○ Large board, which can be clearly seen by all students	○ More comfortable environment ○ Ideal for group work and discussion ○ Easy for teacher to give individual attention, monitor students and provide feedback ○ Marking written work is manageable because there are fewer students ○ Easier to move the furniture
Limitations	○ Difficult to give attention to individuals in the group (e.g., to monitor or give feedback) ○ Difficult to find out/cater to needs of all the students ○ Limited space/difficult to move around ○ Difficult to distribute materials efficiently	○ There is no board to present/record language on (that we can see!) ○ Few peers for students to speak to (e.g., mingling activities won't work) ○ Fewer experiences or points of view amongst the students to discuss or debate

- In **classroom A** the teacher could use the board at the front to quickly and easily present and check language with the students. For instance, he might tell a story to elicit examples of third conditional sentences (e.g., *if he hadn't overslept, he wouldn't have been late*), then put those examples from students on the board in order to encourage them to explore the meaning and form of that target language. The teacher in classroom B doesn't have a board, but she could do something similar with large sheets of paper and a marker pen.

- In **classroom B** the teacher could work on presentation skills with the students, and they would all have the opportunity to present to each other and get peer and teacher feedback. That would be more difficult for the teacher in classroom A, given the number of students and the lack of space, but his students could instead record and upload a digital presentation that classmates could then comment on.

It was perhaps a bit unfair of us to ask what each of the teachers *couldn't* do – while certain things may not be possible in each context, the teachers could probably adapt tasks to achieve the same outcomes. It's this kind of adaptation that you will need to consider for your trainees, and help them to consider, too.

TASK 1.3

You will probably be able to see aspects of novice and expert practice at many different stages of your teaching career. There is a lot to master in language teaching, and you may, for example, have demonstrated some expert practices in relation to vocabulary teaching while still demonstrating novice practices in relation to pronunciation teaching. Teaching skills develop at different rates, and of course different contexts influence the development of teaching skills, too.

The precise mix of skills at varying stages of development will differ between teachers, as no two teachers or teaching contexts are exactly alike. But there is a clear general trend in novice teachers of focusing on trying to establish an identity as a teacher – which can be difficult if you're still learning how to teach! – and only later attending more to student learning than to how they are perceived.

You could also take a look at the Cambridge English Teaching Framework (see Appendix 1) to see other ways in which teacher knowledge and skills develop with expertise.

TASK 1.4

For trainees to get to know their trainer

What's the question?

The trainer puts five or six numbers, dates, places and names on the board/screen (e.g., 1958, 3, Australia, pizza, iPhone) and teachers work in pairs to guess what the information refers to by forming questions.

1958	*When were you born?*
3	*How many children do you have?*
Australia	*Which country would you like to visit?*
pizza	*What's your favourite food?*
iPhone	*What type of phone do you use?*

It does not matter if the teachers get the questions correct. The point is to start a discussion between the trainer and the group and for the teachers to get to know their trainer.

Who am I?

The trainer chooses a number of pictures which provide information about their life, and displays them for everyone to see. Trainees look at the pictures and try to guess what each one tells them about their trainer. It does not matter if the trainees guess correctly. At some point, either during the guessing or at the end, the trainer can reveal the real information about their life.

Of course, with minimal preparation both of these activities could also be adapted and used to help trainees get to know each other!

For trainees to get to know each other

Information recall

Version A: Trainees work in small groups (no more than six). Each person in the group has about 15 seconds to tell the group a few things about themselves. When everyone has had a chance to speak, each group member tries to recall something about the other group members.

Version B: Trainees stand in a line or in a circle (depending on the number of people and room size/arrangement). Each person says TWO things about themselves. Then teachers make pairs and each pair recalls as much as they can about each other and the other people in the room.

'Find someone who . . .' bingo

In our variation of this popular getting-to-know-you activity (see Figure N.1 below), some information that teachers need to find is based on their knowledge of language, teaching and learning, while other information is specific to some of the participants (drawn, for example, from course application documents). The aim is for participants to mingle and talk to each other to complete five boxes in a row, but they should be encouraged to ask follow-up questions to learn more, too.

You can include information about most or all of the participants on the handout, but the bingo element means that there is a natural end to the activity before all the boxes are filled in. The advantage of that is that the activity doesn't go on too long, and trainees have an incentive to keep asking questions to fill in some of the remaining boxes even after the activity is over (e.g., in breaks).

Differences to language teaching

How do these differ from the same tasks in a language lesson? In many ways, they don't. The main aim is the same: for the group to get to know each other and feel comfortable together. The language used will be very similar, too, and the trainer needs to manage the interaction and use of space in the room, as the teacher would. But there are important differences: teachers might need to provide more linguistic support (e.g., sentence stems) to students, and would probably treat these activities as opportunities for diagnostic testing; trainers need to give trainees a chance to reflect on how the activities were set up and managed, and consider how they felt while participating. Trainees should also be prompted to think carefully about how the activities could work with students in their own classrooms, considering what might need to be adapted, and whether or not the outcomes for students would be the same as for them as trainees.

'Find someone who . . .' bingo

Talk to your colleagues to fill the boxes with the names of people who match the given information. When you get five in a row (the names should all be different!), shout 'bingo!'

Find someone who . . .

. . . enjoys going running with no shoes on. *Matt*	. . . can speak Spanish.	. . . has taught children under the age of 6.	. . . knows what CCQ stands for.	. . . used to be in a jazz band.
. . . has used task-based learning in their classes.	. . . has worked in more than two countries.	. . . likes using technology in the classroom.	. . . works in a university.	. . . lives in Poland.
. . . has a cat called Elsie.	. . . has been to an ELT conference.	. . . can explain what an abstract noun is.	. . . finds authentic texts for reading.	. . . has taught exam classes.
. . . teaches one-to-one classes.	. . . has shared a lesson plan online.	. . . studied Art History at university.	. . . has been on TV in Egypt.	. . . can give an example of a third conditional.
. . . knows what an antonym is.	. . . travelled more than 10 hours to be here.	. . . has taught a multilingual class.	. . . can give an example of a discourse marker.	. . . plans to teach in China.

Figure N.1: Example of 'Find someone who . . .' bingo

TASK 1.5

It may be that you don't have any lightbulb moments, which is fine. One of us was asked this as part of a plenary discussion at the early stages of a diploma course, and at that time couldn't think of any lightbulb moments. It felt disappointing not to be able to point to any times where understandings of teaching had developed.

It did prove to be a useful discussion, though. The first benefit was that since then, many lightbulb moments have happened, so perhaps just being aware that they exist makes you more likely to look for them. The second benefit was that listening to other trainees' lightbulb moments was fascinating, and instructive in itself. In fact, as the discussion moved on to other trainees, one of them shared her lightbulb moment. She had worked very hard to prepare a lesson just that week which had been particularly challenging: no matter what she tried, she couldn't find a way to make the plan fun. So when the class finally arrived, she had been surprised to see the students highly engaged, and enjoying the lesson. Her lightbulb moment then was that *the sensation of learning and making progress is fun in itself.*

Hearing this was a lightbulb moment for other trainees in the group too! So consider asking your trainees for their lightbulb moments as a useful discussion at the beginning of a new course.

TASK 2.2

You probably think (consciously or subconsciously) about some or all of the following questions when you plan your lessons:

- What kind of institution will host the lesson, and what are the expectations of that institution? (e.g., is it in a university teaching room, in a small room in a private language school, online, in company offices, is it a one-to-one class in a café, etc.)

- What type of class is it? (e.g., adults/YLs, general English/EAP/exam)

- Is there a syllabus, and what does it prescribe?

- What is to be covered from the coursebook?

- What are the goals for the course?

- What's the goal for this lesson?

- Are there better ways of achieving that goal than using the material I currently have to work with?

- What do the students need to know/do?

- What do they know and what can they do already?

- What will engage the students?

- How much time is available?

- What have we covered in recent lessons?

More or less the same factors will influence your thinking as you design a training session, but you may not have a syllabus or coursebook to work with, and the session may not form part of a course. That can make it more difficult to decide what your intended outcomes should be, so planning lessons without the support of coursebooks is good practice for would-be trainers.

Woodward (2001) has more on how context influences teacher lesson planning in *Planning Lessons and Courses*, Chapter 8.

TASK 2.4

In our experience, it has been a substantial minority (maybe 30%) of the sessions we've attended as teachers that have included both modelling and reflection, but these have unquestionably been the most effective sessions. Modelling of practice is not especially uncommon, but the reflection on it afterwards is often missing, or rushed.

TASK 2.5

The first obvious similarity is the definition of the **parameters for the session**: the description of participants, the resources to be used, and the time available. For teachers, they all represent elements of the teaching context that will guide planning. The same is true for trainers: they have to work within the training context, so it makes sense to sketch out the boundaries of that context first.

The **learning outcomes** for the session are a second element that training plans have in common with lesson plans. There might be two aims for training sessions, as we've discussed in this chapter, but just as an outcome for students should generally include specific examples of language and the situations in which they will use that language, outcomes for training should reference specific examples of new knowledge or skills.

Also very similar to a language teaching lesson plan is the **procedure**, which outlines the sequence of stages and their focus. Trainers, like teachers, need to plan a coherent sequence of activities in order to scaffold and support participants' learning. As a result of completing each stage, participants take steps towards achieving the learning outcomes for the session.

What is different in this training session pro-forma from a lesson template? It's the **title**, which indicates to participants what the focus of the session is, and will probably be communicated to them prior to the session itself, particularly if it forms part of a larger programme of training (see Chapter 9). A well-chosen title will offer a useful shorthand to trainers and participants when looking through a course schedule or when evaluating the impact of a training programme.

TASK 3.1

On the whole, staffroom practices can be easier to set up and manage in the training room, because no students are needed. For that reason, they are sometimes used as a proxy for classroom practices, which is partly the case in Marie's session – she's unable to provide trainees with experience teaching young learners so instead she has them thinking about the YL classroom through a planning activity. Staffroom practices can also be presented in a less trainer-fronted way, using materials such as samples of student work, example lesson plans, exam papers and coursebooks, and these work just as well with very large audiences as they do with smaller groups.

Classroom practices can be difficult to replicate in the training room if it is very dissimilar to the classroom (e.g., in terms of numbers of participants, layout or resources). They are often presented through modelling, which places certain demands on both the trainer and trainees, or through microteaching, which can be difficult to set up and manage. But they are nearly always perceived as highly relevant, they provide a crucial stepping stone towards the application of techniques in trainees' real classrooms, and trainees enjoy both the feeling of progression and the change of pace that a focus on classroom practices can bring.

TASK 3.2

Perhaps the main advantage of loop input is the 'belt and braces' effect: participants learn about a particular aspect of teaching on an intellectual level, but they also experience how it feels. Woodward argues that for some trainees this alignment of content and process makes for a deeper learning experience (Woodward, 2003). Another benefit is that it can be an efficient method of presenting teaching activities that are fairly complex to set up (such as dictogloss or running dictation). Finally, it has the additional advantage of providing, in most circumstances, a record of the activity for participants to take away from the session. This might be written and/or in the form of discussions of what's involved in planning, setting up and running the activity.

The drawbacks of loop input are that it generally requires a classroom-like training room (in terms of size and resources) to work well, and considerable time to unpack the loop into its constituent content and process through reflective discussion after it has taken place; what Woodward refers to as 'decompression time' (2003, p. 302). This is particularly important because even more cognitive load is involved for trainees than might be expected during a standard lesson demonstration.

TASK 3.3

It might be difficult to recall what role discussions have played in the sessions you've attended – it isn't always obvious if you're participating as a trainee. But discussion is often involved in:

- taking part in classroom activities in the role of 'student'

- the process of exploring concepts or ideas from Practical or Professional phases

- brainstorming ideas by thinking about your own teaching and contributing them to the group

When it comes to feelings about discussion, the last of these roles can often seem aimless or a waste of time. There will be trainees who think 'I came here to *get* some teaching ideas, not to give them out!' To make certain that discussions are valuable, then, it is often a good idea to highlight the purpose of the discussion, to respond to trainees' contributions sensitively and fully (see Chapter 4), and to ensure that you add to the ideas that are raised in discussions.

The other feelings raised by discussions probably sit at polar ends of a spectrum. For trainees who attend with friends or close colleagues, discussions are generally very enjoyable – everyone enjoys talking to their friends! But for trainees who are not acquainted with anyone in the group, discussions can be something to dread, because they represent times in the session when everyone around is talking and they feel left out. Avoiding this scenario is one reason for 'getting to know you' activities we mentioned in the Introduction, and for starting your sessions with an interactive activity (Chapter 2). But regardless of whether you have ticked those boxes, it is a good idea to either group trainees yourself or, in large groups, tell trainees to invite those sitting alone to join them. If you include discussion stages in your sessions – and you should – they need to be for every teacher, not just those who are sitting with friends.

TASK 3.4

There is no single correct way to do this, and the personal perspectives of the teacher(s) involved will influence the discussion heavily – that's the point! – so it is perhaps unfair to ask you to analyse this incident without being able to speak to Matthew. Here are his thoughts on this incident and his full analysis of it to compare with your own notes:

I don't remember how I felt about this incident at the time, but it makes me uncomfortable to remember it now. This whole analysis was a really interesting way of unpicking what I was thinking – I'm surprised at what came out of it!

i.

Plus

- I feel like greeting the students by name was a good thing to do; it was a small class.
- I know I got Lin's name right – that wasn't the issue here!

Minus

- Lin was shy, and I think by not just moving on and calling the next name I drew attention to her and probably made her feel even more uncomfortable.
- Insisting on a reply from Lin was a waste of class time that we could have spent learning.

Interesting

- On some level I still don't understand why she didn't just say 'hello' – it makes me wonder what previous classroom experiences she'd had that made her so nervous to speak out. Sadly, if there was a negative experience there,, all I did was add another one.
- Maybe I should think of other ways to take the register or start the lesson – I feel that saying 'hello' is quite non-threatening, but perhaps there are better ways to start.

ii.

Explanation	What values does this reveal? This is quite difficult, but I think it reveals that: ○ I believe students should be expected to speak in class, from the very beginning of the lesson, and especially when they're spoken to. This was the main reason for my insistence, I think. But I hadn't laid this out to the class, or negotiated it with them. ○ I think I also had an idea that it was not a good idea to make an exception for Lin – other students in the class had replied, and I felt like ignoring my greeting wasn't something I wanted to allow from Lin. I guess it felt like a challenge and I didn't want to back down. ○ I don't know if this is a value, but I feel bad about the way I handled this situation. Just on a human level, but also because I'm pretty sure that it turned Lin off English classes even more than she already was – it must have had a negative impact on her learning long term. So as a teaching decision it was really poor, as well as just being insensitive.
Meaning	Why did I do it if I now feel bad about it? ○ I think it was a clumsy way of enacting the values I've mentioned above, but I don't really disagree with those values now. ○ I think it was also maybe a consequence of being too focused on myself and my own agenda, and not empathising enough with the students – they were all teenagers, they were in a beginner class despite having had English for at least a couple of years at school already, and this class took place pretty late in the day – I think 5pm or something like that – at the weekend! So I probably should have had a lot more understanding for how uncomfortable and how unmotivated some of them must have felt.

	○ Thinking through things from the students' point of view like that is something I might have done if I'd spent more time planning, or planned a bit more carefully. I probably was guilty of planning on autopilot a bit for that class. ○ I also think that I should have clarified expectations more explicitly from the outset rather than just believing they would pick up what to do. ○ I'm also thinking would it have been so bad if I'd just said 'OK' and moved on? Of course not, maybe she was having a bad day. I wonder why I saw it as a challenge from Lin. She was a shy student but she wasn't badly behaved.
General significance	What can I take from this? ○ If I was in that situation again I'd give Lin the benefit of the doubt and leave it, and check in with her later when the whole class wasn't watching. ○ More generally, looking at my teaching from the perspective of my students is something I could be doing more, and I need to make time to do that when I'm planning so that I can adjust my lessons in response. ○ Everyone should be able to say 'pass' once in a while if they aren't feeling able to contribute. ○ It's a good idea to be explicit about what I expect from students.

TASK 3.5

This is the text that Sofia plans to use in her session.

CLT is something of an umbrella term (Hall, 2011) and so it is not easy to generalize about how teaching takes place in different contexts. However, a glance at almost any coursebook written for a global market suggests that, across proficiency levels and across publishers, a fairly standard approach to reading is adopted (Cunningham and Moor, 2005; Soars and Soars, 2006; Tilbury, Hendra, Rea and Clementson, 2010; Dummet, Hughes and Stephenson, 2013). A norm has emerged which generally involves a fairly fixed sequence of stages, as listed in the table below:

Pre-reading	○ The teacher builds interest in the topic of the text. ○ The teacher pre-teaches vocabulary that appears in the text.
While-reading	○ The teacher sets a task and the learners read to complete it. ○ The teacher checks that this has been done accurately. ○ The teacher sets a second task and the learners read again to complete it. ○ The teacher checks that this has been done accurately.
Post-reading	○ The teacher sets up an activity that follows on from the text, such as a discussion or a role play.

> Building interest in the text is an opportunity to activate background knowledge. This is important in building expectations of the text and enabling top-down processing. It is also certainly true that learners need to be motivated to read and so building interest would seem a sensible teaching strategy.
>
> Some of the stages outlined above may not be present in every reading lesson. For example, the pre-teaching of vocabulary, essentially a strategy for adjusting the level of the text by providing additional support for bottom-up processing, may be omitted, particularly where a teacher decides that their learners will not need such support to process the text successfully. In addition, after this sequence of stages which focuses on the meaning of the text, there may be further stages that use the text as an object of study. For example, a salient grammar point may be selected and studied, or a lexical set identified. There are great advantages for learners to see language in context in this way. Celce-Murcia and Olshtain (2000) amongst others, point out that language choices frequently depend on contextual demands. However, in the cases where this type of language study stage is included in coursebook material, we may question the extent to which the context is fully explored and exploited. In some cases it seems that the highlighting of a grammar point in a text is little more than a neat segue into a traditional sentence-level analysis and seldom fully considers how the context has impacted on the linguistic choices made.

Figure N.2: P. Watkins, Teaching and developing reading skills (Cambridge University Press, 2018), p. 7

Sofia's objective in choosing this text was to convey the stages of a reading lesson to her trainees, so it makes sense for comprehension questions to focus on an understanding of those stages. Here are some possibilities:

1. Why should teachers aim to build students' interest in the text before they read?

2. How many tasks are normally set during the 'while reading' stage?

3. Are any stages of the process optional? Why?

4. In your experience, are the contexts for the texts you use in class fully explored and exploited?

Making the text more accessible can be done through utilising techniques that teachers typically employ in teaching reading skills, such as using prediction tasks to introduce the text and create a reason for reading, and opportunities for peer checking understanding after reading, or at certain points in the text. Of course, using these techniques wouldn't just benefit the trainees' comprehension of the text, it would also model relevant teaching skills for them.

TASK 4.1

There are four stages in Lydia's plan. In stage one, which is Practical, she *presents* teaching practices. Her trainees don't have an opportunity to try out any of the practical ideas she presents in this session, but that's because they will be able to do that in the teaching practice sessions on their course, so Lydia has chosen to maximise the time available to her for input. At the end of stage one Lydia elicits her trainees' reactions to the demo lesson, and this is a Personal stage in the lesson, even though Lydia hasn't identified it as a separate stage.

Stages two and three in Lydia's plan deal with the Professional – she first ensures they understand the general ideas behind the staging of a listening lesson, then checks their understanding of specific terms. Finally, stage four is Personal, and provides a chance for the trainees to think back over the session and consider what it might mean for their upcoming teaching practice lessons.

TASK 4.2

It's quite possible you found it easier to think of elements that made the PowerPoint presentation *ineffective*, which is fine – it can be as helpful to know what not to do as it is to know what to do!

An effective digital presentation can bring three things to your session. First of all, it can allow you to provide visual input, in the form of video, graphs or diagrams, or photos. As the saying goes, a picture is worth a thousand words, and sometimes you can convey an idea far more effectively through visuals than by trying to describe it. Secondly, presentation slides can provide visual support that helps your audience to follow what you are saying. Thirdly, well-designed slides can help to engage trainees, by adding variety and visual interest.

If you do choose to use a digital slideshow, keep it manageable – less is more when it comes to the number of slides and the amount of content on each one. Indeed, it is unlikely that you will need slides for the whole of your session, so feel free to turn off the projector when it is not needed. Ensure, too, that slides are complementary to your message, and not simply duplicating it. Slides which are packed full of text are not only unnecessary but are usually impossible to read because the size of the font is so small. If large quantities of text are relevant, consider other ways of presenting them (e.g., jigsaw reading) or providing them electronically before or after the session.

Above all, do not sit down at a computer and plan your session on PowerPoint, Keynote or any other presentation software. You should have your session design clear in your own mind before you sit down to create slides. It's usually easy to spot when the session design and the slides are one and the same – the trainer has their eyes glued to the screen at the front of the training room and the trainees are all half asleep!

TASK 4.3

The primary focus of a training session will be on developing teaching practice, not language skills, so interaction in the plan is not there for the benefit of teachers' language abilities (although some may welcome the opportunities for language development that the session provides). Instead, spoken interaction in the training room offers these benefits:

During Professional stages . . .	. . . interaction functions to help **build trainees' identities as teachers**. Part of teachers' professional identity involves participating in discourse about teaching, and the training room is where trainees are introduced to such discourse and are encouraged to take ownership of it. This takes some of the responsibility for professional development off the trainer and puts it onto the participants, who need to step into discussions: 'If teacher-learners [trainees] are not to be merely passive empty vessels into which knowledge is poured, then they need to be able to shape the course of the talk . . . As Danielwicz (2001, p. 168) argues, the course room should be a site where trainees create and experience different representations of themselves' (Singh & Richards, 2009, p. 205). As Professional stages in a training session involve the presentation of new concepts and terms, interaction is a valuable tool for trainers to check understanding among trainees.
During Personal stages . . .	. . . interaction allows the trainer to **elicit teacher beliefs and assumptions** as part of a process of trainee reflection, but also to enable the trainer to work with them. 'Teacher educators need to know their student teachers' conceptions of teaching to make new conceptions of teaching intelligible or create, if necessary, dissatisfaction with existing conceptions which may conflict with those taught' (Almarza, 1996, p. 74).
During Practical stages . . .	. . . interaction offers a way of bridging the gap between the relatively ordered world of the training room and the much more idiosyncratic, unpredictable world that each teacher will go on to practise in once the training session is over. **Discussing how they could apply concepts to their own teaching context** is vital for trainees, as is hearing what adaptations peers plan to make with respect to their contexts. Interaction also provides an **opportunity for trainees to discuss and reflect on how they do what they do**. These discussions frequently provide trainees with as much practical and theoretical material as the tasks designed by the trainer and can have far-reaching effects. With all trainees, then, but particularly with those who have more than a couple of years' experience, it is very important to acknowledge and exploit existing knowledge. And perhaps most simply, interaction in the training room offers opportunities for **modelling teaching techniques and procedures**. That's true not just of the interaction itself, which is an integral part of language teaching, but of how the trainer sets up, manages and feeds back on interactive tasks.

Of course, interaction also makes for a training room that is collegial and supportive, which cannot be underestimated, especially if those relationships continue into subsequent collaborative teacher development activities.

TASK 4.4

There are of course many ways to realise each of the aims, but here are some possible examples. You'll see that they are short and simple, modelling the way in which we would expect a teacher to deliver similar instructions in the classroom.

Aim	Example
Introduce or explain the aims of a session.	'Today I hope that you'll leave the session with a better understanding of what differentiation is and how to do it, and I hope that you *will* go on to do it for your learners!'
Say why the topic might be useful to this group of teachers.	'In all of our classes we have a wide range of abilities, and it can be really difficult to meet the needs of all the learners. So I hope what we learn today will help.'
Link the session to other sessions on the course / at the event.	'We've had recent sessions on adapting the coursebook and on formative assessment, and in many ways this session will build on both of those.'
Signpost a transition between group work and plenary work.	[Raises hand until trainees stop talking] 'Thank you. Now that you've had a chance to discuss your ideas, I'd like you to share them with the whole group.'
Summarising and closing the session.	'So we've seen what differentiation is and some ways of starting to do it with your learners. Let's review our session aims . . .'
Break down instructions, and set a time limit for the next task.	'Now that you've completed the handout, please join your original group and share your answers. Then discuss the three questions you see on the board. You have five minutes.'
Speak to a pair or group who are off task.	'You'll need to put your ideas onto paper for other groups to read, not just discuss them . . .'
Set an extra task for fast finishers.	'Now that you've both finished, can I ask you to compare your answers with each other and justify any differences?'
Give a reminder about time.	'Two minutes left, please!'
Prepare for next stage (e.g., by allocating tasks to different groups before the plenary begins).	[Privately to group] 'When we stop and share ideas as a whole class, would you be happy to start the discussion by being the first group to share your thoughts?'
Prepare participants for plenary work, by giving them a time limit within which to finish their task.	[Privately to group] 'In two minutes I'm going to ask all the groups to share their thoughts with the class, do you think you'll be ready to do that?'

TASK 4.5

Summarised from Guskey (2000).

Trainees' reactions	◦ Questionnaires ◦ Focus groups ◦ Interviews ◦ Personal learning logs
Trainees' learning	◦ Short test/quiz ◦ Microteaching session ◦ Oral or written personal reflections ◦ Portfolio assessment (of lesson plans, essays, or other assignments) ◦ Case study analysis
Organisation support and change	◦ Analysis of school records/documents ◦ Minutes from school meetings ◦ Questionnaires around specific issues ◦ Teacher focus groups
Trainees' use of new knowledge and skills	◦ Teacher lesson plans ◦ Structured interviews with teachers ◦ Teacher reflections, oral or written ◦ Direct observation of trainees
Student learning outcomes	◦ Test results ◦ Portfolio evaluations ◦ Class grades ◦ Affective and behavioural outcomes too (e.g., self-esteem, study habits, attendance)

TASK 5.3

Kavitha

◦ Asking Anita about action points from the previous meeting	Catalytic
◦ Answering Anita's questions	Informative, but could also be catalytic if Kavitha prompts Anita to find her own answers
◦ Discussing what Anita could apply from her reading	Likely to be mostly catalytic; there may be some prescriptive interventions here but Anita probably doesn't need many
◦ Discussing Anita's classroom experiments	Supportive when Anita describes successes, and catalytic when the outcomes of the experiment are less clear; not confronting, as it is Anita (the mentee) raising problems, not Kavitha (the mentor)
◦ Supporting and encouraging	Supportive, perhaps cathartic if Anita needs to talk about the pressures she is experiencing

Kavitha's interventions with Anita are mostly supportive – this reflects their relationship as colleagues and the informal mentoring relationship they have (it was Anita who asked Kavitha for mentor support). The balance towards supportive interventions also reflects Anita's experience – she still has things to learn but she's already been teaching for some time and is clearly able to work on developing her teaching without Kavitha's help for much of the time.

Jason

○ Asking mentees how they are doing	Cathartic
○ Discussing recent lessons	Likely to be mostly catalytic; Jason is aiming to help his mentees develop their reflection and self-evaluation skills
○ Answering mentees' questions	Informative or prescriptive
○ Considering lesson aims and what students are learning	Catalytic – again, to develop mentees' self-evaluation skills
○ Discussing plans for upcoming lessons	Supportive where plans seem logical and well considered, catalytic or even prescriptive when plans appear more problematic
○ Pointing out useful resources	Informative

Jason seems to draw on authoritative interventions more than Kavitha (this label carries no negative connotations for Heron, it simply indicates a directive role for the mentor). Jason explains the reasons for this in Case study 5.5 – his trainees are inexperienced, overwhelmed and not yet used to thinking about their professional development independently. Nevertheless, it's interesting that Jason is very keen to start his meetings with cathartic interventions, retaining a balance between authoritative and facilitative mentor talk (and perhaps thereby creating the conditions for authoritative interventions to be more readily received).

TASK 5.4

There are several things that you could do in this situation. It is highly likely that the trainees will have planned the lesson together, so they should all have some idea of each other's part of the lesson.

1. Ask (or signal to) teacher 1 (currently teaching) if they could continue in place of teacher 2.

2. Ask one of the other three teachers (who are waiting to teach) if they could also teach in place of teacher 2.

3. Decide if teacher 2's part of the lesson is important. If it isn't, then teacher 3 could take over from teacher 1.

4. You take the place of teacher 2 and teach the class.

If one of the other teachers is willing to step in, it should be made clear that their time as a substitute teacher will not be assessed as part of the course – it would simply be an opportunity to get some extra practice and keep the lesson going for the students.

TASK 6.2

Peter asks Theresa five main questions, which can be applied to most pre-observation meetings:

1. Tell me about this group of learners.

2. What are the most challenging aspects of teaching this class?

3. Talk me through what will happen in the lesson.

4. What will make you happy at the end of the lesson? What are you hoping to achieve?

5. What would you find it useful for me to look for and comment on?

The way these prompts and questions are worded is important because of the goal of building trust – the meeting shouldn't feel like an interrogation or a test. Starting the conversation by discussing the learners provides valuable context for the lesson but is also a relatively easy topic to begin with for the teacher. The hope is that by the time the conversation reaches question five, there is enough trust for the teacher to honestly state areas for development and ask for help with them.

TASK 6.3

Do	◦ Walk around the room.	◦ This is an important way of observing learning, but should be agreed with the teacher first.
	◦ Discuss what's taking place with other trainee observers.	◦ Discussions should be saved until the end of the lesson but talking points can be shared in advance, e.g., using Post-it notes.
Don't	◦ Take over the lesson.	◦ This is generally acceptable only if the teacher is unwell, or in the unlikely event that the safety of students or teachers is at risk.

Maybe	○ Speak to students.	○ This should be agreed with the teacher first, and done to gather evidence of learning, not to teach or chat.
	○ Make faces to indicate approval or disapproval.	○ On the whole we try to strike a balance between encouragement and not giving too much away. Disapproving looks are not helpful.
	○ Take photos of the classroom during the observation.	○ This can be a useful way of recording teaching and learning, but must be agreed with the teacher and the students beforehand.
	○ Stay longer than you previously agreed with the teacher.	○ Sometimes lessons unfold slightly differently than planned, and it is probably better to leave at the very end of a lesson stage than in the middle or when the teacher is setting up something new.
	○ Give a thumbs up when you leave.	○ A thumbs up is ambiguous but it is polite to thank the teacher when leaving.

TASK 6.4

Peter: *My favoured method of taking notes during an observation for developmental purposes is to write directly onto the teacher's lesson plan. This for me not only saves time but also allows me to respond to exactly what I see and hear without having to think about under which heading I should be writing something. In the case of Theresa's lesson, this was a short lesson without too many stages, and I actually needed fewer notes to support my discussion with the teacher after the lesson. In other situations I might use an observation template, similar to the examples in Chapter 6, if specific criteria need to be addressed (such as lesson planning, classroom management or use of resources).*

STAGE	NOTES
1 Vocabulary	○ Very friendly introduction, rapport quickly established ○ Supportive, encouraging style ○ Confident use of tech including the board – perhaps students could have written their ideas for free time activities, rather than Theresa ○ Timing a little longer than planned

2 Speaking preparation	◦ Very clear instructions for the speaking task ◦ Instructions checked with one student ◦ Students given time to think and then indicate readiness using Zoom reactions ◦ Timing a little longer than planned
3 Speaking task	◦ Students in breakout rooms which Theresa monitored ◦ Good discussions and decisions
4 Speaking task (repeat)	◦ Pairs told other pairs about their decisions for day out/free time activity ◦ Support given during this stage when students struggled ◦ Students gave some good ideas and others enjoyed listening and asking questions
5 Feedback on content	◦ Lovely idea to ask students to vote on their favourite free time activity ◦ Some students gave reasons for their choices – this could have been expanded to provide more opportunity for fluency practice
6 Feedback on form	◦ Good idea to share right/wrong sentences for students to identify and correct ◦ More focus on pron errors, e.g., *bowling, canoeing*

TASK 7.2

Method of assessment	Example	Comments
Observation	Any good teaching qualification	Practical
Lesson plans	Delta M2	Practical
Test of knowledge	e.g., TKT, Delta M1, DipTESOL unit 1	Professional
Portfolio tasks/ assignments	e.g., CELTA, DipTESOL unit 2	Professional/Personal *Good for ongoing assessment*
Interview	DipTESOL unit 3	Professional/Personal
Journal/diary	Delta M2, DipTESOL unit 4	Personal *Builds reflection skills, good for contextualising learning*
Project	e.g., Delta M3	Practical/Professional/Personal *Integrates knowledge and skills from various areas*

TASK 7.3

1. If reflecting in writing isn't something that teachers are used to, then the effort that should go into reflection is instead spent on trying to write well. That leads to superficial reflection that doesn't offer any insights to the teacher, and often creates the sense that reflecting on teaching is difficult and unproductive. The ultimate aim of reflecting on teaching is to learn how to better notice and describe classroom activity, and then to evaluate it and consider alternative courses of action that might improve learning. Achieving that aim doesn't require teachers to write, but assessing reflection means capturing those thought processes somehow.

2. Apart from writing, teachers might choose to reflect by:

   - Speaking – they could do this alone and record their thoughts on a mobile phone, or they could speak to a friend or colleague and record the conversation.

   - Using their L1 – teachers might find that they reflect differently when they can use their first language, rather than reflecting in English.

   - Acting – teachers might take on a role, such as that of a student in the room, and reflect from that person's perspective. Again, this could be done alone or with a colleague.

   - Drawing – teachers might find that the process of reflecting by creating an image helps them consider things that they would not have thought about if writing or speaking.

If written reflection is necessary for assessment purposes, teachers who struggle with it could be encouraged to reflect in one of the other ways listed above first, and then record their thoughts in writing afterwards.

TASK 8.1

Intensive preservice training course (e.g., CELTA)

- Trainees have no prior teaching experience, so the trainer is clearly the more knowledgeable party (*promotes hierarchy*).

- Over the course of an intensive course, trainers and trainees can get to know each other quite well (*promotes equality*).

- Observer is in the role of trainer, employed by the training centre and approved by the certificating body (*promotes hierarchy*).

- Preservice context means trainees are unlikely to have preconceptions as to how lesson observation and feedback should be conducted (*promotes hierarchy*).

- Number and length of observations and format of feedback determined by the certificating body (*promotes hierarchy*).

- Criteria for 'good teaching' specified in some detail and available to trainee (if they wish) (*promotes equality*).

- Lessons assessed and graded by the trainer (*promotes hierarchy*).

Peer observation between two colleagues

- Age and experience may not differ much (*promotes equality*).

- Teacher and observer probably know each other quite well (*promotes equality*).

- Observer probably has no formal title (*promotes equality*).

- In-service context means that both teacher and observer bring preconceptions about how observation and feedback should be conducted (*promotes equality*).

- No administrative requirements at all (*promotes equality*).

- No benchmark as to what is considered 'good teaching' (*promotes hierarchy – because the benchmark tends to be set by the person in the role of observer and becomes subjective*).

- No assessment, grading, or reporting of details to others (*promotes equality*).

Routine observation of a teacher by their academic manager

- Age and experience may not differ much (*promotes equality*).

- Teacher and observer probably know each other quite well (*promotes equality*).

- Observer has the title of academic manager (*promotes hierarchy – a lot!*).

- In-service context means that both teacher and observer bring preconceptions about how observation and feedback should be conducted (*promotes equality*).

- Administrative requirements set by the institution probably determine the length and frequency of observations, and the format that feedback takes. They may also link observation feedback to pay, contract renewal or career progression (*promotes hierarchy – a lot!*).

- There's often no benchmark for what constitutes good teaching, or there may be rigid benchmarks of observable behaviours designed to make the observer's job easier (e.g., the teacher must call upon every student to answer a question at least once) (*promotes hierarchy*).

- Details of the observation will be saved in the teacher's personnel file and made available to the senior leadership team (*promotes hierarchy*).

TASK 8.2

- For individual feedback, schedule the feedback meeting with the teacher. Try not to leave a long gap after the lesson, and make sure that there's not the pressure to curtail the meeting too soon (e.g., because of teaching commitments).

- (When fixing the date and time for individual feedback) give the teacher a reflection sheet to complete and tell them when to return it.

- Read the teachers' reflections so that you can refer to them in feedback.

- Consider having written feedback ready to give to the teachers once the discussion has ended.

- If working on a course, running frequent feedback sessions (weekly or more), try to vary the format so that you're not doing the same thing every time.

- Consider how to set up the meeting space, especially seating. The priority is somewhere quiet and private.

- Get all paperwork ready – lesson plan, materials, the teachers' reflection, and your written feedback; possibly student work from the lesson too.

TASK 8.3

Approach	Example	Comments
State the issue and give your evaluation of it.	'One thing that we haven't covered is the way that you dealt with errors in this lesson, which I thought was very effective.' 'Let's turn to timing for a moment – you ended up with very little time for your final stage.'	To the point and saves time, but reinforces the idea that feedback is the sole domain of the trainer and doesn't encourage the trainee to reflect.
Raise the general theme and invite the trainee(s) to pinpoint what was relevant.	'How about instructions, any thoughts on those?' 'Last time we talked about how you were using the board – did you think today was better or worse in that respect?'	Prompts the trainee to think (may be useful in group feedback situations for comparing the approaches of different teachers to the same issue), but there is a danger that it becomes a guessing game rather than a genuine moment of reflection.

Refer to the student reaction and elicit the teaching actions or decisions that caused it.	'When you gave the students that controlled practice task there was quite a lot of muttering in L1 – why do you think that was?'	Encourages the trainee to focus on student outcomes and to notice student behaviours, but some may not be able to make those connections yet.

TASK 8.6

Peter: *With written feedback I tend to favour bulleted notes rather than lengthy prose, as this makes the information more easily accessible to the teacher. Lengthy feedback can be overwhelming (even if it is mostly positive) and in my experience fewer comments can be more useful and impactful. Less experienced teachers will generally be more comfortable with feedback that they can quickly understand. However, in some cases, longer feedback may be more appropriate, for example in an observation where specific criteria need to be commented on.*

Teacher	Theresa Dyer	Observer	Peter Lucantoni
Lesson date/time	Thursday, 30 September 40 minutes	Class name	-
Classroom	-	No. of students	6

Course and lesson planning

Strengths	Think about
◦ Clear, achievable main and sub aims ◦ Very comprehensive and detailed plan ◦ Perceptive anticipated problems with solutions ◦ Clear, logical staging	◦ Stage descriptions could be more detailed (e.g., 'vocabulary' – is this presentation? practice?). ◦ Your personal aim was to focus on error correction, but there were few opportunities to focus on form in the plan.

Classroom management

Strengths	Think about
◦ Very pleasant and welcoming style ◦ Great rapport quickly established ◦ Students quickly put at ease ◦ Smooth transitions between various stages ◦ Activity instructions checked	◦ Perhaps have an example for Slide 3 (a couple of the students were quite weak). ◦ There were obvious differences in levels – ideas for differentiation?

Use of resources and materials

Strengths	Think about
○ Confident use of the technology, including whiteboard and breakout rooms	○ Think about asking students to write on the WB (rather than doing it yourself).

Subject knowledge

Strengths	Think about
○ You had plenty of examples of free time activities. ○ You gave a clear explanation of the use of the present perfect tense (during the right/wrong activity).	○ Consider addressing pronunciation errors (e.g., *bowling*, *canoeing*) straight away.

Understanding of learners

Strengths	Think about
○ You appreciated the challenges your students faced in learning online. ○ While monitoring you were ready to provide help when needed, particularly with vocabulary.	○ Consider ways to differentiate activities for students needing support.

Overall

○ Considering the challenging circumstances for this lesson (i.e., unknown students, unknown number of students, teaching online), I think you performed extremely well.

○ Your students were engaged and enthusiastic and performed confidently with your support.

○ They obviously felt comfortable because of the very positive rapport that you established early on.

○ Students were able to plan and talk about free time activities and used appropriate vocabulary.

Action points

○ As two of the students were less confident than the others, it might have been useful to think about ways to offer them more support during the speaking activity. Consider planning differentiated tasks to cover all eventualities when you are working with an unfamiliar group.

○ Your personal aim around error correction was not really actioned – you could use the lesson recording to highlight potential areas for correction (seeing if there was anything you missed during the class) and address them in the next lesson.

TASK 9.1

For most teachers, programmes will be the least common type of training that they have attended and many will never have participated in a programme at all. Examples of such programmes might be a national programme of teacher training organised by a ministry of education, or a programme of training implemented by a large institution that wishes to introduce a new teaching methodology in its classrooms.

All teachers ought to have completed a course to qualify initially and begin teaching, and some may have taken further courses to gain qualifications at higher levels or to fill gaps in their expertise. For both of us, the majority of our training experiences as teachers were standalone events that didn't form part of a course or programme, and if you are lucky enough to work in an institution that values teacher learning and staff development, the same may be true for you.

TASK 9.2

The first thing that stands out is Yi's schedule – it is extremely intensive, for the trainees as well as for her. The days when Yi is observing will be particularly hard work, because observing lessons requires great concentration and it is difficult to sit at the back of a classroom for two hours, let alone all day! The schedule also doesn't allow time for Yi to have a face-to-face feedback discussion with the teachers after their observations, so the only feedback they receive is written, and therefore much more open to ambiguity or misinterpretation. The very condensed course timetable is ultimately due to financial constraints imposed by Yi's institution, which wants to minimise the time that teachers are in the training room because it means that they are not teaching paying students.

Yi's trainees have a similarly demanding teaching schedule outside the course, therefore, so she often finds that they have not completed the online component of the course by the time she arrives to deliver the face-to-face workshops (or that those who have did so in a hurry). This means that Yi sometimes has to allow time for questions or filling in gaps in knowledge, and her workshops can feel rushed as a result. On the other hand, Yi sometimes finds that the trainees' 'book knowledge' (*Knowing about*) of certain topics is very strong as a result of their previous training experiences, which have tended to be online, and she can move quickly into more practical tasks in her sessions.

Yi mentioned that when there is a large number of trainees she works with another trainer, and this presents its own challenges: they will need to standardise their assessments of the teachers and the feedback that they give to them, and as the lead trainer Yi will need to ensure that administrative tasks are completed so that the trainees receive their certificates. Working with another trainer brings many advantages, however – the trainees are able to receive more individual attention than they would in a large group, Yi has the opportunity to share thoughts and ideas with her co-trainer and the admin work can be split between them, saving time.

TASK 10.2

Of course, every trainer's development profile is different, and needs will depend to some extent on the demands of the local training context. But frameworks like those in Table 10.1 provide an important yardstick, in this case for trainers, but also for teachers (e.g., using the Cambridge English Teaching Framework, see Appendix 1). Being able to diagnose development needs is a vital skill for teachers, because they need to be able to take charge of their own development. So if you have successfully used the frameworks in Table 10.1 to highlight areas that you could work on, consider how you could help trainees to use a teaching framework to do the same thing for themselves.

TASK 10.3

One way of looking at development is to consider it in terms of relationships with different groups of people, so this may have been the way that you decided to group the activities. Teaching and learning are social endeavours (Johnson & Golombek, 2011), so the groups of people that we interact with as teachers and as trainers can play a significant role in the development of our practice. Duncan Foord suggests that teachers think about their development in terms of five concentric circles of development: at the centre is the individual teacher, surrounded by, in turn, teacher and students, teacher and colleagues, teacher and school, and teacher and profession (Foord, 2009, p. 14). This approach highlights the opportunities for development in routine interactions with all these groups, and places the teacher at the centre of their development plan. It also allows for progressively more ambitious activity as the teacher's development extends further from their own classroom experience.

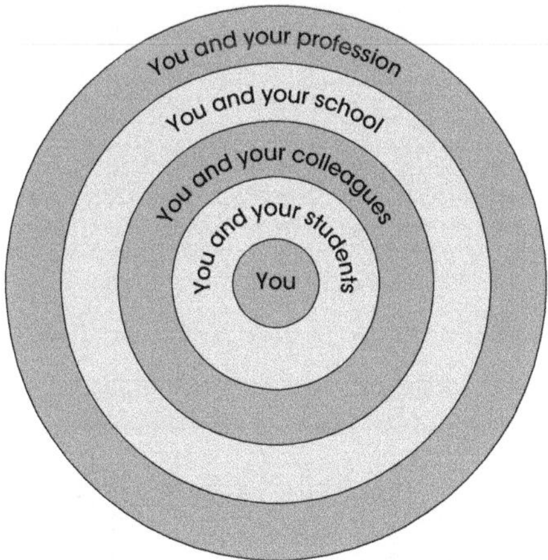

Figure N.3: Foord's five circles of development (Foord, 2019)

Cambridge English Teaching Framework – at the heart of professional development

We developed the Cambridge English Teaching Framework: to help teachers identify where they are in their professional career to help teachers and their employers think about where they want to go next and identify development activities to get there.

Stages	Foundation	Developing	Proficient	Expert
Learning and the learner	Has a basic understanding of some language–learning concepts. Demonstrates a little of this understanding when planning and teaching.	Has a reasonable understanding of many language–learning concepts. Demonstrates some of this understanding when planning and teaching.	Has a good understanding of many language–learning concepts. Frequently demonstrates this understanding when planning and teaching.	Has a sophisticated understanding of language–learning concepts. Consistently demonstrates this understanding when planning and teaching.
Teaching, learning and assessment	Has a basic understanding of some key principles of teaching, learning and assessment. Can plan and deliver simple lessons with a basic awareness of learners' needs, using core teaching techniques. Can use available tests and basic assessment procedures to support and promote learning.	Has a reasonable understanding of many key principles of teaching, learning and assessment. Can plan and deliver lessons with some awareness of learners' needs, using a number of different teaching techniques. Can design simple tests and use some assessment procedures to support and promote learning.	Has a good understanding of key principles of teaching, learning and assessment. Can plan and deliver detailed lessons with good awareness of learners' needs, using a wide range of teaching techniques. Can design effective tests and use a range of assessment procedures to support and promote learning.	Has a sophisticated understanding of key principles of teaching, learning and assessment. Can plan and deliver detailed and sophisticated lessons with a thorough understanding of learners' needs, using a comprehensive range of teaching techniques. Can design a range of effective tests and use individualised assessment procedures consistently to support and promote learning.
Language ability	Provides accurate examples of language points taught at A1 and A2 levels. Uses basic classroom language which is mostly accurate.	Provides accurate examples of language points taught at A1, A2 and B1 levels. Uses classroom language which is mostly accurate.	Provides accurate examples of language points taught at A1, A2, B1 and B2 levels. Uses classroom language which is consistently accurate throughout the lesson.	Provides accurate examples of language points taught at A1–C2 levels. Uses a wide range of classroom language which is consistently accurate throughout the lesson.
Language knowledge and awareness	Is aware of some key terms for describing language. Can answer simple learner questions with the help of reference materials.	Has reasonable knowledge of many key terms for describing language. Can answer most learner questions with the help of reference materials.	Has good knowledge of key terms for describing language. Can answer most learner questions with minimal use of reference materials.	Has sophisticated knowledge of key terms for describing language. Can answer most learner questions in detail with minimal use of reference materials.
Professional development and values	Can reflect on a lesson with guidance and learn from feedback. Requires guidance in self-assessing own needs.	Can reflect on a lesson without guidance and respond positively to feedback. Can self-assess own needs and identify some areas for improvement.	Can reflect critically and actively seeks feedback. Can identify own strengths and weaknesses as a teacher, and can support other teachers.	Consistently reflects critically, observes other colleagues and is highly committed to professional development. Is highly aware of own strengths and weaknesses, and actively supports the development of other teachers.

See the full version of the framework for detailed competency statements: cambridgeenglish.org/teaching-framework

Appendix 2 Lesson plan

Theresa Dyer
September 19, 16.20–17.00
School in Rome, Italy

Main aim	By the end of the lesson, the Ss will have developed their fluency in the planning and choosing of a fun free time activity to do as a class.
Sub aim	By the end of the lesson, the Ss will have expanded their range of vocabulary related to free time activities.
Personal aims	To evaluate the effectiveness of error correction techniques I use in the lesson, in terms of ∘ when I error correct, ∘ which errors I choose to focus on.
Class profile	I don't know very much about this class because it's their first lesson together. However, their level is roughly a high intermediate level (B1+/B2) and they are a mixture of Italian and Spanish native speakers. Most of the Ss are women (there is one man registered), but their ages range from 16 to mid-40s. There should be between 6 and 8 Ss. Some of them are students (at high school and university) and some are teachers. There may also be other professions present. They are generally studying English to help them in their studies, e.g., to gain entry to university programmes, or for work. They have been studying English online for some time now, so they are used to the online learning environment and can use most Zoom tools efficiently.
Assumptions	Since this lesson is their first one together, the purpose is also largely diagnostic, i.e., to find out what the Ss can do in English and where their problems lie. I can assume that they will have some basic vocabulary to describe free time activities and they should have enough language to have a discussion that entails making suggestions, agreeing and disagreeing. I can also assume that the task should be quite engaging and relevant to all the Ss since everyone has something they enjoy doing in their free time.

Anticipated problems and solutions	1. Ss may be limited in the number of free time activities they can name in English, so at the brainstorm stage, I will prompt them and try to elicit some, e.g., activities you can do indoors: playing board games, ice skating, or activities you can do outdoors, e.g., fishing, trekking.
	2. Not knowing exactly how many Ss there will be will have some impact on the timing and the interaction patterns I set up: if there are only a few Ss, I will ask them to do the initial speaking task in pairs. If there are more of them, I will set up small groups. Pair work will be quicker than group work so I may have to make timing adjustments as I go along.
Materials	*Evolve 3 Student's Book*, Unit 12.5, 2019, Cambridge University Press (adapted)
	T-produced PowerPoint slides
	Word document: Right or Wrong?
Time	40 minutes

Stage	Stage aim	Procedure	Timing and Interaction
Vocabulary	To find out what free time activities Ss know in English To provide ideas for the speaking task	Show Ss the slide with images from *Evolve 3* and elicit what the free-time activities are. Concept-check paddle boarding (if necessary): *Where do people do this? The sea, river, lakes.* *Is it like surfing? The board is similar.* *Can they do this when the water is calm or not? Calm.* Screen-share the Zoom whiteboard and ask Ss for more fun free time activities. Write them on the WB. Tell Ss they may use some of these ideas in the next stage.	5′ T–Ss

Speaking preparation	To provide the Ss with 'thinking time'	Set the Speaking task: tell the Ss we want to plan a fun day out for the class and that they are going to suggest an activity. Provide the Ss with prompts to think about: where to do the activity, cost, what we need, how easy/difficult it is, why it would be enjoyable. Give Ss time to think of an activity (possibly from the previous vocabulary brainstorm). They can take notes, if they want. Check instructions: *Do you need to write sentences? No.* *Can you just write some ideas? Yes.* Ask Ss to raise their hands using Zoom reactions when they have some ideas.	5' S
Speaking (task)	To promote fluency To provide Ss with a first 'rehearsal' of the speaking task	Tell the Ss they are going to share their ideas with a partner/s and they have to decide on the best idea to propose to the class. Put Ss in BORs [breakout rooms]. Monitor and input language/correct mistakes as necessary without infringing too much on Ss' opportunity to develop their fluency. Close BORs when the Ss have had enough time to choose the best idea in the group (broadcast Ss a message to choose the best suggestion, as a reminder).	5'–10' S–S or Ss–Ss

Speaking (task repetition)	To promote fluency To provide Ss with an opportunity to improve on their first attempt at the speaking task	Tell the Ss they're going to tell the class what the best suggestion for a day out together was. The other Ss have to listen because they will vote on the activity they would like to do, at the end. They can ask each other some questions for more information, if they want. Nominate different Ss to present their ideas. Listen with video off and take notes of good samples of language and common mistakes.	10' Open class Ss–Ss (T moderates)
Feedback on content	To provide a communicative purpose for the task and fulfil the outcome: choosing a free time activity for the class to do together	Ask Ss to vote on the free time suggestion they liked best by using the 'raised hand' Zoom reaction and get some reasons for Ss' choices.	5' T–Ss
Feedback on form	To focus on accuracy and stave off 'fossilisation'	Screen-share the Word document 'Right or Wrong' and ask Ss to identify the correct sentence/s and to correct mistakes in the other sentences.	5' T–Ss

References

Almarza, G. G. (1996). Student foreign language teacher's knowledge growth. In D. Freeman & J. C. Richards (Eds.), *Teacher learning in language teaching* (pp. 50–78). Cambridge: Cambridge University Press.

Anderson, J. (2017, Spring). CAP – Context, Analysis, Practice: A lesson planning model for language teacher education. *Teacher Training and Education SIG Newsletter*, 15–18.

Bailey, K. M. (1996). The language learner's autobiography: Examining the 'apprenticeship of observation'. In D. Freeman & J. C. Richards (Eds.), *Teacher learning in language teaching* (pp. 11–29). Cambridge: Cambridge University Press.

Bailey, K. M. (2001). Observation. In R. Carter & D. Nunan (Eds.), *The Cambridge guide to teaching English to speakers of other languages* (pp. 114–119). Cambridge: Cambridge University Press.

Bartels, N. (2009). Knowledge about language. In A. Burns & J. C. Richards (Eds.), *The Cambridge guide to second language teacher education* (pp. 125–134). New York: Cambridge University Press.

Beaumont, B. (2019). Contextualised CPD: bringing equality to teaching and professional qualifications. *IATEFL Conference*. Liverpool, UK.

Borg, S. (2009). English language teachers' conceptions of research. *Applied Linguistics, 30*(3), 358–388.

Borko, H., Jacobs, J., Eiteljorg, E., & Pittman, M. E. (2008). Video as a tool for fostering productive discussions in mathematics professional development. *Teaching and Teacher Education, 24*(2), 417–436.

Brown, J. D., & Coombe, C. (2015). Introduction: Research in language teaching and learning. In J. D. Brown & C. Coombe (Eds.), *The Cambridge guide to research in second language teaching and learning* (pp. xiii–xx). Cambridge: Cambridge University Press.

Burns, A. (1999). *Collaborative action research for language teachers.* Cambridge: Cambridge University Press.

Cambridge English Language Assessment. (2016). Cambridge English Trainer Framework. Retrieved from www.cambridgeenglish.org/Images/297310-cambridge-english-trainer-framework-introduction.pdf

Chandler, J. (2003). The efficacy of various kinds of error feedback for improvement in the accuracy and fluency of student writing. *Journal of Second Langue Writing, 12*(3), 267–296.

Childs, S. S. (2011). 'Seeing' L2 teacher learning: The power of context on conceptualizing teaching. In K. E. Johnson & P. R. Golombeks (Eds.), *Research on second language teacher education: A sociocultural perspective on professional development* (pp. 68–85). New York: Routledge.

Chong, C. S. (2012). What does a CELTA tutor do? *ET Professional, 83*, 52–54.

Cordingley, P., Higgins, S., Greany, T., Buckler, N., Coles-Jordan, D., Crisp, B., Saunders, L., & Coe, R. (2015). *Developing Great Teaching: Lessons from the international reviews into effective professional development.* Teacher Development Trust.

Davies, B., & Northall, N. (2019a). No one told me that! 6. *ET Professional, 122*, 49–51.

Davies, B., & Northall, N. (2019b). 'No-one told me that!' Top tips for new trainers. *IATEFL 2018: Brighton conference selections* (pp. 218–220). Faversham: IATEFL.

Delaney, J.-A. (2019). Assessment and feedback. In S. Walsh & S. Mann (Eds.), *The Routledge Handbook of English Language Teacher Education* (pp. 385–401). Abingdon: Routledge.

Dewaele, J. M. (2018). Why the dichotomy 'L1 versus LX user' is better than 'native versus non-native speaker'. *Applied Linguistics, 39*(2), 236–240.

Diaz Maggioli, G. (2012). *Teaching language teachers.* Plymouth: Rowman & Littlefield.

Doff, A. (1996). *Teach English.* Cambridge: Cambridge University Press.

Doff, A., Jones, C., & Mitchell, K. (1984). *Meanings into words.* Cambridge: Cambridge University Press.

Dörnyei, Z., & Kubanyiova, M. (2014). *Motivating learners, motivating teachers.* Cambridge: Cambridge University Press.

Dragas, T. (2019). Professional development for teacher trainers: A neglected area? *IATEFL 2018: Brighton conference selections* (pp. 230–231). Faversham: IATEFL.

Duff, T. (1988). *Explorations in teacher training.* London: Longman.

Edge, J. (1985). The Somali oyster – Training the trainers in TEFL. *System, 13*(2), 113–118.

Eken, D. K., Çeltek, S., & Bosson, A. (2015). Observation-related professional development. *ET Professional, 98*, 53–56.

Ellis, R. (1990). Activities and procedures for teacher education. In J. C. Richards & D. Nunan (Eds.), *Second language teacher education* (pp. 26–36). Cambridge: Cambridge University Press.

Ellis, R. (2005). Principles of instructed language learning . *System, 33*(2), 209–224.

Fanselow, J. F. (1987). *Breaking rules: Generating and exploring alternatives in language teaching.* New York: Longman.

Farrell, T. S. (2013). *Reflective practice in ESL teacher development groups.* Basingstoke: Palgrave Macmillan.

Farrell, T. S. (2015). It's not who you are! It's how you teach! Critical competencies associated with effective teaching. *RELC Journal, 46*(1), 79–88.

Farrell, T. S. (2018). Second language teacher education and future directions. In *The TESOL Encyclopedia of English Language Teaching* (pp. 1–7). doi:https://doi.org/10.1002/9781118784235.eelt0922

Foord, D. (2009). *The developing teacher.* Peaslake: Delta.

Fortune, J. C., Cooper, J. M., & Allen, D. W. (1967). The Stanford Summer Micro-Teaching Clinic, 1965. *Journal of Teacher Education, 18*(4), 389–393.

Freeman, D. (1989). Teacher training, development, and decision making: A model of teaching and related strategies for language teacher education. *TESOL Quarterly, 23*(1), 27–45.

Freeman, D. (2009). The scope of second language teacher education. In A. Burns & J. C. Richards (Eds.), *The Cambridge guide to second language teacher education* (pp. 11–19). New York: Cambridge University Press.

Freeman, D. (2016). *Educating second language teachers.* Oxford: Oxford University Press.

Freeman, D., McBee Orzulak, M., & Morrissey, G. (2009). Assessment in second language teacher education. In A. Burns & J. C. Richards (Eds.), *The Cambridge guide to second language teacher education* (pp. 77–90). New York: Cambridge University Press.

Gebhard, J. G. (1990). Models of supervision: Choices. In J. C. Richards & D. Nunan (Eds.), *Second language teacher education* (pp. 156–166). Cambridge: Cambridge University Press.

Grinder, M. (2006). *Charisma: The art of relationships.* Michael Grinder & Associates.

Guskey, T. R. (2000). *Evaluating professional development.* Thousand Oaks, CA: Corwin Press.

Harmer, J. (2007). *The practice of English language teaching* (4th ed.). Harlow: Pearson.

Hatano, G., & Inagaki, K. (1986). Two courses of expertise. In H. Stevenson, H. Azuma & K. Hakuta (Eds.), *Child development and education in Japan* (pp. 262–272). New York: W. H. Freeman.

Hobson, A. J., Ashby, P., Malderez, A., & Tomlinson, P. D. (2009). Mentoring beginning teachers: What we know and what we don't. *Teaching and Teacher Education, 25*(1), 207–216.

Holmes, A. (2017). Training is teaching. *ET Professional, 111*, 49–51.

Howatt, A. P., & Widdowson, H. G. (2004). *A history of English language teaching* (2nd ed.). Oxford: Oxford University Press.

Hughes, J. (2015). *A practical introduction to teacher training in ELT.* Hove: Pavilion.

Huling, L., & Resta, V. (2001). Teacher mentoring as professional development. *ERIC Digest* (ED460125). Retrieved from https://files.eric.ed.gov/fulltext/ED460125.pdf

Ingersoll, R. M., & Strong, M. (2011). The Impact of Induction and Mentoring Programs for Beginning Teachers: A Critical Review of the Research. *Review of Educational Research, 81*(2), 201–233.

Ingvarson, L., Meiers, M., & Beavis, A. (2005). Factors affecting the impact of professional development programs on teachers' knowledge, practice, student outcomes & efficacy. *Education Policy Analysis Archives, 13*(10), 1–26.

Johnson, K. E., & Golombek, P. R. (2011). A sociocultural theoretical perspective on teacher professional development. In *Research on second language teacher education: A sociocultural perspective on professional development* (pp. 1–12). New York: Routledge.

Johnson, R. K. (1990). Developing teachers' language resources. In J. C. Richards & D. Nunan (Eds.), *Second language teacher eduation* (pp. 269–281). Cambridge: Cambridge University Press.

Kirkham, D. (2015). Developing teacher development. *ET Professional, 97,* 4–6.

Kirschner, P. A. (2017). Stop propagating the learning styles myth. *Computers & Education, 106*, 166–171.

Lamb, M. (2019). Flipping training. *ET Professional, 124*, 45–48.

Leahy, S., & Wiliam, D. (2012). From teachers to schools: Scaling up professional development for formative assessment. In J. Gardner (Ed.), *Assessment and learning* (pp. 49–71). Sage Publications.

Lortie, D. (1975). *Schoolteacher: A sociological study.* Chicago: University of Chicago Press.

Lubelska, D., & Robbins, L. (1999, November). Moving from teaching to training. *IATEFL Teacher Trainers' SIG Newsletter*, 7–9.

MacBeath, J. (2013). Learning and Teaching: Are they by any chance related? In C. McLaughlin (Ed.), *Teachers learning: Professional development and education* (pp. 1–20). Cambridge: Cambridge University Press.

Magloff, L. (2020, January). Teach in teacher training. *EL Gazette*, pp. 34–35.

Malderez, A. (2003). Observation. *ELT Journal, 57*(2), 179–181.

Malderez, A. (2009). Mentoring. In A. Burns & J. C. Richards (Eds.), *The Cambridge guide to second language teacher education* (pp. 259–268). New York: Cambridge University Press.

Malderez, A., & Bodóczky, C. (1999). *Mentor courses.* Cambridge: Cambridge University Press.

Malderez, A., & Wedell, M. (2007). *Teaching teachers: Processes and practices.* London: Continuum.

Mann, S. (2005). The language teacher's development. *Language Teaching, 38*(3), 103-118.

Mann, S., Davidson, A., Davis, M., Gakonga, J., Gamero, M., Harrison, T., Mosavian, P., & Richards, L. (2019). *Video in language teacher education.* London: British Council.

Mayne, R. (2019). *Taboo 2.* Retrieved from https://evidenceinformedelt.net/2019/10/06/taboo-2/

Moss, P. A., Girard, B. J., & Haniford, L. C. (2006). Validity in educational assessment. *Review of Research in Education, 30*, 109–162.

Parrott, M. (1991). Teacher education: Factors relating to programme design. In R. Bowers & C. Brumfit (Eds.), *Applied linguistics and English language teaching* (pp. 36–46). London: Macmillan.

Randall, M., & Thornton, B. (2001). *Advising and supporting teachers.* Cambridge: Cambridge University Press.

Richards, J. C. (2017). *50 Tips for teacher development.* Cambridge: Cambridge University Press.

Richards, J. C., & Farrell, T. S. (2011). *Practice Teaching: A reflective approach.* New York: Cambridge University Press.

Richardson, S., & Díaz Maggioli, G. (2018). *Effective professional development: Principles and best practice.* Cambridge: Cambridge University Press.

Rossner, R. (2013). Assessing language teaching competences - why and how? *English language teacher education in a diverse environment* (pp. 115–121). British Council.

Schön, D. (1983). *The reflective practitioner: How professionals think in action.* New York: Basic Books.

Scrivener, J. (2011). *Learning teaching* (3rd ed.). Oxford: Macmillan.

Scrivener, J. (2012). *Classroom management techniques.* Cambridge: Cambridge University Press.

Sherin, M. G., & Van Es, E. A. (2009). Effects of video club participation on teachers' professional vision. *Journal of Teacher Education, 60*(1), 20–37.

Shulman, L. S. (1988). A union of insufficiencies: Strategies for teacher assessment in a period of educational reform. *Educational Leadership, 46*(3), 36–41.

Shulman, L. S., & Shulman, J. H. (2004). How and what teachers learn: a shifting perspective. *Journal of Curriculum Studies, 36*(2), 257–271.

Simons, D. J., & Chabris, C. F. (1999). Gorillas in our midst: sustained inattentional blindness for dynamic events. *Perception, 28*(9), 1059–1074.

Singh, G., & Richards, J. C. (2009). Teaching and learning in the course room. In A. Burns & J. C. Richards (Eds.), *The Cambridge guide to second language teacher education* (pp. 201–208). New York: Cambridge University Press.

Smith, R. C. (2007). *Lawrence Faucett's life and career*. Retrieved from https://warwick.ac.uk/fac/soc/al/research/collections/elt_archive/halloffame/faucett/life

Thaine, C. (2010). *Teacher Training Essentials: Workshops for Professional Development*. Cambridge: Cambridge University Press.

Thornbury, S. (1991). Metaphors we work by: EFL and its metaphors. *ELT Journal, 45*(3), 193–200.

Thornbury, S., & Watkins, P. (2007). *The CELTA Course: Trainee Book*. Cambridge: Cambridge University Press.

Tripp, D. (1993). *Critical incidents in teaching.* Abingdon: Routledge.

Tripp, D. (1994). Teachers' lives, critical incidents, and professional practice. *Qualitative Studies in Education, 7*(1), 65–76.

Tsui, A. B. (2009). Teaching expertise: Approaches, perspectives, and characterizations. In A. Burns & J. C. Richards (Eds.), *The Cambridge guide to second language teacher education* (pp. 190–197). New York: Cambridge University Press.

Ur, P. (2012). *A course in English language teaching* (2nd ed.). Cambridge: Cambridge University Press.

Van Es, E. A., & Sherin, M. G. (2008). Mathematics teachers' 'learning to notice' in the context of a video club. *Teaching and Teacher Education, 24*(2), 244–276.

Vilches, M. L. (2015). Becoming a trainer: The experience of Philippine English teachers in the Primary Innovations Project. In T. Wright & M. Beaumont (Eds.), *Experiences of second language teacher education* (pp. 269–295). Basingstoke: Palgrave Macmillan.

Wajnryb, R. (1992). *Classroom observation tasks.* Cambridge: Cambridge University Press.

Wallace, M. J. (1991). *Training foreign language teachers: A reflective approach.* Cambridge: Cambridge University Press.

Waters, A. (2005). Expertise in teacher education: Helping teachers to learn. In K. Johnson (Ed.), *Expertise in second language learning and teaching* (pp. 210–229). Basingstoke: Palgrave Macmillan.

Watkins, P. (2018). *Teaching and developing reading skills.* Cambridge: Cambridge University Press.

Weintraub, E. (1989). An interview with Ephraim Weintraub. *The Teacher Trainer, 3*(1), 1.

Weir, C., & Saville, N. (2015). Series editors' note. In R. Wilson & M. Poulter (Eds.), *Studies in language testing 42: Assessing language teachers' professional skills and knowledge* (pp. viii–xii). Cambridge: Cambridge University Press.

Wendt, J. R. (1984). DIE: A way to improve communication. *Communication Education, 33*, 397–401.

Westerman, D. A. (1991). Expert and novice teacher decision making. *Journal of Teacher Education, 42*(4), 292–305.

Weston, D., & Clay, B. (2018). *Unleashing great teaching: The secrets to the most effective teacher development.* Abingdon: Routledge.

White, R., Hockley, A., van der Horst Jansen, J., & Laughner, M. S. (2008). *From teacher to manager.* Cambridge: Cambridge University Press.

Widdowson, H. (1984). The incentive value of theory in teacher education. *ELT Journal, 38*(2), 86–90.

Williams, M., & Burden, R. L. (1997). *Psychology for language teachers.* Cambridge: Cambridge University Press.

Willingham, D. T., Hughes, E. M., & Dobolyi, D. G. (2015). The scientific status of learning styles theories. *Teaching of Psychology, 42*(3), 266-271.

Wilson, R., & Poulter, M. (2015). *Studies in language testing 42: Assessing language teachers' professional skills and knowledge.* Cambridge: Cambridge University Press.

Woodward, T. (1991). *Models and metaphors in language teacher training: Loop input and other strategies.* Cambridge: Cambridge University Press.

Woodward, T. (2001). *Planning lessons and courses.* Cambridge: Cambridge University Press.

Woodward, T. (2003). Loop input. *ELT Journal, 57*(3), 301–304.

Wragg, E. C. (1999). *An introduction to classroom observation* (2nd ed.). London: Routledge.

Wright, T. (2009). 'Trainer development': Professional development for language teacher educators. In A. Burns & J. C. Richards (Eds.), *The Cambridge guide to second language teacher education* (pp. 102–112). New York: Cambridge University Press.

Wright, T., & Bolitho, R. (2007). *Trainer development.* Self published.

Index

Locators in **bold** refer to figures and tables.